THE ART OF
THE POSSIBLE

The Art of the Possible

Booker T. Washington and Black Leadership in the United States, 1881–1925

Kevern Verney

Routledge
New York and London

Published in 2001 by
Routledge
29 West 35th Street
New York, NY 10001

Published in Great Britain by
Routledge
11 New Fetter Lane
London EC4P 4EE

Routledge is an imprint of the Taylor & Francis Group.

Printed in the United States of America on acid-free paper.

Library of Congress Cataloging-in-Publication Data

Verney, Kevern, 1960–
    The art of the possible : Booker T. Washington and black leadership in the United
States, 1881–1925 / Kevern Verney.
        p. cm.
    Includes bibliographical references and index.
    ISBN 0-8153-3723-X
    1. Washington, Booker T., 1856–1915. 2. Washington, Booker T., 1856–1915 —
Friends and associates. 3. Washington, Booker T., 1856–1915 — Political and social
views. 4. African Americans — Biography. 5. Educators — United States — Biography.
6. African American leadership — History. 7. African American intellectuals —
History. 8. African Americans — History — 1863–1877. 9. African American —
History — 1877–1964. I. Title.

E185.97.W4 V47 2001
370'.92 — dc21
[B]   2001019236

Contents

Series Editor's Foreword

In the past thirty years, scholars in the field of African-American studies have produced some of the most compelling and original books in American letters. Research on black leadership, labor, community, resistance and intellectual tradition have blossomed into a field of inquiry of paramount importance. There has been a steady increase in historical scholarship, with younger academics reaching out in new directions and using innovative methodologies such as race and gender analysis. In works on all eras of American history, from each region of the country and even abroad, scholars today carry on the vigorous pursuit of knowledge and analytic interpretation that have always characterized African-American studies.

Crosscurrents in African-American History aspires to publish the best and most recent research in the field. Routledge is proud to present distinguished books that offer contemporary interpretations of the black experience in the United States. The topics in the series have been carefully chosen to fulfill this mission and to advance our knowledge of this critical field. Now and in the future, Routledge will publish volumes that create new paradigms in African-American historical scholarship, while resting securely on the accomplishments of established work in black studies.

Graham Russell Hodges
Margaret Washington

Acknowledgments

Preparing a 90,000 word book manuscript is a demanding task at the best of times. Moving house twice, and contracting chicken pox, during the period of writing provided less than optimum conditions. I am grateful to the individuals and organizations below for helping to ensure that a challenging project did not become an insurmountable one.

In the United Kingdom, Edge Hill College funded two research visits to the United States, without which this book could not have been written. The support of Head of History, Chris Parker, for a partial research sabbatical during 1999 and 2000 was equally important. I am also indebted to *Borderlines* for permission to publish chapter 3, the original version of which appeared as: '"Roads Not Taken": Booker T. Washington and Black Leadership in the United States, 1895–1915', *Borderlines*, 3, No. 2 (Winter, 1996–97), 144–58.

In the United States it is not possible to give individual recognition to everyone involved in the production process at Routledge, but I am grateful to all concerned for their professionalism, patience and enthusiasm.

On a personal note my parents, Neville and Susan Verney, gave both moral and practical support. This was also true of my partner, Juliet Hadley, who provided encouragement when it was needed most and endured the countles hours I spent on my P.C. without complaint.

CHAPTER 1

Introduction

African-American History, 1865–1925

The Reconstruction era, 1865–1877, that followed the end of the American Civil War was the best of times and the worst of times for African Americans.

It was the best of times because the passage of the Thirteenth Amendment to the U. S. Constitution in 1865 confirmed the emancipation from slavery of four million blacks in the American South. In a dramatic period of change this achievement of freedom was only a beginning. The 1866 Civil Rights Act and the Fourteenth and Fifteenth Amendments to the Constitution, ratified in 1869 and 1870, respectively, went further and promised ex-slaves equal citizenship and voting rights.

In national politics the Republican Party, which had initiated these measures, retained unbroken control of both houses of Congress and the U.S. Presidency during the administrations of Andrew Johnson, 1865–1869, and Ulysses S. Grant, 1869–1877. At the local level the enfranchisement of freed slaves, voting disabilities imposed on former Confederates, and the choice of many southern whites not to participate in the political process led to the election of Republican state administrations throughout the South for the first time. Political life in the southern states was controlled by an alliance of northern newcomers to the region; the "Carpetbaggers," southern converts to the Republican Party, the "Scalawags," and elected black politicians.

In economic terms emancipation gave freed slaves the potential opportunity to work for themselves, rather than their old masters, and the hope of becoming independent, self-sufficient farmers. Throughout the South blacks strived to acquire their own smallholdings or, as in the Sea Islands off South Carolina and Georgia, joined land cooperatives run by freedmen.

Socially, freed slaves gained the right to move freely around the country, to select their own marriage partners, and the peace of mind that came from knowing that their children would not grow up to a life of servitude. In the years 1865–1866 ex-slaves participated in a large interregional migration within the southern states. In part this was a psychological assertion of freedom or a return to their old neighborhoods by blacks dislocated from their homes during the Civil War. Often it was a search by freedmen and women for loved ones from whom they had been separated under slavery. Emotional reunions between husbands and wives, parents and children, took place throughout the South, in some cases after 20 or 30 years loss of contact.

Despite the gains, Reconstruction was also a time of disappointment and disillusionment for blacks. Although slavery was abolished, national and state Republican administrations provided little in the way of practical help or material assistance to enable ex-slaves to prosper in their new condition. In Congress land redistribution schemes, involving a grant of 40 acres and a mule to each family of freed slaves, were discussed but never implemented. The 1866 Southern Homestead Act did open up federally owned land for cheap purchase and settlement, but most freed slaves lacked the money and resources to take advantage of such an opportunity.

The most important initiative of the federal government to help blacks in the transition from slavery to freedom was the creation of the Bureau of Abandoned Lands, Refugees and Freedmen in 1865. More commonly known as the Freedmen's Bureau, the agency was headed by the union army general, Oliver Otis Howard. He was a good choice. Genuinely sympathetic to the needs of the freedmen, he went on to found Howard University in Washington, D. C., one of the earliest and most prestigious institutions of higher education for blacks in the United States. Under Howard the Bureau aided blacks in the South with free transportation and provided assistance in meeting their educational needs. Local Bureau agents helped ex-slaves find work, and acted as mediators in disputes with their new employers.

Despite the provision of such services the overall scale of the Bureau's operations was strictly limited. The laissez-faire values of the late nineteenth century ensured that the Bureau provided a minimum in charitable aid, lest this create a culture of dependency. The supply of food, clothing, and shelter was often restricted to cases of extreme need, and even then was not always forthcoming. If the Bureau made available school buildings for black education, teaching staff had to be provided by private charities and philanthropic organizations such as the American Missionary Association (AMA).

Length of tenure, as well as scale of operation, was also a problem. Although the Bureau survived until 1872, most of its operations were wound up by 1869. Throughout its life the continued existence of the agency was subject to annual review and renewal, encouraging a philosophy of short termism.

A factor that was constant was chronic understaffing and insufficient resources. John De Forest, a Bureau agent in South Carolina, was given an area to administer that was two-thirds the size of Connecticut. To maximize economy Bureau agents were neither specially selected nor trained. Instead, as in the case of De Forest, they were typically army officers who were allocated Bureau work in addition to their military duties, and without extra pay. From the onset many agents thus had every reason to feel resentful of the Bureau tasks they were expected to carry out. Often agents held strong racial prejudices and sided with southern whites against the interests of freedmen.[1]

In the absence of economic assistance from federal and state authorities, and lacking capital and resources of their own, most freed slaves were forced to enter into labor contracts with former masters or other planters in their locality. This resulted in the emergence of sharecropping, which spread rapidly to become the dominant form of labor for blacks in the South from the 1870s until the 1930s. Under this system planters provided black families with small plots of land to farm, seed, livestock, food, and other provisions. At harvest time when the crop, invariably cotton, was gathered in the planter claimed a share of the proceeds, supposedly ranging from one-third to one-half, as a return for his investment.

On the surface such agreements represented a natural market compromise between the economic interests of freed blacks and white landowners. Black agricultural laborers aspired to be independent small farmers but lacked the capital to achieve this goal. Planters owned plentiful supplies of land, but lacked the cash resources to employ farm laborers to cultivate it. In theory, the sharecropping system thus partially satisfied the aspirations of both groups.

In practice things usually turned out rather different. Illiterate and economically naïve, ex-slaves were systematically cheated by one-sided contracts. They were obliged to purchase food and provisions on credit from plantation stores run by landowners that provided goods at grossly inflated prices and exorbitant interest rates. At the end of the year this accumulated expenditure meant that sharecroppers frequently owed 100 percent or more of the value of their crops. In subsequent years they were obliged to work without hope of any financial reward in a vain attempt to pay off ever mounting debts.

Often groups of planters in an area came together to form planter associations to ensure that there was no variation in local labor contracts. Black farmers who questioned the fairness of what was on offer, or who sought to escape exploitation by moving from one plantation to another, found it impossible to obtain work. The predominantly rural nature of the South with a lack of any alternative employment in industry only added to the constraints. In consequence debt peonage became endemic among black sharecroppers by the 1880s and the 1890s. Many were reduced to a form of serfdom that was scarcely better than their former slave condition.

The political rights gained by southern blacks during Reconstruction proved to be no more secure than their economic liberties. In states like Virginia and Tennessee, which had mainly white populations, white Democrats easily ousted local Republican administrations. In states like Louisiana, Mississippi, and South Carolina, with natural black voting majorities, more extreme tactics were employed to restore white supremacy. During the so-called "Redemption" campaigns, which began in 1875, wholesale fraud, violence, and intimidation were used to restore Democratic Party rule throughout the South. In 1877 the Republican administration in South Carolina became the last state government to fall, marking the end of the Reconstruction era.

Nationally the Republican Party continued to retain control of the Presidency and both Houses of Congress, but chose not to interfere in events in the South. After 12 years of Reconstruction the mood within the Party, and the nation at large, had changed. There was no longer the same level of concern over the welfare of ex-slaves. Voters were tired of the "annual autumnal insurrections" that accompanied elections in the South, and were unwilling to support the continued use of military force to safeguard black voting rights in the region.

In the late 1870s and in the 1880s the white planter class, or "Bourbon aristocracy" as it was commonly known, consolidated its political control of the South. Continued use of fraud and coercion, combined with gerrymandering, relentlessly reduced the electoral power of black voters. Other gains made by blacks during Reconstruction were also systematically reversed. The provision of separate schools for whites and blacks enabled state administrations to systematically reduce levels of public expenditure on black education while leaving white pupils unaffected. In South Carolina in 1890 the annual expenditure of the state on the education of white children was three times that allocated for blacks of school age.[2]

During the early 1890s the rise of the People's Party briefly threatened the supremacy of the planter class. Generally known as "Populists," supporters of the new party were mainly small farmers in the South and West of the country. They became increasingly frustrated at the depressed state of the rural economy and the failure of the Republican and Democratic parties to support measures to alleviate their growing poverty and distress. Perceiving themselves as the victims of a monied conspiracy of businessmen and financiers who had corrupted the existing party machines, they sought relief in the creation of a third national political party to champion their interests.

In the South many white yeoman farmers broke with their traditional deference to the planter aristocracy that controlled the organization of the Democratic Party in the region. Seeking to build a new alliance, on class rather than racial lines, white Populist leaders like Tom Watson of Georgia openly appealed to African-American voters for their support.

Initially successful, this challenge to the status quo was ultimately unsustainable. Racial enmities proved too deep as poor whites found it impossible to cooperate with black sharecroppers. The entrenched power of the Bourbon aristocracy was also too great. Planters used economic coercion to ensure the political loyalty of white tenant farmers and black sharecroppers by threatening to expel them from their lands and homes.

By 1896 the Populist challenge had collapsed. Nationally what remained of the movement was subsumed into the Democratic Party. Within the South state governments moved to exclude blacks from political life altogether, thus ensuring that any future electoral divisions would not pose a threat to continued white supremacy in the region. New laws were introduced that required applicants for voter registration to pass literacy tests or demonstrate a "good understanding" of selected passages from state constitutions. "Grandfather" clauses limited registration to those applicants whose ancestors had been U. S. or state citizens in 1860.

In the case of *Williams v. Mississippi*, in 1898, the Supreme Court held that such measures were permissible under the U. S. Constitution. The new laws did not violate the equal citizenship rights of blacks under the Fourteenth and Fifteenth Amendments to the Constitution because they supposedly applied to all voters regardless of race. In practice this was not the case. Within a few years of the *Williams* decision the vast majority of blacks in the South were effectively denied all voting rights while white voter participation remained largely unaffected. Black disfranchisement brought about by such means continued largely unchecked until as late as the 1960s.

In 1896, in another far-reaching decision, the United States Supreme Court recognized the constitutionality of legally enforced racial segregation in the case of *Plessy v. Ferguson*. By an 8–1 majority the justices on the court accepted the notion of "separate but equal." Segregated facilities or accommodations for whites and blacks did not infringe black citizenship rights under the Fourteenth and Fifteenth Amendments to the U.S. Constitution because the mere act of separation was deemed not to imply the superiority or inferiority of either race.

Following this ruling racial segregation under the law quickly spread throughout the South and impacted or nearly all aspects of daily life. Seating and accommodation in hotels, theaters, restaurants and diners, railway carriages, public toilets, schools, hospitals, factories, and businesses were all affected. Racial segregation was rigidly enforced in work, in play, and even in death, with mandatory segregated white and black burial plots. In sharp contrast to the Hans Christian Andersen logic of the *Plessy* ruling the facilities available to blacks were almost always grossly inferior.

The *Williams* and *Plessy* decisions marked a worsening in U. S. race relations. During the 1890s white attitudes toward blacks generally became more negative, as was reflected in the popular literature of the day. Earlier literary portrayals of African Americans, such as Harriet Beecher Stowe's *Uncle Tom's Cabin* (1851), and *The Songs and Sayings of Uncle Remus* (1880), compiled by the southern white journalist Joel Chandler Harris, had been marred by crude racial stereotyping. At the same time the black characters in these works, if comical and intellectually inferior to whites, were also affable and benign in disposition. By the turn of the century more sinister imagery began to dominate, most notably in the writings of the popular novelist Thomas Dixon. In books such as *The Leopard's Spots* (1902) and *The Clansman* (1905) blacks were represented as bestial in nature, ruled by instinct rather than reason. Black men were menacing brutes whose insatiable sexual lust posed a constant threat to the purity of white womanhood.

Dixon's lurid imaginings typified the myth of the black rapist that became common in southern white society around the turn of the century. One consequence of this was the growth of lynching. The unlawful killing of a suspected criminal or wrongdoer by vigilantes, lynching in the Reconstruction era had been a national problem that claimed both black and white victims. By the late 1880s it was a mainly southern phenomenon with the large majority of lynch victims being black. Between 1889 and 1893, 839 people were lynched in the United States; 705 of these incidents were in the South and 579 of all lynch victims were black. From 1894 to 1898, 680 of the 774 lynchings in the nation took place in the South and 544 of those killed were blacks.[3]

In the first two decades of the twentieth century the numbers of lynchings noticeably began to decline. Nonetheless, as late as 1919–1923 a black American was still lynched on average every week in the southern states. Moreover, if the numbers of lynchings fell the manner of the killings frequently became more horrific. Early lynch victims were commonly put to death by hanging, sometimes openly, sometimes clandestinely. Later victims were increasingly denied such a comparatively quick end. They were routinely tortured in the most appalling, sadistic fashion for hours on end before dying. Castration, maiming, and burning alive, often one limb at a time to maximize the suffering, became a common practice. Lynchings, or burnings as they might be more accurately described, also became more public. Large crowds often gathered to watch the ghastly spectacle and encourage those responsible in their work. All ages and all classes in southern white communities appeared to regard the occasion as some kind of macabre public festivity. Adults dressed in their Sunday best, courting couples, and even children attended such events. When the day's events were over the remains of the victim, toes, fingers, and other bodily parts, were routinely cut off as souvenirs of what had taken place. [4]

The most frequent justification for such protracted and unnatural cruelty was that the deceased had been guilty of rape or attempted sexual assault against a white woman. Local whites had become so enraged by the unspeakable nature of the violation that they were unable to restrain themselves from seeking immediate retribution against the alleged offender. Ironically, the apologists for lynchings thus attributed to white lynch mobs the same susceptibility to savage animal behavior that, in other contexts, was seen as a racial weakness exclusively confined to African Americans. An alternative justification was that the accused rapist was put to death in order to spare the victim of his assault from having to relive her experience in court before a judge and jury. The fact that the individual lynched was often later exonerated from rape or any other crime was an unfortunate side issue.

In contrast to the thin public apologies, the real motivations for lynchings were many and complicated. Despite the rape mythology many of those lynched were never even accused of sexual assault. Often victims were put to death for minor transgressions of racial etiquette rather than any unlawful act. The extreme punishment meted out for such misdeamors served a variety of purposes. The rigid unwritten racial codes of the South were publicly and dramatically reaffirmed. White solidarity was reinforced, and the large crowds that attended a lynching or burning demonstrated the complicity and approval of the local white community in what was done. It was thus unheard of for lynch mobs or their ringleaders to ever be brought to trial for the crimes they committed.

For blacks in the region the regular reporting of lynching across the South instilled a sense of terror and anxiety, and served as a constant reminder of their inferior position in society. Every new account of a lynching demonstrated the inability of the law to protect African Americans in their daily lives, even from the most appalling violations of their rights.

Extreme conditions require exceptional leadership. The two most important black American spokespersons in the late nineteenth century were Frederick Douglass and Booker T. Washington. Each rose to prominence from humble beginnings.

Born a slave in Maryland in 1817 or 1818, Douglass escaped to freedom in 1838. During the 1840 and the 1850s he became a leading figure within the abolitionist movement, befriending the radical abolitionist William Lloyd

Garrison. In 1845 the publication of his memories of slave life, *The Narrative of the Life of an American Slave*, turned Douglass into a nationally and internationally known celebrity. This was confirmed by his prolonged tour of Britain and Ireland from 1845 to 1847 to further the abolitionist cause.

On his return to the United States Douglass launched two abolitionist journals of his own, *The North Star*, 1847–1851, and *Frederick Douglass's Paper*, 1851–1860. During the 1850s Douglass became a convert to the newly created Republican Party because of its outspoken opposition to slavery. In the Civil War, 1861–1865, he vigorously campaigned for an end to slavery, or the "Peculiar Institution" as it was commonly called, and supported the creation of black regiments to fight for the preservation of the Union. A new journalistic undertaking saw the publication of *Douglass's Monthly* from 1860 to 1863. In these years Douglass also enjoyed the trust and respect of Republican President Abraham Lincoln, to whom he acted as an unofficial advisor on racial issues.

In some respects the defeat of the South, and the abolition of slavery in 1865, marked the culmination of Douglass's life work, despite the fact that he was still only 47 years old. During the Reconstruction period Douglass continued to be a loyal supporter of the Republican Party and was the proprietor of yet another journal, *The New National Era*, from 1870 to 1873. In 1874 he unwisely accepted the position of President of the Freedmen's Bank, a commercial venture publicly endorsed by the national Republican administration of President Ulysses S. Grant, to attract the savings of former slaves. Within a few months of Douglass taking office the Bank collapsed as a result of fraud and incompetence, taking with it the savings of most of its black investors. Although personally blameless of any impropriety, Douglass was greatly embarrassed by the affair.

Following the end of Reconstruction, in 1877, Douglass held minor political office, firstly as U.S. Marshall for the District of Columbia, 1877–1881, and later as Recorder of Deeds for the District of Columbia, 1881–1886. His last official posting came in the Diplomatic Service as Change D'Affaires in Haiti between 1889 and 1891. Despite his advancing age, and the worsening racial conditions within the United States during these years, Douglass continued to be an outspoken defender of black civil and political rights down to his death on 20 February 1895.

Booker T. Washington filled the leadership vacuum left by the death of Douglass. Born a slave in 1856 in Virginia, Washington was the last great black American leader to have had direct experience of slavery. From 1872 to 1875 Washington was educated at the newly founded Hampton Institute run by Samuel Armstrong in Virginia. Armstrong became a surrogate father figure for Washington and had a major impact on his thinking. His race and inexperience notwithstanding, Washington was appointed Principal of his own college, Tuskegee Institute in Alabama, in 1881 with

Armstrong's enthusiastic support. Starting with virtually no teaching resources, and only a few dilapidated outbuildings, Washington transformed Tuskegee into the best known black educational institution in the South. By 1915 the institute had expanded to the point where it worked on an annual operational budget of $100,000.[5]

Washington and his mentor Armstrong were both converts to the philosophy of industrial education. Fashionable in the late nineteenth century and early twentieth century, this emphasized the importance of teaching practical and vocational skills to black children and poor whites. The study of subjects like carpentry and rural science was advocated for boys, with domestic science and needlework for girls, rather than more academic disciplines like literature and the arts.

The idea of industrial education became popular in educational circles for a variety of reasons. It fitted in with the business values that strongly influenced American social thought at the turn of the century. In respect to black Americans it was seen as a necessary corrective to the kind of education that had been given to ex-slaves and their children after the Civil War. In the 1860s and the 1870s northern missionary teachers in the South had sometimes paid too much attention to religious instruction and the teaching of subjects like Latin and algebra rather than meeting the more obvious needs of illiterate ex-slaves.

Less positively, industrial schooling reflected the cultural and racial prejudices of late nineteenth-century America. The children of the poor would not be educated above their station in life or be given unrealistic social expectations. Similarly, African-American pupils would not be educated beyond what was perceived to be the limited capacity for learning of nonwhite races in respect to the higher curriculum of life. Instead they would be prepared for a life as agricultural laborers or domestic servants. Such implicit social subordination meant that some, though not all, southern whites who had previously opposed any education for blacks were prepared to support industrial schooling. This was particularly true of the planter class. Comprised of former slaveholders and their descendents, members of this group retained some paternalistic feelings toward the families of their ex-slaves, provided the latter did not seek to transgress the social and racial codes of the South.

During the 1880s and the early 1890s Washington quietly consolidated and expanded the educational facilities at Tuskegee Institute. He succeeded in winning the approval of local whites by his polite, deferential manner, abstemious, puritan life-style, and strict public noninvolvement in any issue of political controversy. The same strict constraints on personal conduct were also expected of all staff and students at the institute.

In 1895 Washington gained national status and recognition following his Atlanta Compromise speech at an international cotton exposition in

Georgia. Conservative and pragmatic by nature, Washington acknowledged the deteriorating state of race relations in the United States. In a much-publicized oration he appeared to accept the inevitability of segregation, arguing that the white and black races could be as "separate as the fingers" in "all things that are purely social," but "one as the hand in all things essential to mutual progress." He called on black Americans to strive for education and economic advancement rather than agitate for civil and political rights. The address led to Washington receiving widespread praise from northern and southern whites, and established him as the leading black spokesperson in the United States, a status he retained until his death in November 1915.

In 1901 Washington's autobiography, *Up From Slavery*, became an instant success, both in the United States and Europe, securing him international acclaim as an educator and race leader. At the height of his powers, he became an unofficial advisor on race relations to the Republican Presidents Theodore Roosevelt, 1901–1909, and William Taft, 1909–1913.

Despite, and perhaps in part because of, his rapid rise to fame Washington did not achieve universal support. Extremist southern white politicians such as James Vardaman and Theodore Bilbo, both of Mississippi, remained hostile to, and suspicious of, any program for black racial uplift, however conservative. Within the African-American community more radical black spokespersons denounced Washington for being too accommodationist and subservient to white opinion. The most vociferous criticism came from well-educated blacks in the North. William Monroe Trotter and George Washington Forbes regularly attacked Booker T. Washington, often in personally offensive terms, in the columns of their newspaper, the Boston *Guardian*. In 1903 Trotter, and a small group of his supporters disrupted a speech given by the Tuskegeean in the city. Dubbed the "Boston Riot" by the press, the incident was one of the first notable signs of public black opposition to Washington.

Trotter's voluble and provocative behavior notwithstanding, the most influential and persuasive of Washington's black critics was the multitalented academic, W.E.B. Du Bois. Born in Great Barrington, Massachusetts in 1868, Du Bois's early life was very different from that of the Tuskegeean. He came from the first generation of blacks born after the abolition of slavery. Although not able to escape prejudice altogether, Du Bois's childhood was free from the intense racism that prevailed in the South. A gifted pupil at school, Du Bois went on to study at the all black Fisk University in Tennessee in 1885, and then at Harvard in 1888, gaining a Ph.D. in 1895 for a thesis on the suppression of the international slave trade from Africa to the United States. From 1897 to 1910 he was employed as Professor of Sociology and History at the black Atlanta University in Georgia.

Initially supportive of Booker T. Washington, over time Du Bois came to have increasing misgivings about the Tuskegee philosophy. These doubts first attracted public attention in an influential essay, "Of Mr Booker T. Washington and Others" published in Du Bois's book *The Souls of Black Folk* in 1903. In a critical, but balanced, appraisal of Washington's program Du Bois argued that overemphasis on industrial education led to the neglect of higher learning. This weakness, combined with inaction in respect to civil and political rights, meant that Washington was in effect condemning blacks to political, social, and economic subordination.

In January 1904 an attempt by Du Bois to reconcile Washington with his critics at a private conference at Carnegie Hall in New York ended in failure when the Tuskegeean conspired to pack the meeting with his own supporters. Following this incident the rift between the two men widened. In 1905 Du Bois launched the Niagara Movement, a small, all black, organization comprised mainly of intellectuals who were opposed to the Tuskegee philosophy.

The group met with little success. In part this was because of internal disagreements between Du Bois and Trotter. The Movement also suffered from the exclusion of whites and its elitism, reflecting Du Bois's belief in the need for an autonomous racial leadership provided by the "talented tenth," a select cadre of educated and professional blacks.

Washington also did his best to sabotage the efforts of the new body. Black newspapers owned or controlled by him published negative reports of the Niagara Movement or ignored it altogether. Washington employed spies to infiltrate and report on the organization. He used the Tuskegee Machine, a network of influential black and white contacts in the North and South, to discourage recruitment to Niagara and deter potential financial donations. In 1909 the Movement collapsed having achieved little, if anything, of note.

Despite early setbacks, northern black opposition to Washington steadily increased. In the same year that Niagara folded Du Bois became a founding member of the new biracial civil rights organization the National Association for the Advancement of Colored People (NAACP). Du Bois was chosen to be editor of the NAACP journal, *Crisis*, a position he held until 1934. With the exception of Du Bois the early leadership of the NAACP was almost exclusively white. This included liberal and progressive reformers such as Mary White Ovington, William Walling, and Moorfield Storey. Several of the founder members came from an abolitionist family background, most notably the New York City newspaper proprietor Oswald Garrison Villard, who was a grandson of William Lloyd Garrison.

During the last years of his life Washington's leadership was increasingly challenged by the NAACP. Although he did his best to stop the growth of the new organization it steadily expanded between 1909 and 1915. The negative tactics of the Tuskegee Machine were less effective against the white leaders of the NAACP who were generally affluent and enjoyed considerable status in their own right. There was also a sense that the time for change was overdue. African-American communities, particularly in the North, lost patience with Washington's conservative style of leadership.

Perhaps sensing this new mood, or possibly in an attempt to head off the threat posed to his position by the NAACP, Washington himself became less accommodationist. He attacked the excesses of imperialism abroad and became more outspoken in his criticism of segregation at home. This new-found assertiveness may also have stemmed from personal experience. In the Ulrich affair of 1911 Washington was attacked and badly beaten in New York for supposedly peeping through a window at a white woman in one of the less salubrious districts of the city. Unexplained circumstances surrounded the incident, most notably the reason for Washington's presence in such an undesirable neighborhood. Nonetheless his assailant, Ulrich, was known to be of doubtful character and an individual whose testimony lacked credibility. The Tuskegeean protested his innocence and undertook legal proceedings against his tormentor. Despite Washington's impeccable reputation, built up over many years, Ulrich was acquitted. The impact of the whole ordeal on the Tuskegeean is difficult to assess. However, it may have made him feel less optimistic about the state of U. S. race relations, and more inclined to speak out publicly against racial injustice.

The year 1915 was a significant one for black Americans. In November the death of Booker T. Washington marked an end to the conservative style of racial leadership associated with him. The Tuskegee Machine went into a rapid decline. Robert Russa Moton, who succeeded Washington as Principal of Tuskegee Institute, was an able educator but had no ambitions to emulate the role of his predecessor as a national spokesperson. At the Amenia conference of 1916 leading supporters of Washington were reconciled with the NAACP, ending a mutually damaging seven-year rift.

World War I, 1914–1918, had important consequences for the U.S. economy and society in general, and black Americans in particular. Between 1880 and 1914 the United States experienced major changes. Rapid industrialization and urban growth transformed the economy, especially in the North. The population of New York City grew from 1.2 million in 1880 to 5.6 million by 1920. In the same period Chicago saw its population rise from just over 500,000 to 2.7 million. The population of Detroit rose from 116,340 to just under one million, and that of Pittsburgh from 235,071 to 588,343. Individual cities developed strong associations with particular industries. Chicago, in addition to being a gateway to the West, became a center for meatpacking, Detroit became the unofficial capital of the car industry, and Pittsburgh became established as a center for steel production.[6]

At first black Americans were comparatively unaffected by these changes. At the start of the twentieth century around 90 percent of African Americans still resided in the South. Although some southern cities, such as Richmond, Virginia, Atlanta, Georgia, and Birmingham, Alabama, experienced significant growth between 1880 and 1920, the region as a whole remained mostly rural. Cotton production and the sharecropping system continued to be the mainstay of the southern economy.

Initially industrial expansion in the North offered little in the way of alternative opportunities for southern blacks. Most of the new jobs created were taken by immigrants from southern and eastern European countries, such as Russia, Poland, Italy, and Greece. Between 1880 and 1919 over 23.5 million immigrants arrived in the United States. The influx peaked in the early years of the twentieth century, with more than eight million immigrants arriving between 1901 and 1909, and over 2.4 million in 1913–1914 alone. Although the newcomers suffered from mounting cultural bigotry and ethnic prejudice at the hands of native white Americans, industrial employers still hired them in preference to black Americans. The emerging U.S. labor movement, with blacks regularly being excluded from trade union membership, reinforced this discrimination. Often the only good employment opportunities for African Americans came as a temporary strike breaking labor force during a period of industrial conflict.[7]

Barriers to black migration within the South reinforced poor job prospects in the North. "Antienticement" laws passed in some southern states prevented northern labor agents from recruiting among black workers in the region. Blacks themselves were generally reluctant to leave loved ones and familiar home surroundings in favor of the uncertainties of city life in the North.

The outbreak of war in Europe in 1914 was the catalyst that finally prompted a major exodus of blacks from the South to the North. Increased wartime demand provided an added stimulus to the already booming industrial northern economy. At the same time immigration to the United States was effectively curtailed as European governments conscripted their populations into the armed forces and erected legal barriers to stop emigration being a way to escape military service. Often immigrants already in the United States chose to return to their former homeland out of a sense of patriotic duty.

In an attempt to fill the labor shortages created by these developments, northern industrialists began to hire significant numbers of black workers for the first time. "Antienticement" laws notwithstanding, northern employers actively recruited southern blacks into their labor force with promises of high wages, accommodation, and cheap rail fares.

For a variety of reasons blacks themselves were also more attracted by job opportunities in the North. The war years coincided with a period of hardship and uncertainty in southern agriculture as cotton crops were ravaged by a new insect pest, the boll weevil. First arriving in Texas from Mexico, in 1892, the weevil steadily moved eastward, reaching Georgia and North and South Carolina in the early 1920s. In any one year up to half of all cotton crops in the states affected could be destroyed by the new pest. Between 1892 and 1918 total weevil damage was estimated at $250 million, or a loss of around 4.5 million bales of cotton. Black share-croppers, who enjoyed little prosperity even at the best of times, inevitably suffered most.[8]

Social conditions in the South reinforced the economic incentives of African Americans to leave the region. Segregation, lynchings, and daily racial oppression offered little encouragement to stay. This was particularly true for younger generations of blacks who, without first hand memories of slavery, were less willing to tolerate the injustices endured by their parents and grandparents.

All factors combined resulted in 1.25 million blacks leaving the South for the North in the Great Migration of 1915 to 1925. The majority of migrants relocated to a small number of large cities. From 1910 to 1930 the black population of Chicago rose from 44,103 to 233,903, and that of New York from 91,709 to 327,706. Cleveland, Detroit, Indianapolis, Philadelphia, and Pittsburgh also experienced large increases in the size of their black communities.[9]

Once underway, the migration developed a self-sustaining momentum. Migrants wrote letters home to friends and relatives praising the comparatively relaxed pattern of race relations in the North and the high rates of pay on offer. Typically, northern factory workers could earn between $2.25 and $3.25 a day as opposed to just 75 cents a day for farm laborers in the South. Early migrants provided latercomers with a friendly face and a first place of accommodation on their arrival in a city.[10]

Black newspapers, most notably the Chicago *Defender*, run by Tuskegee graduate Robert Abbott, reinforced the positive message. The *Defender* listed employment opportunities in the North and expressed outrage at the injustices suffered by blacks in the South. Such was the paper's perceived impact that some southern states outlawed its sale and distribution.

Ironically, one consequence of the Great Migration was a deterioration of race relations in the North. Before World War I few northern cities had a sizable black population. Small in number, urban blacks were also disproportionately middle class and in professional occupations. For these reasons there was a general absence of the rigidly enforced racial segregation that existed in the South.

The influx of black migrants during the war years changed this situation. African-American communities became large enough to attract white attention and concern. The arrival of black families in previously all white neighborhoods triggered hostility and resentment among existing residents. Violence, intimidation, and the refusal of white landlords to lease property to black tenants led to African Americans being forced to live in overcrowded and unsanitary all black ghettos, such as Harlem in New York and the South Side in Chicago. Often families were forced to live in cramped and badly maintained single room "kitchenette" apartments.

In a wider context, segregation became an established, widespread feature of northern city life for the first time. The end of World War I, in November 1918, added to racial tensions as demobilized white and black soldiers returned home and found themselves in competition for jobs, both with each other and recent black migrants. The consequences were predictable. During the "Red Summer" of 1919 there were more than 25 race riots in cities across the United States. The worst of these was in Chicago during July when at least 15 whites and 23 blacks were killed, 537 people injured, and over 1,000 black families left with nowhere to live when their homes were burnt by white mobs.[11]

The impact of the Great Migration on black cultural life was more positive, though no less profound. The ghettos of the North attracted a talented young generation of black artists and intellectuals in a cultural flowering that became known as the Harlem Renaissance. Black authors and poets such as Langston Hughes, Claude McKay, and Jean Toomer saw their works lionized in fashionable white middle-class artistic circles. This was despite the fact that their writings were often sharply critical of U.S. race relations.

In popular music black cabaret artists and musical reviews regularly achieved both critical and commercial success on Broadway. The Cotton Club in Harlem became a center of New York nightlife with its all black dancers and musicians, including Jazz legends like Duke Ellington, Dizzy Gillespie, and Cab Calloway.

Despite the musical innovations of the Jazz age, in a wider context the United States entered a period of social and cultural conservatism in the 1920s. Violent labor conflicts within the United States and the 1917 Bolshevik Revolution in Russia led to fears of left wing political extremism. The end of the war revived earlier anxieties and prejudices of white Americans over the prospect of renewed mass immigration. Nativist sentiments culminated in the 1924 National Origins Act. This limited immigration to the United States to just 165,000 people a year, a quota that was moreover largely restricted to immigrants from northern and western Europe.[12]

Strict immigration controls helped to ensure continued job opportunities for black migrants, but the overall impact of the "New Era" of conservatism in the 1920s was negative for African Americans. Perhaps most depressing of all was a major revival of the Ku Klux Klan. First formed in Pulaski, Tennessee, in 1866, the original Klan had numbered around 500,000 members at its peak and had terrorized blacks and Republican voters across the South in the late 1860s and early 1870s. Ultimately suppressed by the federal authorities, the order was effectively extinct by 1872.[13]

In 1915 a defrocked Methodist minister, William Joseph Simmons, resurrected the Klan in Atlanta, Georgia. The revival was sparked off by the murder of a local white girl Mary Phagan and by the glamorous portrayal of the Reconstruction Klan in D.W. Griffiths's film *Birth of a Nation* that was released the same year.

Over the next 10 years the Klan experienced unprecedented growth. Its membership rose to 100,000 by 1921, and over four million by 1924, the height of its popularity. There were several reasons for this success. "Kleagles," full-time recruitment agents working for commission, aggressively sold Klan membership on a door-to-door basis. The Klan appealed to a range of common prejudices of the day. Although still an antiblack organization, it was also xenophobic, antisemitic, anti-Catholic, antitrade union, and anticommunist. Individual Klan branches, or "Klaverns" as they were called, tailored their bigotries to reflect the anxieties of their own locality. Partly for this reason, the Klan revival was not just confined to the organization's traditional southern heartland. The order also enjoyed popularity in cities like Chicago, by attuning itself to northern concerns over immigration and black migration.[14]

In such a climate it continued to be difficult for individuals and organizations to provide effective civil rights leadership. Looking to meet the needs of urban black migrants a new body, the National Urban League (NUL), was created in 1911. Founded out of two earlier groups, the National League for the Protection of Colored Women and the Committee for Improving the Industrial Conditions of Negroes in New York, the League was dominated by affluent white liberals. The nature of its leadership, and its focus on practical self-help issues, meant that the League was an essentially conservative organization.

More vigorous campaigning in defense of black civil and political rights was left to the NAACP, which pursued its goals through a legalistic strategy, challenging racial discrimination and segregation in the courts, and lobbying for federal antilynching legislation. In the 1910s and 1920s these efforts brought only modest success. In the case of *Buchanan v. Warley*, in 1917, the United States Supreme Court held that city ordinances enforcing residential segregation were unconstitutional, but the manner of the victory was less than complete. The ruling of the judges stemmed less from concerns over racial fairness than from the belief that such measures violated the property rights of homeowners. Worse was to follow. The major NAACP initiative during the 1920s, an attempt to secure the passage of a federal antilynching law, the Dyer bill, ended in failure.

Despite setbacks the NAACP did start to develop genuine grass roots black support, with over 300 branches or chapters, and some 9,000 members by the 1920s. In a symbolic breakthrough, James Weldon Johnson, a former supporter of Booker T. Washington, served as the first black Executive Secretary of the NAACP between 1920 and 1930. However, the organization still lacked a genuine mass membership in this period and it was unable to completely fill the void in race leadership created by the death of Booker T. Washington.[15]

In the event, the unlikely successor to Washington as the dominant race leader of the day was a West Indian newcomer to the United States, Marcus Garvey. Born in 1887, Garvey spent his early life in Jamaica. His father, a small farmer, was descended from the Maroons, a mountain community of runaway slaves who had proudly defended their hard won freedom. In 1901, aged 14, the younger Garvey left school to take up an apprenticeship in the printing industry, but was sacked following his involvement in an abortive strike in 1907.

Without settled employment, Garvey embarked on extensive foreign travel between 1910 and 1914, visiting Central and South America and Europe, settling in London. During this period he became familiar with Booker T. Washington's autobiography, *Up From Slavery* (1901), a work that strongly influenced him. Returning to Jamaica in 1914, he sought to develop a program of industrial education on the island and created his own organization, the Universal Negro Improvement Association (UNIA) for this end. Looking to Tuskegee as a role model, Garvey entered into a periodic correspondence with Washington, seeking his support and financial help. In 1916, still short of funds, Garvey visited the United States in what was originally intended as a lecture tour to raise money. Addressing audiences across the United States, Garvey displayed considerable ability as an orator and soon became well known in many black American communities. In 1917 he decided to settle in the United States and established a branch of the UNIA in New York City that attracted around 1,000 members by the end of the year.[16]

A skilful self-publicist, in 1918 Garvey launched his weekly newspaper, the *Negro World*, in the United States. The paper soon gained a wide circulation, first among black Americans, and later overseas in Central and Southern America and Africa.

Garvey built on these early achievements with a succession of new ideas and ventures that helped to maintain the growing momentum of the UNIA movement. In 1919 he began a series of economic initiatives with the creation of the Negro Factories Corporation (NFC), which established a chain of black shops and businesses. Reflecting the growing scope of

Garvey's ambition, the Black Star Line (BSL), formed in the same year, marked the creation of an intended international black steamship line. Initially, three ships were purchased, the *SS Yarmouth*, the *SS Kanawha* and the *Shadyside*, from a $750,000 fund raised by the sale of share certificates to small black investors. Started as a business venture, Garvey ultimately hoped that the BSL would help fulfill his wider vision of uniting black peoples across the world in international commerce.[17]

Garvey's economic self-help initiatives were another indication of his affinity with the ideas of Booker T. Washington. At the same time, by the early 1920s Garvey had become an independent thinker in his own right, and increasingly distanced himself from the Tuskegee philosophy in many key respects. Most notably, he rejected the possibility of successful long-term integration of blacks into U.S. culture and society. Instead he became a black nationalist, advocating racial separation and the founding of an independent black state in Africa.

In August 1920 delegates from over 25 countries attended the first UNIA International Convention of the Negro Peoples of the World, held in Harlem, New York. The Convention elected Garvey as Provisional President of his envisaged new African Republic, and adopted its own red, green, and white flag together with a national anthem "Ethiopia, Thou Land of Our Fathers." Garvey also went on to create his own black nobility, the Knights of the Nile, and began to set up a national organizational infrastructure in waiting with the formation of groups like the African Legion, the Garvey Militia, the Black Eagle Flying Corps, and the Universal African Motor Corps.

By 1923 UNIA membership had reached over one million in the United States alone, with a further 120,000 members in Central and South America, and 30,000 members in Africa. The unprecedented success of the Garvey movement can be explained by a variety of factors. Garvey himself was a forceful orator and skilful propagandist. His various initiatives combined appeals to black racial pride with practical and material self-help. UNIA Liberty Halls in northern cities served as local community centers and provided free temporary accommodation and food for urban newcomers, as well as spreading Garvey's nationalist message. UNIA members could hope for employment in NFC businesses, while purchasers of BSL shares could look for financial dividends as well as demonstrating their racial solidarity.[18]

In northern cities the creation of large semiautonomous black communities, as a result of the Great Migration, made natural recruiting areas for the UNIA. The formation of all black ghetto neighborhoods made racial separatism appear a realistic possibility. The rise of organizations like the Ku Klux Klan, and the racial conservatism of the 1920s made it seem a desirable one. In New York City, the effective headquarters of the

Garvey movement, the Jamaican Garvey benefited from the presence of a sizable West Indian population. Between 1900 and 1930 almost 40,000 West Indians of African descent settled in Harlem.[19]

In a worldwide context, Garvey's calls for an end to colonialism were attractive to many young blacks in Africa and the Third World. The mutual fratricidal destruction of the leading colonial powers in Europe during World War I also created hopes that the age of imperialism might be approaching an end.

Within the United States relations between already established African-American spokespersons and civil rights groups with the Garvey movement were difficult and generally poor. Some individuals, such as Timothy Thomas Fortune, William Pickens of the NAACP, and the social-ist and labor leader Asa Philip Randolph, were initially prepared to afford Garvey cautious approval. This backing effectively came to an end in 1922 when Garvey met with leaders of the Ku Klux Klan in a self-styled racial summit. Garvey himself justified the event as a meeting of equals between proud black men and race-conscious whites. Most black American leaders were left unconvinced. NAACP officials and prominent African-American spokespersons criticized Garvey.

Other race leaders also distrusted Garvey on other grounds. His "Back to Africa" scheme was seen as fanciful and impractical. There were doubts about the financial soundness of his economic ventures, most notably the Black Star Line. Jealousy of Garvey's success, and xenophobic distrust of his West Indian origins, were other, less principled, sources of opposition. Garvey was frequently subjected to highly personalized criti-cism in black journals and newspapers. Between 1920 and 1923 W. E. B. Du Bois embarked on a sustained campaign against Garvey in the NAACP journal *Crisis*. Pickens and Randolph joined with other black spokesper-sons in urging the United States government to investigate the finances of the Black Star Line. In 1923 a "Garvey Must Go" campaign called for his prosecution for fraud and deportation from the United States.

The impact of this sustained criticism is difficult to gauge. Although obviously damaging in some ways, in part such attacks rebounded to Garvey's advantage, affording him publicity and giving him the appear-ance of a persecuted martyr. The fact that many of Garvey's critics seemed to be academic, middle class, and elitist helped to reinforce this impression.

More damaging was the possibility that in his attempts to silence his detractors, Garvey was encouraged to pursue ever more ambitious and grandiose projects that realistically had little prospect of any immediate success. By 1922 the Black Star Line was in a state of financial ruin with almost no realizable assets, following a series of poor investments and dis-astrous commercial undertakings. Worse was to follow. In 1925 Garvey him-self was convicted of fraud for continuing to advertise shares in the line.

Jailed for two years, he was released in 1927 and deported. Settling first in Jamaica, and then in England, Garvey never succeeded in fulfilling his vision of an independent black African republic. He died in London in 1940, a largely forgotten figure. In the United States, the UNIA was unable to survive Garvey's departure, and went into a sharp decline.

In a parallel development, the national membership of the Ku Klux Klan suffered a similar collapse from 1925 onward. Changing public perceptions of the Klan, following shocking revelations about corruption and criminality in the organization, led to Klan membership falling to just 45,000 by 1930. The fall of both the Klan and the UNIA was as sudden, and unexpected, as their meteoric rise.[20]

CHAPTER 2

The Lion and the Lamb

Frederick Douglass and
Booker T. Washington

The year 1895 was a significant one for African Americans. It saw both the death of Frederick Douglass and the emergence of Booker T. Washington as a national race leader. Douglass was the best known, and most influential, black spokesperson in the United States during the 50-year period 1845 to 1895. Washington was the dominant race leader for the 20 years that followed, between 1895 and 1915. It was, perhaps, inevitable that contemporaries, as well as later historians, should compare and contrast the lives and careers of the two men.

For critics of Washington, Douglass has provided an alternative, more radical, more appealing, role model for black leadership. The black intellectual, Kelly Miller, who knew both men personally, was able to empathize with the philosophy of each. In a thoughtful 1908 essay, "Radicals and Conservatives," he considered their respective attributes. "Douglass was like a lion, bold and fearless," he observed, whereas "Washington is lamblike, meek and submissive." Continuing his analysis, in terms clearly unfavorable to the Tuskegeean, he summed up the respective characteristics of the two leaders:

> Douglass escaped from personal bondage, which his soul abhorred; but for Lincoln's Proclamation, Washington would probably have arisen to esteem and favor in the eyes of his Master as a good and faithful servant. Douglass insisted upon rights; Washington insists upon Duty. Douglass held up to public scorn the sins of the white man; Washington portrays the faults of his own race. Douglass spoke what he thought the world should hear; Washington speaks only what he feels it is disposed to listen to. Douglass's conduct was actuated by principle; Washington's by prudence.[1]

Friends and supporters of Washington, like the black New York journalist Timothy Thomas Fortune, also compared the Tuskegee educator with Douglass, but instead sought to stress the ideas the two men held in common, with the implication that Washington was the natural heir to the Sage of Anacostia as a race leader. In a speech at Houston, Texas, the Tuskegeean's Personal Secretary, Emmett J. Scott, thus informed his audience that "long before" he had met Washington "I had hailed him as the successor of the mighty Douglass."[2]

Such statements, coming from Washington's close and trusted associates, suggest that the Tuskegeean himself favored his leadership being compared with that of Douglass. A reading of Washington's own writings reinforces this view. A common ploy of the Tuskegee educator was to honor the memory of Douglass as a way of indirectly praising his own achievements. In his autobiographical *My Larger Education* (1911) Washington thus recalled "the wonderful life and achievements" of Frederick Douglass, and how as a boy "I had wished to go to school and learn to read" so "that I might read for myself what he had written and said."

In similar vein he recalled how, in 1888 or 1889, he first heard Douglass deliver a speech, which left Washington "profoundly impressed, both by the man and the address," though "I did not dare approach even to shake hands with him." The literary groundwork completed, Washington proceeded to inform his readers how, in 1892, Douglass had visited Tuskegee Institute to deliver a commencement address. Superficially venerating the oratorical abilities of Douglass, a no less obvious point of the two anecdotes was to highlight the considerable rise in status of Washington himself in the intervening period. From being an unknown, star-struck member of the audience, "a mere three or four years later" his achievements at Tuskegee were such that even the mighty Douglass was prepared to accept an invitation to be a guest speaker at the institute.

A little further on in the text Washington ingenuously reminded his readers that "Frederick Douglass died in February 1895," while "In September of the same year I delivered an address in Atlanta at the Cotton States Exposition." The implication was clear, that the Tuskegeean himself had now supplanted the departed Douglass as a race leader.

Lest any reader fail to draw the obvious conclusion, Washington continued by noting how, in the wake of the Atlanta speech, he was surprised at "the number of letters, telegrams, and newspaper editorials that came pouring in upon me from all parts of the country demanding that I take the place of 'leader of the Negro people' left vacant by Frederick Douglass's death, or assuming that I had already taken this place."

In a tactful display of humility the Tuskegeean emphasized his point by making it clear that "until these suggestions began to pour in upon me, I never had the remotest idea that I should be selected or looked upon, in any such sense as Frederick Douglass had been, as a leader of the Negro people." Indeed, as a mere "Negro school teacher in a rather obscure industrial school" he was "not a little embarrassed" when he "first began to appear in public," and was continually referred to as "the successor of Frederick Douglass." After this display of self-effacement any reader who had not previously thought of the humble Washington as a race leader of comparable stature to Douglass could, by now, hardly fail to make such a connection.[3]

In addition to honoring Douglass as an indirect way of commending himself, as the only black leader of his generation of comparable stature, Washington also sought to find in Douglass's actions and experiences tacit approval of his own policies.[4]

In *Up From Slavery* (1901) he thus recalled "a conversation which I once had with the Hon. Frederick Douglass." The latter spoke of an experience while traveling in the state of Pennsylvania when he was forced, on account of his color, to ride in the baggage car of a train, despite having paid the same fare as other passengers. Rather than seek a confrontation with the railway authorities Douglass opted for dignified resignation, reflecting that "the soul that is within me no man can degrade, I am not the one that is being degraded on account of this treatment, but those who are inflicting it upon me."[5]

If the great Douglass chose to act in such a manner then this clearly implied justification for Washington's own "separate but equal" strategy of avoiding any direct public confrontation over racial segregation. Moreover, the manner by which Washington knew of the incident, as a traveling companion in personal conversation with Douglass, provided further proof of his closeness to the Sage of Anacostia.

In a later passage in *Up From Slavery* Washington recalled how, when crossing the Atlantic in 1899, "I found a life of Frederick Douglass, which I began reading." The implicit suggestion that Washington himself was a national and international race leader of comparable stature to Douglass was thus again placed in the mind of the reader.

The inference was reinforced by Washington's observation that in his travels throughout England he met "those who had known and honoured the late William Lloyd Garrison, the Hon. Frederick Douglass, and other abolitionists." In respect to the sea voyage, he contrasted his own comfortable passage with the transatlantic crossing of the *S.S. Cambria* in 1847, on which Douglass had been confined to steerage accommodation. The contrast, Washington concluded, provided clear evidence that race relations in America were improving and, by unspoken implication, justified his policy of patient conservatism.[6]

Autobiographical reminiscences were only one of a variety of ways in which Washington sought to link himself with the work and achievements of the Sage of Anacostia. In 1906 he was credited as the author of a biography, *Frederick Douglass*. In fact the account, like many works purportedly written by the Tuskegeean, was ghost written. The "ghost" in this instance was Samuel Laing Williams, a black lawyer from Chicago born in 1859. Williams was a good choice for the task. He had not only known Douglass personally, but was also a close ally of Washington who could be relied on to write nothing that might make Washington's work at Tuskegee appear in an unfavorable light. In an added precaution, Washington himself played an active role in editing and revising the text for publication.[7]

Not surprisingly, the book was quick to make clear that the militant Douglass had, in the main, lived and worked in a "period of revolution and liberation." It was a time of "war and controversy, and of fierce party struggle," in which the task "assigned to him was, on the whole, one of destruction and liberation, rather than construction and reconciliation." This was, of course, in contrast to the "period of construction and readjustment" that prevailed in Washington's own era. Douglass's vigorous defense of black civil and political rights was thus safely accounted for and explained away.[8]

Potentially more awkward were the harrowing scenes of slave life that Douglass so often evoked. These ghastly accounts did not square easily with Washington's own reminiscences of slave life. The accommodationist Washington more typically wrote in nostalgic terms about his memories of slavery in order to flatter, and win the approval, of the southern planter class.[9]

The inventive Tuskegeean found a simple means to explain the apparent contradiction. Until the age of seven the young Douglass would "have felt few of the privations of slavery," Washington assured his readers. The childhood days of a slave were probably "as happy and carefree as the white children in the big house. At liberty to come and go and play in the open sunshine, his early life was typical of the happier side of Negro life in slavery." Coincidentally, Washington himself was just six or seven years of age at the time of Lincoln's Emancipation Proclamation on 1 January 1863, and only nine years old at the end of the Civil War in 1865. His benign personal memories of slavery, in sharp contrast to those of Douglass, could therefore be explained away as the joyful naiveté of a child untouched by the realities of adult life.[10]

Despite its careful emphasis on the major differences between the era of Douglass and that of the early twentieth century, the biography was quick to point up the lessons that could be drawn from Douglass's life where these were favorable to Tuskegee and its work. Washington and Williams noted that during his early years as a free man, Douglass was prepared to accept any kind of work, however humble. If the "employment was hard, and the pay small, yet it did not seem so to this newly emancipated slave." If Douglass was not too proud to undertake manual labor then other African Americans not far removed from slavery, some 60 years later, should have no qualms about it either, was the clear message.[11]

Elsewhere, in discussing Douglass as a mature race leader, it was pointed out that "Naturally there were those of his color who envied him; who sought to discredit his worth and work," and "who felt that so long as he lived and spoke none other could be known, or disagreement heard." Envy, and resentment of success, rather than principle, it might thus be inferred, were the motives of Washington's own growing numbers of black critics by 1906–1907. Rather than raising serious doubts about his policies such malicious attacks were, as in the case of Douglass, ultimately testimony to his achievement and greatness.[12]

In the light of such logic it was ironic that as the years passed, and the memory of Douglass faded, Washington himself was inclined to be more critical of his illustrious predecessor. Secure and established as a national and international race leader in his own right, he had less need to appropriate the mantle of Douglass to justify his words and actions. Washington's early writings, like the *Story of My Life and Work* (1899), and *Up From Slavery* (1901), generally referred to Douglass in respectful, if not reverential terms. The later biographical study, *Frederick Douglass*, if still strongly positive about its subject, was no longer unremittingly so. The passage of the years, and his supposed role of objective historian, enabled Washington to indirectly hint at possible shortcomings in the great man.

In respect to the Reconstruction era, it was noted that "during his later years" Douglass "came to understand that the problem on the work of solving which he and others had entered with such high hopes" had been "longer and more complicated than it at that time seemed."[13]

The subject most overtly criticized was Douglass's second marriage, in 1884, to a white woman, Helen Pitts, who, ironically, had earlier worked as a teacher at Washington's old college, Hampton Institute in Virginia. The marriage "caused something like a revulsion of feeling throughout the entire country." Moreover, Douglass's "own race especially condemned him, and the notion seemed to be quite general that he had made the most serious mistake of his life." The sentiments of both whites and blacks alike "against amalgamation" had "never been so clearly demonstrated as in this case."[14]

By the time of his 1911 work, *My Larger Education*, Washington was prepared to criticize Douglass directly, rather than in the guise of an impartial chronicler recording past facts and events. Expressing his personal viewpoint, Washington asserted that Douglass's "long and bitter political struggle . . . against slavery" had left him ill prepared for "the equally difficult task of fitting the Negro for the opportunities and responsibilities of

freedom. The same was true to a large extent of other Negro leaders."
Ostensibly highlighting the failings of these other, unnamed spokespersons,
Washington effectively criticized Douglass as well. "At the time when I met
these men and heard them speak I was invariably impressed," he noted, but
"there was something lacking in their public utterances." The Tuskegeean
"felt that the millions of Negroes needed something more than to be
reminded of their sufferings and of their political rights; that they needed
to do something more than merely to defend themselves."[15]

By this time Washington was inclined to bury Douglass rather than to
praise him, both symbolically as well as philosophically. He became
actively involved with the efforts of the Pen and Pencil Club, a group of
around 40 leading black Americans who sought to pay off the outstanding
mortgage on Cedar Hill, Douglass's former home. The scheme was linked
with a plan by the Frederick Douglass Memorial and Historical
Association, of which Washington was a trustee, to turn the house into a
national museum to honor the work of Douglass and the abolitionist
movement.[16]

Washington himself personally launched an appeal on behalf of the
endeavor in January 1909. An obvious connotation of this initiative was
that the central role played by Washington was a natural one for him to
undertake as Douglass's successor as a race leader. In another sense the
celebration of Douglass's work in a museum firmly consigned his achievements to the dead past, in contrast to the present day efforts of Washington
himself.[17]

Booker T. Washington clearly relied on a selective reading of
Frederick Douglass's life and career to provide justification for his own
work at Tuskegee. At the same time he was, in part, able to do this only
because there were some genuine similarities in the thoughts and actions
of the two men. Douglass, like Washington, had a long-standing commitment to the idea of industrial education. In 1853 he cooperated with the
abolitionist, and author of *Uncle Tom's Cabin*, Harriet Beecher Stowe, in
an attempt to establish a black industrial school in the United States. "We
must become mechanics; we must build as well as live in houses; we must
make as well as use furniture," Douglass wrote to Stowe in advising her of
the needs of black Americans. Continuing in language that could have
been used by Washington himself, he noted that:

> We need mechanics as well as ministers. We need workers in iron, clay
> and leather. We have orators, authors, and other professional men, but
> these reach only a certain class, and get respect for our race in certain
> select circles. To live here as we ought, we must fasten ourselves to our
> countrymen through their every-day cardinal wants. We must not only
> be able to black boots but to make them.[18]

In the light of such statements Washington was quite reasonably able to claim that Douglass had advocated industrial education almost 30 years before Tuskegee was founded.[19]

In any event, Douglass's 1853 initiative with Stowe failed to reach fruition because of lack of funds.[20] Despite this setback Douglass continued to be a consistent supporter of industrial education for the remainder of his life. During his last years he showed a more than passing interest in Tuskegee itself. In addition to speaking there, in 1892, in 1894 he helped to secure a donation of $242.75 for the institute. In February 1895 he wrote to Booker T. Washington about a new invention for the preservation of food-stuffs that might prove of benefit to black farmers in the South.[21] It was entirely in character that one of Douglass's last initiatives was to help found a black industrial school at Manassas in Virginia.[22]

Significantly, the subject of Douglass's commencement address at Tuskegee was "Self-Made Men," a typically Washingtonian theme that emphasized the values of thrift and hard work as the best means of advancement for blacks in the South. "WORK! WORK!! WORK!!! WORK!!!! Not transient and fitful effort, but patient, enduring, honest, unremitting and indefatigable work, into which the whole heart is put," was the key to individual success.

Douglass's choice of topic was, in part, influenced by the nature of his audience. He delivered the same address to students at an Industrial School at Carlisle, Pennsylvania, in March 1893.[23] At the same time the speech also reflected his genuine commitment to laissez-faire values and a belief in individual self-help. First written and delivered in 1859, Douglass gave his "Self-Made Men" lecture over 50 times to audiences across the United States during the remaining 46 years of his life. Reflecting the con-servative social values of his day, it was one of his most popular addresses. Although he updated the speech from time to time, to give it added topi-cality; the essential message of the oration remained remarkably unchanged over time. Despite his eulogy to the virtues of hard toil, Douglass himself was clearly resolved to put in no more work than was necessary when it came to writing his own lectures, even if freshness and originality had to be sacrificed as a result.[24]

Like Booker T. Washington, Douglass believed that the best prospects for the large majority of blacks lay in agricultural employment within the southern states of America. He was consistently opposed to emigration schemes to resettle African Americans outside of the United States. Although black leaders like the churchman Alexander Crummell, and the abolitionist and Republican politician, Martin R. Delany, periodically sup-ported such projects between the 1850s and the 1870s, they held no appeal for Douglass. Africa was too geographically remote, and most black Americans did not want to go there anyway. Even if they did, the "navy of all the world would not be sufficient to remove our natural increase to that far-off country," and "removal to any of the territories" was equally "out of the question."[25]

Less positively, Douglass shared the prejudices of many nineteenth century Americans, including Booker T. Washington, in his perceptions of African culture and society. "Under the palm trees of Africa" it was possible to find "food, raiment and shelter" with little or no efforts. The native African was thus lazy and uncivilized, "Nature has done all and he has done nothing." The result, Douglass believed, was "that the glory of Africa is in her palms, and not in her men."[26] Given such views it is not surprising that Douglass shared with Booker T. Washington a belief in the idea of the "White Man's Burden," and felt that colonialism was the best means of advancement for African tribal societies.[27]

Within the United States, Douglass believed that the South was "the natural home of the colored race," and that it was there that "the destiny of that race be mainly worked out." At times, as with his opposition to emigration overseas, this led him into conflict with other leading black American spokespersons.[28]

The most notable instance of this came in 1879–1881, when Douglass was critical of the Exoduster Movement. Initiated by two blacks, Henry Adams and "Pap" Singleton, this venture sought to settle blacks from the southern states in Kansas, enabling migrants to escape debt peonage and to become independent small farmers in their own right.

In a speech in Baltimore, Maryland, "The South Knows Us," given in May 1879, Douglass condemned the Exoduster project, and presented a favorable image of the opportunities open to blacks in the South. Similar in tone to the "Cast down your buckets where you are" rhetoric of Booker T. Washington's 1895 Atlanta Compromise Address, Douglass's intervention led to him being criticized by younger, more radical, black speakers. In particular he was accused of failing to recognize the dire social and economic conditions suffered by most southern blacks.[29]

Invited to debate the Exoduster phenomenon before the American Social Science Association in September 1879, Douglass was sufficiently shaken by the attacks on him that he declined to attend to give his prepared talk, "The Negro Exodus from the Gulf States." Displaying an uncharacteristic lack of courage, he claimed prior commitments as an excuse for nonparticipation and his speech was read by a stand in.[30]

The ultimate failure of the Exodus, with many of the unfortunate migrants succumbing to illness and starvation, provided a partial, albeit unwelcome, vindication of Douglass's views. At the same time, the charges of naiveté, in respect to his view of black living conditions in the South, were also justified. In a tour of Georgia and South Carolina, in March 1888, Douglass saw first hand the suffering and deprivation of black sharecroppers, and tacitly acknowledged that his earlier perceptions of black life in the region had been too optimistic. In a speech in Washington, D.C., "In Law Free: In Fact a Slave," the following month, Douglass denounced the evils of debt peonage in the South.[31]

Fresh insights did not, however, lead Douglass to abandon his general opposition to black migration. In the last years of his life he was at best willing to support only a limited departure of blacks from the South to prevent the build up of a surplus labor force as "men, like trees, may be too thickly planted to thrive."[32]

Despite some genuine similarities in their views, and Washington's best propaganda efforts, many contemporaries of the two men, and the majority of subsequent historians, have perceived the racial leadership of Douglass as bold and militant, and that of Washington as timid and conservative.[33]

In a variety of respects this view is justified. Washington advocated industrial education as an alternative to agitation for civil and political rights. Douglass envisaged the development of industrial schooling in conjunction with civil rights protest as part of a two-pronged strategy. Hard work and the acquiring of manual laboring skills alone were not enough. Why should "hoeing and planting corn" or "digging potatoes and raising cabbages" be seen as the "preferable and most effective" means of countering "the unjust, anti-Republican and disgraceful race restrictions imposed upon us," Douglass noted in 1855.[34]

In October 1883, Douglass was quick to vent his anger when, by an 8–1 majority, the United States Supreme Court held the 1875 Civil Rights Act to be unconstitutional. One of the most radical pieces of legislation passed by Congress during the Reconstruction era, the act had stipulated that all persons, regardless of race or color, were entitled to full and equal access to public accommodations and facilities. The Court ruled that this violated the constitutional rights of proprietors to refuse service to customers, or provide it on such terms as they saw fit. In a protest meeting that followed in Washington D.C., Douglass condemned the actions of the Court as a decision that had "humbled the nation."[35]

In one of his last major speeches, "The Lessons of the Hour," delivered in Washington, D.C., in January 1894, Douglass was equally vigorous in his denunciation of lynching, "the epidemic of mob law and persecution." In forthright terms he denounced the "blood chilling horrors and fiendish excesses perpetrated against the colored people by the so-called enlightened and Christian people of the South."[36]

Douglass was not only more outspoken on black civil and political rights than Booker T. Washington, he also supported other reforming causes of his day, including the temperance movement, Irish home rule, and the living conditions of the poor. In July 1848 he spoke in support of women's rights at the first Women's Rights Convention at Seneca Falls in

New York. He remained committed to this cause for the remainder of his life. In a speech in Boston, Massachusetts, in May 1888, he declared himself still proud to be "a radical woman suffrage man." His "special mission in the world, if I ever had any, was the emancipation and enfranchisement of the negro," he informed his audience. "Your mission is the emancipation and enfranchisement of women." This was "a much greater cause since it comprehends the liberation and elevation of one-half of the whole human family." It was fitting that on the day of his death, 20 February 1895, Douglass's last public engagement was to attend a women's suffrage rally in Washington, D.C.[37]

In contrast to the more radical Douglass, Booker T. Washington was rarely willing to take outspoken positions on any of the great controversial issues of his day, outside of race relations. Although, like Douglass, he personally abstained from alcohol he did not become an active campaigner for the temperance movement.[38]

In 1910 and 1911 Washington did undertake a six week tour of Europe to study the living conditions of the poor, but the trip was not intended to highlight injustice, still less advocate radical reform. Instead, the record of his visit that resulted, *The Man Farthest Down: A Record of Observation and Study in Europe* (1911), reflected the conservative sociological thinking of the times. Typically, the book stressed thrift, hard work, and self-help as the best means to escape poverty, and contrasted the economic opportunities of blacks in the American South with the plight of the most disadvantaged groups in European countries.

In respect to women's rights, Washington was equally reticent. "I am in favour of every measure that will give to woman, the opportunity to develop to the highest possible extent, her moral, intellectual, and physical nature so that she may make her life as useful to herself and to others as it is possible to make it," he guardedly informed one enquirer in December 1908. However, lest such a statement appear too bold, the cautious Tuskegeean went on to note:

> I do not, at the present moment, see that this involves the privilege or the duty, as you choose to look upon it, of voting. The influence of woman is already enormous in this country. She exerts, not merely in the homes, but through the schools and in the press, a powerful and helpful influence upon affairs. It is not clear to me that she would exercise any greater or more beneficient influence upon the world than she does now, if the duty of taking an active part in party politics were imposed upon her.

Eager to please, and unwilling to offend, Washington concluded his letter with diplomatic evasion, reflecting that the issue was one "which it seems to me, the women know better than the men, and I am willing to leave it to their deliberate judgement."[39]

Any comparison of the careers of Douglass and Washington is complicated by the changing values of late nineteenth-century America. In the decades that followed Reconstruction, the United States became increasingly conservative in terms of social, economic, and political thought. This was particularly true of race relations. To contrast the radicalism of Douglass between the 1840s and the 1870s with the later accommodationism of Booker T. Washington is thus unfair and ahistorical. All black Americans living in the 1880s and 1890s had to take note of the worsening racial climate and adjust their aims and expectations accordingly. This included Frederick Douglass himself.

In the last 20 years of his life Douglass made a number of compromises that he might have resisted in earlier years. In 1877 he accepted the position of U.S. Marshall for the District of Columbia from Republican President Rutherford B. Hayes. This was despite the fact that the post was stripped of its ceremonial duties, which included attending formal White House functions and presenting guests to the President. Seen as a snub by many blacks in Washington, D.C., Douglass nonetheless resisted calls for him to resign in protest, and continued to serve as Marshall until the end of Hayes's term of office.

In 1881 Douglass endured a further humiliation when the incoming Republican President, James Garfield, removed him from the position of Marshall and offered him the lesser post of Recorder of Deeds. Once again, Douglass chose to accept rather than resign, and served as Recorder of Deeds until 1886, when he was removed by the Democratic President, Grover Cleveland.[40]

Despite the growing conservatism of the Republican Party in the 1880s and 1890s, Douglass, like Washington, continued to remain loyal to the Party of Lincoln. In 1892 he rejected the call of younger black spokesmen to support the newly formed Populist Party, and instead campaigned for the reelection of Republican President Benjamin Harrison.

In his third, and final, autobiography, *Life and Times of Frederick Douglass,* first published in 1881, Douglass defended his decision to serve as U.S. Marshall and, somewhat unconvincingly, denied that the truncated duties of the office implied any racial insult. The book, which appeared in a revised and updated second edition in 1893, was a further sign of Douglass's growing conservatism. His first two autobiographies, *Narrative of the Life of Frederick Douglass, an American Slave* (1845), and *My Bondage and my Freedom* (1855), were the works of a radical abolitionist voicing his personal sense of outrage, and the anger of African Americans in general, at the institution of slavery. *Life and Times* was notably different in tone, reading more like the reminiscences of an elder statesman recalling with satisfaction past glories rather than focusing on present evils still to be overcome.[41]

Life and Times reflected the material prosperity and middle-class life-style enjoyed by Douglass at Cedar Hill, and its nine-acre estate in Anacostia in Washington, D.C., in the last years of his life. One symbol of this affluence was an extended tour of Europe and North Africa under-taken by Douglass and his second wife, Helen, between September 1886 and August 1887. From 1845 to 1847 Douglass had journeyed through Britain and Ireland as an abolitionist orator, and a radical spokesman for other social and political causes, such as women's rights and Irish inde-pendence. His return visit, some 40 years later, was in marked contrast, more in the style of a grand European tour of the type undertaken by pros-perous Americans.[42]

If a fitting reward for a lifetime of achievement, such success had a price. Douglass became less sensitive to, and less aware of, the needs and problems of the mass of ordinary black Americans in the South. His initial lack of empathy with the Exoduster migrants, in 1879–1881, was one sign of this growing detachment. Similarly, despite his forthright language in "The Lessons of the Hour," he was at first slow to fully appreciate the hor-rors of lynch law in the South. It was not until he met with, and read the writings of, the young militant black woman activist and journalist Ida B. Wells, in 1892, that he realized the need for urgent action on the issue. [43]

Booker T. Washington and Frederick Douglass clearly had shared beliefs on a variety of issues. Writing in 1900 Washington was accurately able to assert that "Mr. Douglass had the same idea concerning the impor-tance and value of industrial education that I have tried to emphasize." Moreover, "He also held the same views as I do in regard to the emigra-tion of the Negro to Africa, and was opposed to the scheme of diffusion and dissemination of the Negro throughout the North and Northwest." Instead, Douglass believed "as I do that the Southern section of the coun-try where the Negro now resides is the best place for him."[44]

In Douglass's last years the similarities between the two men, if any-thing, became more pronounced. The conservative climate of the 1880s and 1890s, and the Sage of Anacostia's own cultivated life-style, had a mel-lowing effect on Douglass's former radicalism. These considerations notwithstanding, there also remained important differences between the two race leaders.

Like most members of the human race, Douglass did not enjoy public criticism of his beliefs, but unlike Washington, he did not systematically resort to covert persecution of those African-American spokespersons who disagreed with him. Actuated by principle himself, Douglass was bet-ter able to understand that there were members of the black community who disagreed with his ideas out of genuine conviction. He believed that they had a right to hold such views even if he thought them misguided. In contrast to the paranoid Washington, he did not see all criticism as akin to a personal vendetta, and a plot against his own leadership. In consequence, he showed a greater flexibility of mind than the Tuskegeean. He was more able to admit when he was wrong, and modify his views accordingly. This was indicated in his changing perceptions of black living conditions in the South, following a tour of Georgia and South Carolina in 1888, and his heightened awareness of the problem of lynching after meeting with Ida B. Wells in 1892.[45]

Even in old age Douglass was more willing to speak out against political and social injustice than Booker T. Washington, and, with a broader humanitarian vision than the Tuskegeean, did not confine his statements to issues involving race. Douglass did not seek to appease whites by blaming blacks themselves for the problems they suffered, rather than segregation and discrimination. Similarly, he did not regularly reinforce negative white stereotypes of African Americans by resorting to audience-pleasing anecdotes about the propensity of blacks to steal chickens and watermelons, or laze in the sun.

Not surprisingly, such contrasts have generally made Douglass appear the more appealing of the two men, both as an individual and a race leader, to later generations of historians and African Americans alike. If the conservative Washington has often seemed unattractive by comparison it is because the period of history during which he lived is also less appealing than the decades of more radical change that preceded it. Individuals, whatever their abilities, are more a product of their times than the values of their era are a product of them. "Douglass lived in the day of moral giants; Washington lives in the era of merchant princes," noted Kelly Miller in 1908:

> The contemporaries of Douglass emphasized the rights of man; those of Washington, his productive capacity. . . . The equality of man was constantly dinned into Douglass's ears; Washington hears nothing but the inferiority of the Negro and the dominance of the Saxon. Douglass could hardly receive a hearing today; Washington would have been hooted off the stage a generation ago. Thus all truly useful men must be, in a measure, timeservers; for unless they serve their time, they can scarcely serve at all.[46]

Douglass, bold by nature, spoke the truths that the cautious Washington declined to utter. Simple differences in character and personality are, however, insufficient to explain this contrast. It was not that Washington felt oppression and discrimination less keenly than Douglass. If anything, residing in the rural South, rather than a leafy middle-class neighborhood in the District of Columbia, he was probably more sensitive to it. Washington's accommodationist philosophy derived from the fact that as a pragmatic race leader he chose to strive for what was possible, rather than what was right and just.

Stirring and courageous as the speeches of Douglass often were, they had no discernible impact in limiting the spread of debt peonage, lynchings, and segregation during the 1880s and the 1890s. To the contrary, these evils became more widespread and intensive during these years. Washington may have empathized with the public statements made by Douglass, but he also realized that white Americans, particularly in the South, were not prepared to heed them.

Writing to the liberal New York newspaper proprietor, and future NAACP founder, Oswald Garrison Villard, in January 1904, Washington acquainted him with the case of a black man recently burned to death in Pineapple, Alabama. Carried away by emotional frenzy, the lynch mob had accidentally set fire to neighboring buildings, and much of the business section of the town had been destroyed. "Now the whole country is aroused on the subject of lynching," Washington noted, but "of course, the feelings of the majority of the people . . . have been aroused because of the burning houses rather than the lynching of a Negro."[47]

Living and working in the Deep South at a time when such distorted values prevailed, it was understandable that Washington advocated a program of racial uplift that stressed economic self-help and only covert or indirect challenges to racial discrimination and segregation. Simple survival instincts, let alone considerations as to what was practical, left room for few other options. Washington may have lacked the courageous defiance of Frederick Douglass, but in the repressive racial conditions of the Progressive era it was better to be a living lamb than a dead lion.

CHAPTER 3

Roads Not Taken

Booker T. Washington
as a Race Leader

Despite the heroic endeavors of Professor Louis Harlan, not all modern historians find Booker T. Washington, with his accommodationism and peasant conservatism, an attractive area of research. Seemingly implicit in this viewpoint is the value judgment that alternative, more successful, or at least less harmful, strategies could have been pursued by Washington.

Harsh judgments have been predicated "on Booker T. Washington on the assumption that he ought to have embraced another and better set of moral choices," noted one 1974 commentator, but what "these choices were is seldom made clear ... certainly they could not have been those of the 1950s or 1960s." This key question clearly deserves fuller consideration. Realistically, did Washington have the scope to pursue more challenging policies? If so, in specific practical terms, what more could he have actually done to advance the interests of black Americans in the years 1895–1915?[1]

The risks of a more outspoken strategy were all too clear, as was demonstrated in the careers of other race leaders of the day. Like Washington, Timothy Thomas Fortune was born a slave in 1856, in Marianna, Florida. Largely self-educated, he gained a growing reputation as a journalist after moving to New York City in 1879. By 1887 he owned his own newspaper, the New York *Age*.

Although a close friend of Washington from the 1880s, Fortune was clearly more radical in outlook. In 1889 he cofounded the National Afro-American League, an all black civil rights organization committed to the defense of black civil and political rights by peaceful agitation. Viewed for a time as an heir to Douglass as a race leader, Fortune's later career failed to live up to its earlier promise.

In 1893 the National Afro-American League, lacking in white patronage and any widespread black support, collapsed through lack of funds and interest. By 1907–1908 continuing financial problems forced Fortune to sell his shares in the *Age*. Beset by personal problems he succumbed to alcoholism, depression, and nervous breakdown at this time. Although gradually recovering from this lowpoint, Fortune spent the remaining years of his life largely dependent on the patronage of first Booker T. Washington and later Marcus Garvey. From 1923 Fortune was editor of the UNIA newspaper the *Negro World*, a post he retained until his death in 1928.[2]

William Monroe Trotter, one of Washington's earliest and most outspoken critics, enjoyed a more comfortable start in life. Born in Boston, Massachusetts in 1872, Trotter benefited from a good schooling and went on to study at Harvard University. In 1901 he founded his own newspaper, the Boston *Guardian*, with fellow black journalist George Washington Forbes.

Deeply hostile to the conservative Tuskegee philosophy, Trotter attracted national attention in 1903 by heckling a speech given by Washington in Boston. After the "Boston Riot," as it became known, Trotter for a while seemed to be the leading black opponent of Tuskegee. In 1905 he joined with W.E.B. Du Bois in founding the Niagara Movement, and later launched his own civil rights organization, the National Equal Rights League, in 1908.

Ultimately, frustration, rather than fulfillment, was the keynote in Trotter's life. The National Equal Rights League never attracted any mass following and was effectively moribund by 1921. During the 1920s Trotter was marginalized as a race leader and suffered increasing financial hardships in his efforts to keep the *Guardian* in print. He died in penury and all but forgotten in 1934.[3]

If giving pause for thought, the experiences of Fortune and Trotter provide less than conclusive proof that any black leader who advocated a vigorous defense of black civil and political rights was doomed to failure. Personal weaknesses contributed to the setbacks suffered by both men: mental frailty and alcoholism in the case of Fortune and a quarrelsome nature and an inability to work well with others on the part of Trotter. The clandestine sabotage of the Tuskegee Machine also added considerably to Trotter's problems.

In the 1880s and the 1890s the career of the North Carolina educator Joseph Price provided tantalizing evidence that a more assertive strategy than that embraced by Washington might have been viable. Born to a free black mother and a slave father in 1854, the life of Price in many ways mirrored that of the Tuskegeean.

In 1882 Price became President of Zion Wesley Institute, later renamed Livingstone College, in Salisbury, North Carolina. He demonstrated considerable ability in securing white patronage for black education and achieved a growing reputation as an orator and educator.

In the early 1890s Price probably had a greater national status as a racial spokesman than Washington in Alabama. In comparison to the Tuskegeean, Price was more vigorous in defense of black civil and political rights, and attached equal importance to a liberal arts education and industrial training. It is possible that Price's premature death from Bright's disease, in 1893, deprived African Americans of an individual who, had he lived, might have been more assertive and more effective as a race leader than the Wizard of Tuskegee.[4]

In respect to Washington himself, his own meteoric rise as an interracial diplomat, in the years after 1895, derived largely from the acclaim heaped upon him by white society, not from any mass black following. Prior to 1895 Washington was little known outside of Tuskegee, let alone Alabama. Even after his achievement of celebrity status, it is questionable whether Washington ever managed to build up any widespread grass roots organizational support, despite his claims to speak for the majority of black southerners. Paradoxically, the very success of Tuskegee Institute made him more vulnerable to the withdrawal of white financial support. By 1915 Tuskegee's expansion meant that Washington needed to raise a minimum of $100,000 a year to meet the running costs of the institute.[5]

On two occasions, when Washington did seem to depart from his script laid down at the 1895 Atlanta Cotton Exposition, the resulting storm of southern white indignation forced him into an ignominious retraction. In a speech on the Spanish-American War, at the National Peace Jubilee in Chicago, on 16 October 1898, Washington spoke of racial prejudice as "a cancer gnawing at the heart of the Republic," in particular "in the Southern part of our country." The heated reaction of the southern press placed Washington in a situation in which he felt obliged to backtrack on his position less than a month later, in a letter to the editor of the Birmingham *Age-Herald*.[6]

Washington's status as a race leader seemed briefly to be similarly threatened in 1901, following his appearance as a dinner guest at the White House at the invitation of President Roosevelt. Historically, such an occasion was not without precedent. Less than 40 years earlier Frederick Douglass had been received at a White House reception by Abraham Lincoln. However, the more repressive racial environment at the turn of the century made Washington's presence at the dinner seem an intolerable affront to many white southerners. "For days and weeks I was pursued by reporters in quest of interviews," the older, wiser, Washington later recalled of the incident. "I was deluged with telegrams and letters asking for some expression of opinion or an explanation; but during the whole of this period of agitation and excitement I did not give out a single interview and did not discuss the matter in any way."[7]

Washington's sympathizers have advanced both the Chicago and White House incidents as proof of his precarious position. The evidence is, however, subject to more than one interpretation. Both incidents came relatively early in Washington's national career, when his position as a race reader was less entrenched than in later years. If Washington was dependent on white support then arguably, over time, this was an increasingly reciprocal relationship. White Americans invested emotional as well as financial capital in Washington, which, hallowed by the passage of the years, could not be so easily withdrawn.

Later sources of unpleasantness in Washington's career, when his position as a national black leader had been secured, provoked less heated southern reactions. When, on 14 August 1905, the Tuskegeean dined with the millionaire businessmen John Wanamaker in a Saratoga hotel, and was reported in the southern press as having been so bold as to escort one of the young ladies of the family into dinner on his arm, there was a predictable minor outburst in the South, but it was nowhere near as intense as that following the Roosevelt dinner of 1901.[8]

Even the unfortunate Ulrich affair of 19 March 1911, when Washington was accused of peeping through a keyhole at a white woman and accosting her as "sweetheart" late one night in one of the less salubrious districts of New York City, did not seriously tarnish Washington's public reputation in the long term. A by then aging and physically drained Washington may have suffered intense private and psychological trauma from which he never fully recovered. However, his influential white backers were prepared to give Washington the benefit of the doubt, despite a number of unresolved questions surrounding the incident. The Tuskegee trustee, Seth Low, seemed to sum up the feelings of many when he concluded that the allegations made against Washington were "entirely unworthy of belief." Washington's accusers had "shown themselves to be untrustworthy, and their word is not to be accepted against the word of an honorable man like Booker T. Washington." If the 1898 Chicago speech, the 1911 Ulrich affair, and the intervening White House and Wanamaker dinners attested to Washington's vulnerability, they equally provided evidence of his durability.[9]

It is one thing to suggest that Washington could have pursued a more outspoken strategy without taking unacceptable risks, but what tangible gains could such a policy have offered? Clearly, it would be expecting a great deal to believe that Washington could have had any significant impact in checking the tides of segregation and racial injustice that swept over African Americans at the start of the twentieth century.

Nonetheless, it is arguable that the act of voicing such protest would not have been without benefit. A more dynamic course of action might have served to unite, rather than divide, black opinion, and to develop more fully in the mass of black Americans a sense of injustice at the racism of white society. Washington's accommodationist stance tended toward the opposite effect, splitting black leadership in the nation, and reinforcing feelings of inadequacy in ordinary blacks.

Equally, the Washington program buttressed white bigotry and assuaged potential latent white guilt at the treatment of blacks in a society committed to democratic and republican values. Washington's anesthetic words helped ensure that this contradiction was safely sedated out of the conscious thoughts of white Americans.

Some commentators, most notably Professor Louis Harlan, have sought to revise Washington's conservative reputation by focusing attention on his "secret life" of more assertive civil rights activity. This hidden strategy can, however, be seen as fundamentally flawed. Simply put, any white self-doubts, so carefully nurtured by Washington's covert support of antisegregation lawsuits and editorials, could be laid to rest by the riposte that segregation could not be considered unjust precisely because, in public, Washington appeared to accept it.[10]

In one sense, Washington himself was the principal victim of the accommodationist philosophy that he so assiduously pursued. The largesse that white benefactors bestowed on Tuskegee was purchased at an unquantifiable psychic cost, to Washington the man, of adopting a position of constant servility and the repression of his own feelings.[11]

A forthright stand against racial injustice in his public writings and speeches was one potential path not taken by Washington. A second avenue that might have been pursued more vigorously by the Tuskegee educator was a greater emphasis on, and awareness of, African-American culture and history, in short a sense of black consciousness.

On numerous occasions, especially when addressing all black audiences, Washington did talk of the need for a pride in racial identity. Speaking to blacks at the Alabama State Normal School on 17 January 1890, he stated that "I would not change my color if I could." In private correspondence with George Washington Cable the same year, the Tuskegee principal expressed his irritation at "the disposition on the part of many of our friends to consult *about* the Negro instead of *with* — to work *for* him instead of *with* him." The Tuskegeean felt a close rapport with ordinary blacks living and working in the Cotton Belt and it is possible, as some studies have suggested, that his endeavors on their behalf have not been given due recognition by historians.[12]

Washington also stressed, from time to time, the need to develop the study of African-American history and a sense of pride in black achievement. "We must have pride of race. We must be as proud of being a Negro as the Japanese is of being a Japanese," he advised members of the National Negro Business League in Philadelphia on 20 August 1913. "Let us go from this great meeting filled with a spirit of race pride; rejoicing in the fact that we belong to a race that has made greater progress within fifty years than any race in history."[13]

The very existence of the Business League, and Washington's urgings to blacks to patronize African-American businesses, can indeed be seen as signs of a nascent black nationalism in Washington's philosophy. Nonetheless, it is a moot point as to how fully Washington ever thought through the full implications of this tendency. His more oft-stated argument was that blacks could achieve economic advancement despite the existence of racial prejudice precisely because consumers would bestow their custom on a value-for-money basis rather than on grounds of racial solidarity.[14]

Sporadic references to the need for a pride in racial identity aside, Washington was, in the words of one biographer, "first and last an American," in contrast to W. E. B. Du Bois who was "first and last a Negro." The former's underdeveloped sense of race consciousness was reflected in his use of stereotyped "darkey" anecdotes to white audiences. Easy oratorical ploys to win the empathy of his listeners, Washington never seemed to consider the negative aspects of such racist anecdotes in "subliminally reinforcing white bigotry and a sense of inferiority among blacks."[15]

"It may be foolish of me to think of such things, and to want you to tell me what you think about it," Leola Chambers, a black correspondent, wrote to Washington in February 1914, "but do you suppose if we should stop telling so many jokes about our chicken stealing, the white people would soon think we had quit stealing and began to raise our own?" The Tuskegeean's reply to this enquirer, that "if we treat a joke merely as a joke, people will at least recognize that we have a sense of humor," hardly convinces. The fact that it was not the use of humorous anecdotes in his speeches, but their racist form to which the writer objected, seemed to have escaped him.[16]

Washington's perceptions of black culture and black history could be equally shortsighted. The study of the past was important less as a means to reinforce a vibrant, living, black culture than to find out "the true history of the race" and collect "in some museum the relics that mark its progress."[17]

The existence of a distinct African-American heritage had limited meaning for the Americanized Washington. Until the Civil War, "the life of the Negro was so intimately interwoven with that of the white man that it is almost true to say that he had no separate history," he declared in *The Story of the Negro*. "To the slave on the plantation the 'Big House' where the master lived was the center of the only world he knew."[18]

Publicly, the Tuskegeean accepted the southern white notion that slavery had served as a "civilizing school" for blacks, rescuing them from savagery and ignorance. When addressing a northern audience at the Brooklyn Academy of Music, on 23 February 1903, Washington pithily remarked that "I confine myself to a statement of cold bare facts when I say that when the Negro went into slavery, he was a pagan; when he ended his period of bondage he had a religion." Moreover, "When he went into slavery he was without anything which might properly be called a language; when he came out of slavery he was able to speak the English tongue with force and intellect."[19]

Given such attitudes, it is not surprising that Washington never appeared to develop any deep and lasting interest in black Africa, or indeed to perceive race relations in a wider global context. For all his visits overseas, Washington never journeyed to Africa, Asia, or even the West Indies. A series of triumphal progresses through the courts of Europe, topped by afternoon tea with Queen Victoria, was not matched by a reciprocal resolve to visit the area of the world from where that most English of beverages originated. The closest Washington came to a first-hand experience of Africa was in conversations with the famed explorer H. M. Stanley in the environs of the British House of Commons. In contrast to the romantic Du Bois, the pragmatic Tuskegeean typically emerged from these interviews not with any misty-eyed nostalgia for the Dark Continent, but rather "more convinced than ever that there was no hope for the American Negro's improving his condition by emigrating to Africa."[20]

Washington did, sometimes, express a symbolic empathy with blacks outside the United States. Writing in July 1907, he observed that there was "always a peculiar and scarcely definable bond that binds one black man to another black man; whether in Africa, Jamaica, Haiti, or the United States." He was also, at times, surprisingly outspoken against imperial excesses, particularly in respect to the atrocities committed in the Belgian Congo. Moreover, Washington was a vigorous campaigner for U.S. aid to the independent black republic of Liberia, and a smattering of Tuskegee graduates sought to re-create their mentor's vision of industrial education variously in Togo, Nigeria, the Sudan, and the Congo, albeit with limited success.[21]

Interestingly, for a leader not renowned as a black internationalist, Washington even participated in the planning of the first Pan African Conference in London while visiting England in 1899. More characteristically, he did not attend the Conference itself, held in 1900, or any of the other worldwide race conferences of his day. Washington's views on imperialism were more aptly symbolized by his meeting with Stanley than his sometime journalistic outbursts, that in any case often originated from the pen of his white ghostwriter Robert Park. Possessing no real appreciation of tribal culture and society, the Tuskegeean essentially accepted the doctrine of the "White Man's Burden" in respect to European colonization of

Africa. Putting philosophy into practice, he periodically cooperated openly with imperial authorities in the African colonies.[22]

During a visit to Berlin in 1910, with a conviction undiminished by the contradictory facts, Washington went so far as to praise German imperial administration in Africa as a model for other nations, since Germans did "not seek to repress the Africans, but rather to help them that they may be more useful to themselves and to the German people." In reality, German colonialism was "arbitrary, exploitative, and disruptive, blatantly ignoring local African customs and culture."[23]

In his 1901 autobiography, *Up From Slavery*, Washington gently rebuked his white readers with the thought that "no white American ever thinks that any other race is wholly civilized until he wears the white man's clothes, eats the white man's food, speaks the white man's language and professes the white man's religion." In his own life and career, Washington both consciously and unconsciously internalized these values all too readily.[24]

Washington's relationship with his contemporary black critics is an aspect of his leadership that has been tacitly accepted, even by sympathetic commentators, as being capable of improvement. Washington's relentless hounding of black spokespersons who had the temerity to disagree with him has been well catalogued. In the name of the greater good, Washington regularly infiltrated opposition groups with spies and saboteurs, sought to have critics dismissed from their employment, even imprisoned, and attempted to eliminate hostile black newspapers by circulation wars and malicious lawsuits. Given these covert activities, a full understanding of the Tuskegeean's "secret life," on balance, arguably further tarnishes, rather than restores, his historical reputation. Irrespective of the moral issues raised by such unsavory measures, Washington's tactics divided black leadership in America at a time when it most needed to be united, and arguably retarded the development of effective black civil rights protest.[25]

In his defense, in as much as he was ever prepared to admit to the rough handling of opponents, Washington justified his actions on the grounds of necessity. In short, vociferous protest by black militants was not only foolhardy but worse, might threaten Washington's own endeavors—and the well being of blacks generally—by alienating the support of white moderates.

There are several problems with this reasoning. In the first instance, it could be argued that militant black protest could have the opposite effect, strengthening rather than weakening white support for the Tuskegee program. The more incendiary other black leaders appeared, the more white Americans might have been prepared to look to Washington as the voice of black moderation. Publicly, for this very reason, it clearly benefited Washington to distance himself from more radical black spokespersons. His covert sabotage of their efforts may, however, have been less judicious if their presence actually served to reinforce white support for Washington.

Equally, if outspoken northern blacks did sometimes hinder the advancement of blacks in America as a whole, the harsh, purgative cures adopted by Washington in dealing with them could be worse than the ailment itself. In April 1908, Washington sabotaged a dinner between liberal whites and northern black leaders at the Cosmopolitan Club in New York by leaking details of the engagement to hostile press reporters. The lurid newspaper reports that ensued, replete with heavy sexual innuendo and scaremongering headlines about miscegenation and racial intermarriage, hardly did anything to facilitate the development of more harmonious race relations. The public mood in the weeks that followed was such that one of the dinner guests, Mary White Ovington, later to be a founding member of the NAACP, received such distressing and obscene hate mail that she felt compelled to have her daily correspondence opened by male relatives.[26]

At heart, it would seem that Washington became so obsessive in stifling militant black protest not because he thought this protest would be counterproductive, but because of a paranoid tendency to see such action as a direct, personal attack on himself. In private correspondence he referred to black leaders who advocated a more assertive strategy as "the little crowd who are opposing me" and "largely actuated by motives of jealousy." In August 1906, Washington wrote to Richard Greener, whom he had employed to infiltrate the Niagara movement, that "the whole object" of that organization was "to defeat and oppose everything I do."[27]

The fact that it was a paranoid fear for his personal position that primarily motivated Washington was indicated by his good relations with black leaders like Charles Chesnutt, Robert Russa Moton, and Thomas Fortune, who though all, at times, inclined to a more radical stance than the Tuskegeean, succeeded in reassuring him of their personal support. The forthright editorials that appeared from time to time in black newspapers like the New York *Age*, which were safely in the Tuskegee camp, support the view that Washington did not necessarily object to protesting too much, provided that it was not possible to see in such protest any implicit criticism of his own policies.[28]

Washington's inability to listen to points of view different from his own, or to accept even the most mild and diplomatic questioning of his policies, was no less apparent in his day-to-day running of Tuskegee Institute. The *Booker T. Washington Papers* are peppered with complaints by Tuskegee staff and students about Washington's authoritarian management. Moreover, it is probable that recorded grievances represented but a small proportion of the discontent, for individuals who allowed their doubts to become public risked hurtful letters of rebuke from Washington. In some cases, Tuskegee staff found themselves, with no prior warning, in receipt of a letter of immediate dismissal, without so much as the courtesy of a personal interview with Washington. Even a previous record of good and long service was not always sufficient to safeguard against such draconian treatment.[29]

Washington presided over Tuskegee more in the style of a dictator than a college principal, even allowing for the more authoritarian styles of leadership that may have prevailed in southern educational institutions at the end of the nineteenth century. Unable to trust, or delegate to, those around him, he sought to control almost every day-to-day action of staff and students. Teachers risked being publicly rebuked for missing evening prayers, chewing gum, or smoking in the street. Office staff were expected to answer all correspondence on the same day that it arrived from the post office, even if it was necessary to remain at work until the early hours of the morning to do so. Students were forbidden to leave the grounds of the institute without first seeking permission.[30]

Whether at Tuskegee, or in the wider black community, Washington appeared incapable of accepting the fact that those individuals who disagreed with him could be motivated by principle rather than personal malice. Ever compelled to bear equivocation and snubs from vacillating, but influential, white supporters, Washington was never able, or willing, to show tolerance to other leaders in the black community.[31]

Washington's lack of generosity of spirit was a personal weakness of the man himself, not a result of the social and political climate of his era, except in so much as Washington's own personality was, in part, shaped by that climate. Other black leaders, no less the products of the same society, were notably more magnanimous in their attitudes toward the Tuskegeean. As late as the Carnegie Hall Conference of January 1904, W. E. B. Du Bois still hoped to reach an amicable accord with Washington, only to find that the latter had surreptitiously packed the meeting with his own supporters.[32]

From 1909 onward, Oswald Garrison Villard repeatedly sought to maintain a spirit of goodwill between the newly formed NAACP and the Tuskegee Machine, only to find himself cold-shouldered by Washington. Gestures of goodwill, rather than being reciprocated, were imbued with sinister hidden meaning by the ever-suspicious Tuskegeean. When, in January 1911, Villard informed Washington that the NAACP had separated from the Constitution League of John Milholland, following attacks by the later on the Tuskegee philosophy, Washington saw this action only as a ploy to win his sympathy while freeing Milholland to redouble his criticism.[33]

The passage of the years led Washington to conclude that what was good for himself was good for black America. This philosophy led him into a relentless persecution of all who sought to question his judgment. In the long term, Washington's perception of himself as the sole repository of wis-

dom and virtue may, ironically, have done more to bring about the demise
of the Tuskegee philosophy than all his real or imagined enemies. The abso-
lutist rule Washington enjoyed over Tuskegee meant that the institute was
too dependent on him personally. In the ten years that followed
Washington's death in 1915, the Tuskegee Machine fell rapidly into disre-
pair and ruin. The NAACP, in contrast, endured. A capacity to survive in
adversity was an essential ability for any civil rights organization conceived
during Washington's stewardship of black leadership in America.[34]

The racial climate of the Progressive era was a depressing one.
Precisely because of these bleak conditions effective civil rights leadership
was all the more crucial. Washington sincerely sought to fill this vacuum
and, in some respects, was an able spokesperson. Moreover, the stress he
placed on industrial education and avoidance of political activity was not
unique to him but had strong roots in African-American society.[35]

There is, however, a logical inconsistency in the argument that seeks
to reaffirm Washington's greatness as a race leader by emphasizing the
manifest difficulties that confronted him. It is a viewpoint that, at times,
comes close to reducing Washington's role in history to that of a gesticu-
lating puppet, well meaning but incapable of effective independent
thought and action. The net result of this perspective is to diminish rather
than enhance Washington's historical stature. Indeed, by this viewpoint
Washington appears to be not only marginalized, but also wrongheaded, in
his policies. An accommodationist strategy may be justified if it ultimately
results in tangible gains, or at the very least short-term damage limitation.
It is less easily defended if it is accepted that the scope for such gains or
limitation was minimal, bordering on nonexistent.

The attention that both Washington's contemporaries and later historians have devoted to his life and career belies the accuracy of this inef-
fectual stereotype. The work of a marionette would hardly warrant such
extensive debate. An essential attribute of greatness, the potential for
which Washington surely possessed, must be the ability to transcend difficulties rather than succumb to them. In the words of one biographer,
"whatever his dreams and failures," Washington "was a man of tremendous force, which he exerted on black and white America at a time when
both were still capable of changing under the thrusts of strong, determined
individual leaders." Washington's failure to achieve more than he did was
not just because of the *zeitgeist* of his age but also because "having become
respectable and powerful, the man whose first home was a slave's cabin
grew more disposed to look backward at the distance he had come than to
look ahead at the way there yet remained to go."[36]

Clearly, Washington's accommodationist strategy was aimed at the
long-term, not just short-term results. The philosophy underpinning this
approach can, though, be seen as a source of weakness as well as one of

strength. Washington's concept of the long haul could all too easily lead to the deferral, and ultimately avoidance, of constructive action that might otherwise have been undertaken. If the Tuskegeean's achievements during his own lifetime were limited, it was not just because of the constraints imposed by American society, but also because of the boundaries for action set by Washington himself. Accomodationism "in nature," as the historian Michael West has noted was "aimed primarily" at "shoring up Southern American Jim Crow and minimizing resistance to it."[37]

Washington has frequently been judged severely because of the assumption that a set of more positive, untried, policies was open to him. In this context, an examination of alternative, albeit untested, initiatives that may have been available to the Tuskegeean is a useful exercise. Whether such strategies would, or would not, have been more effective than those actually chosen by Washington is, by definition, impossible to judge, precisely because they remained untried. Nonetheless, identifying alternative actions that might have been open to him, and that might have offered some hope of success, even in the context of the repressive racial atmosphere of his era, still serves a purpose. If nothing else, it casts doubt on the validity of the view that the Tuskegeean pursued every realistic option available to him, and that he could have done no more.

In terms of specific roads not taken it is possible to identify at least three areas in which Washington's leadership could have been more dynamic. First, the Tuskegeean could have adopted a more forthright public stance against segregation and racial injustice. This was particularly the case from 1906 onward, by which time Washington's national status as a race leader had become more secure.

Moreover, Washington's failure to moderate Theodore Roosevelt's harsh treatment of the black soldiers involved in the 1906 Brownsville episode had indicated the limitations of an accommodationist strategy. This was even more forcefully delineated by the clearly unsympathetic attitudes of the Taft and Wilson administrations to black civil rights issues.[38]

In the limited extent to which Washington did adopt a more assertive program, the shift was not discernible until 1911, and then usually only to the most perceptive observer. Greater frankness on the part of Washington may not have had an immediate or wide-reaching effect, but it could have served to raise the self-esteem of the wider black community and could have forced those whites who were prepared to listen to confront the contradictions between a democratic, republican society and the way in which African Americans were treated in that society.[39]

A second area of activity in which Washington could have shown more dynamism was in fostering a greater awareness of African-American culture and identity, and in placing the black struggle for civil rights in a global, Pan-African context. The racial pride and consciousness of black

Americans might thus have been enhanced, together with an appreciation that blacks in America were not alone in striving for greater civil and political rights.

It is also possible that Washington could have responded in more positive ways to his black and liberal white critics after 1900. The existence of growing numbers of more militant civil rights spokespersons, rather than jeopardizing the work of Tuskegee, may even have benefited it, by reinforcing Washington's image as the sweet voice of moderation to the ears of conservative whites.

Equally, a leader other than the Tuskegeean may have perceived alternative strategies not as a threat, but simply as different methods of advancement toward the same mutually desired objective. The essential tragedy of Washington was perhaps that unlike the still disagreeing black leadership of later generations, he was unable to see that the various civil rights groups of his era could be "as separate as the five fingers" in the programs they advanced, but "as one as the hand" in their mutual desire for black advancement in a segregated and racially unequal society.

CHAPTER 4

As Separate as the Five Fingers

Booker T. Washington and the Age of Jim Crow

Booker T. Washington's publicly held views on racial segregation were most clearly stated in his address at the Cotton Exposition in Atlanta, Georgia on September 18 1895. Directed to an audience of northern and southern whites, black Americans, and business delegations from overseas, the speech was a, if not the, defining moment in Washington's life and career. It was the first time that an African American had been invited to speak from the platform at such an event.

Previously little known outside of Alabama, the oration transformed Washington into a nationally and internationally acclaimed race leader, a status he was to retain until his death in 1915. The ideas put forward by the Tuskegee educator in 1895 were equally unchanging. Outlining his social and economic philosophy, Washington's openly declared views on race relations in the United States at Atlanta remained, in many respects, unaltered during the last 20 years of his life.

Delivered during a period of worsening race relations in the United States, most particularly in the South, the Atlanta speech highlighted Washington's considerable abilities as an interracial diplomat. In emotive and nostalgic terms he reminded southern whites of the record of loyal and steadfast service by blacks in the region, "the most patient, faithful, law abiding and unresentful people that the world has seen." Notwithstanding the upheavals of civil war and emancipation, black Americans would remain constant in their devotion, "nursing your children, watching by the sick bed of your mothers and fathers, and often following them with tear-dimmed eyes to their graves."

Similarly, recent changes would not lead African Americans into harboring unrealistic expectations that would disrupt the existing status quo. "The wisest among my race understand that the agitation of questions of social equality is the extremist folly, and that progress in the enjoyment of all the privileges that will come to us must be the result of severe and constant struggle rather than of artificial forcing." In the most oft-quoted sentence from the address Washington even seemed to give his tacit approval of racial segregation, noting that "in all things that are purely social we can be as separate as the fingers, yet one as the hand in all things essential to mutual progress."[1]

His southern white listeners suitably reassured, Washington offered a message of hope to the black section of the audience. African Americans should aspire to economic self-help "in agriculture, mechanics, in commerce, in domestic service, and in the professions." In this endeavor they could expect benevolent encouragement from whites, for "whatever other sins the South may be called to bear, when it comes to business pure and simple," it was "in the South that the Negro" was "given a man's chance in the commercial world." Still adjusting to "the great leap from slavery to freedom" it was true that most blacks had to begin "at the bottom of life" rather than "at the top." Nonetheless, from these humble beginnings the potential for progress was unlimited, for "no race that has anything to contribute to the markets of the world is long in any degree ostracized." Fittingly, for a spokesman to be later labeled the Moses of his race, Washington concluded his speech with biblical imagery of a promised land, "a new heaven and a new earth" in "our beloved South."

Warmly applauded by his immediate listeners, whites on the platform, led by the Governor of Georgia, rushed to shake Washington's hand at the conclusion of his speech. The congratulations were enthusiastic and prolonged to the point that he found it difficult to make an exit from the building. The address was equally well received by white newspapers and politicians, both in the North and the South.

Significantly, the first reactions of many African-American commentators were also positive. Such enthusiasm, by Washington's own admission, did not last. After further reflection more radical spokespersons in the black community, particularly in the North, came to view the oration as too conservative and accommodationist. The speech became known as the Atlanta Compromise address because of its concessions to southern white sensitivities.[2]

Distance has added to the disenchantment with the view, with modern black and white historians generally being critical of Washington's performance. The Tuskegean has been accused of assuaging white guilt feelings over racial discrimination and thus encouraging further repression. His stress on starting at the "bottom of life" has been seen as limiting black economic expectations to employment as servants and agricultural laborers.

Similarly, the address reinforced negative white racial stereotypes of black Americans by highlighting the perceived frailties of freed slaves.

They were "ignorant and inexperienced" and unable to "draw the line between the superficial and the substantial, the ornamental gewgaws of life and the useful." Freedmen had a tendency to steal pumpkins and chickens.[3]

In a broader context, Washington unashamedly played on the popular prejudices of his era. Appealing to the antiimmigrant sentiments that were common in American society in the 1890s, he urged southern whites to "cast down your buckets" among their tried and tested black labor force rather than "look to the incoming of those of foreign birth and strange tongue and habits for the prosperity of the South." Capitalist hostility to emerging trade union organization was appeased by the reminder that African Americans had tilled the fields, "cleared your forests, builded your railroads and cities" all "without strikes and labour wars."

In contrast to the minor flaws Washington identified among southern blacks, he remained silent on the more serious racial injustices inflicted by whites. Debt peonage, the evils of the convict labor system, segregation, discrimination, and lynching were all but ignored by Washington in his Atlanta address. The only hint of reproach to southern white society for such wrongs was limited to a plea for "a blotting out of sectional differences and racial animosities and suspicions, in a determination to administer absolute justice, in a willing obedience among all classes to the mandates of law."

The prime responsibility for racial uplift seemed to rest not with southern whites but blacks themselves who needed to avoid letting their "grievances overshadow their opportunities." They had to develop more thrift and a stronger work ethic, learning to "dignify and glory common labour" and to appreciate that "there is as much dignity in tilling a field as in writing a poem."

Given the worsening racial conditions of the 1890s, any address that made more substantive demands of white society would have achieved little that was positive and would have risked jeopardizing future white philanthropic donations to black industrial education in general, and Tuskegee Institute in particular. Acknowledging this dilemma, one recent commentator has argued that the best option for Washington at Atlanta was to decline to speak at all. The year 1895 was "a time for silence," and Washington should have declined the invitation of the organizers of the Atlanta exposition to give an oration. In doing so he would, by quiet implication, have made a tacit protest against racial injustice. Moreover, he would have denied southern whites a source of release from their uncertainties and insecurities over the changing pattern of race relations.[4]

The difficulty with such a principled approach was its clear limitations as a constructive or practical policy. Outside of Alabama, and some educational circles, Washington was a little known figure before his Atlanta address. If he had declined to speak at the Cotton Exposition it would have done little, if anything, to create angst and self-doubt among white Americans. Unaware of the Tuskegeean's existence, let alone his snubbing of the event, most delegates at Atlanta would probably have viewed his absence with a complacent lack of concern.

Worse, the exposition organizers may have replaced Washington with an even more conservative and accommodationist African-American spokesperson. Any number of black speakers, such as Bishop Abram L. Grant of Texas and Bishop Wesley J. Gaines of Georgia, could have been relied on to address whites in honeyed terms on the subject of race relations in hope of patronage or personal advancement. This would have left whites more, not less, secure in their racial philosophy.[5]

Washington's absence from Atlanta would not only have failed to advance the lot of African Americans in general, but could also have been at considerable personal cost to himself. In his efforts to expand Tuskegee Institute, Washington was always heavily dependent on white philanthropy. A place on the speakers' platform at Atlanta gave him an invaluable opportunity for favorable publicity, and the possibility of new sources of patronage. Absence from the event would only have reduced the prospects of generosity from potential white benefactors who were made aware of his noncooperation.

In the 20 years that followed his Atlanta speech, Washington clearly did enjoy the status of a nationally and internationally recognized race leader. For most of this period he declined to use this opportunity to speak out in forthright terms against racial segregation. He has been reproached both by more radical black contemporaries, such as William Monroe Trotter, and by later historians for his failure to do so. When responding to his critics the Tuskegeean justified his inaction on a variety of grounds.

In the first instance, he argued that consistent public protest would not have achieved anything. Writing to the Progressive white newspaper proprietor, Oswald Garrison Villard, in 1904, Washington acknowledged that some blacks, particularly in the North, saw his strategy as too conservative. It was "very natural" that northern blacks should "chafe and become restless and impatient over conditions which the race has to endure." Washington admitted that he became "just as impatient as they do, and wish just as much as they that I could change conditions." However, "you and I both know that mere wishing will not make a change."[6]

In the racial climate that prevailed in the early years of the twentieth century, southern whites were unlikely to respond positively to black criticism of the status quo. To the contrary, the perception would have been created that black Americans were a race of complainers seeking to blame their disadvantaged position in society on the actions of whites. "There are times when it is wise for us to hold these indignation meetings to protest against injustice that is practiced upon our race," Washington told his students in a Sunday evening talk at Tuskegee on 13 January 1907. However, as might be expected from an address entitled "Looking on the Bright Side of Life," Washington went on to stress that such a strategy had clear limitations:

> no race should depend on its success in life merely upon the publica-
> tion of its wrongs. If it does it is going to fail, because the world grows
> sick of a weak race, of a sick race, just as individuals grow sick of weak
> individuals and sick individuals. There is no pleasure no encourage-
> ment in coming into contact with failure. The world likes to come in
> contact with success. The world does not honor failure. That is true with
> regard to a race, just as it is true with regard to an individual. I speak
> to you as I do because I want you to go out from here prepared to help
> the race learn how to overlook the wrongs and injuries, to hold up its
> head, and go bravely on. Tell the world that your race is going to suc-
> ceed; then the world will hold out its hand and help to encourage it.[7]

Protesting too much might be counterproductive in other ways. It would inadvertently give more publicity and focus to the statements and actions of extreme segregationists at the expense of more sympathetic southern white spokesmen. Typically, Washington used a rustic anecdote, "The Loudest Frog," to make this point. In his favored role as a rural sage the Tuskegeean was fond of telling audiences the story of an elderly freed-man from Alabama who lived near a frog pond. The noise each night from the pond was such that the "old coloured man" was unable to sleep and he became convinced that the neighborhood was overrun by frogs. However, closer inspection revealed the source of the irritation was just one loud and "very large old bullfrog." Making explicit the moral of the tale Washington reassured his listeners with the thought that "our enemies are not so many in number but they make a great deal of noise; we must not be deceived by those bullfrogs."[8]

The difficult balance between criticism and accommodation was high-lighted when an unsigned editorial, penned by Washington, appeared in the black newspaper the Boston *Transcript*. The piece consisted of a vigor-ous attack on new segregationist legislation in Georgia that excluded African Americans from railroad sleeping cars in the state. Prior to publi-cation the black journalist, and confidante of Washington, Timothy Thomas Fortune, added a final sentence of his own that suggested that if other states below the Mason-Dixie line introduced similar measures, it would be very difficult for self-respecting blacks to use the southern rail-roads at all. The addition reinforced the sense of black injustice that was central to the editorial, but left Washington unimpressed. He feared that it might only encourage southern railway authorities, and segregationist legislators, to enact further discriminatory measures precisely because these might deter blacks from railroad travel altogether.[9]

The impact of constant protest and agitation on African Americans, as well as whites, was also unhelpful according to Washington. The effect on black audiences would be to maximize feelings of resentment and injustice, but without providing any practical prospect of redress for their grievances. Radical black orators might develop feelings of bravado and self-importance from the applause of their listeners, but they would have no tangible gains to show for their efforts. Their labor would be better employed in less dramatic, but more rewarding, self-help economic initiatives.

In a November 1913 article, "What I am Trying to Do," published in the *World's Work,* Washington used his familiar anecdotal style to convey his argument. He recounted the experiences of a young black friend who was "exceedingly sensitive" over "the rights of his race" and became a popular speaker in local African American communities. Like many orators "he was strong on quotations from people who have been a long time dead." Over time he began to realize that "indignation meetings" were not providing him or his family with food, clothes and other basic necessities of life.

Fortunately, as with most fairy tales, there was a happy ending. Chastened by poverty, and enlightened by advice from Washington, the hero of the story abandoned political agitation in favor of a career as a small farmer. Predictably his endeavors led to material success and earned him the respect of local blacks and whites alike. The moral was clear. Hard work and economic achievement were the best ways for black Americans to achieve equal rights in society rather than political agitation.[10]

In his public utterances on segregation Washington always maintained a careful balance between articulating black expectations and accommodating to white society. Often he used language that was deliberately ambiguous. If, during his 1895 Atlanta address, Washington expressed the view that the races could be as separate as the fingers "in all things that are purely social" his precise interpretation as to what this actually meant was less clear. In a private letter, written less than one month after the address, Washington noted "that there are a great many things in the South which southern white people class as social intercourse that is not really so." Consequently, "if anybody understood me as meaning that riding in the same railroad car or sitting in the same room of a railroad station is social intercourse they certainly got a wrong idea of my position."[11]

Often, conservative statements made by Washington on closer scrutiny contained careful qualifications that greatly diluted the import of what he was saying. In his Atlanta speech Washington thus stressed that for blacks the "opportunity to earn a dollar in a factory, just now is worth infinitely more than the opportunity to spend a dollar in an opera house." This choice of words gave the deliberate impression that Washington believed that African Americans should confine their immediate aspirations to manual labor. At the same time, the use of the caveat "just now" suggested that he believed that blacks should not be denied the enjoyment of the opera forever. Equally, if blacks should begin "at the bottom of life" Washington was careful to avoid saying that that should be the end point of their journey, even if his southern white listeners chose to place precisely such an interpretation on his words.

On other occasions Washington made use of irony and subtle understatement to make implicit criticism of segregationist practice, while at the same time appeasing southern white sensitivities. Although only nine years old at the end of the Civil War in 1865, he sometimes wrote fondly of his memories of life as a slave boy. On one level such accounts were clearly intended to appeal to southern white nostalgia for the antebellum era, and the romantic mythology of the "Lost Cause" that had developed by the end of the nineteenth century. In other respects, they arguably comprised veiled attacks on restrictive racial practices of more recent origin.

"Christmas Days in Old Virginia," published in 1907, thus recalled the happiness of Christmas past as both slaves and white planters and their families joined together to enjoy shared festivities. These simple pleasures of days gone by, Washington confessed, had more appeal for him than the "stiff and formal customs" of Christmas present. Whether this reference to more modern customs included segregation was a matter left for Washington's readers to judge for themselves. "Stiff and staid" can be seen as a not unreasonable description of a society where most whites would not even admit blacks into their home on a social basis, let alone share yuletide festivities with them.[12]

In *The Story of the Negro*, published two years later, Washington recalled that "until freedom came the life of the Negro was so interwoven with that of the white man that it is almost true to say that he had no separate history." For plantation slaves the "Big House" where the master lived was the center of the only world they knew. Simultaneously appeasing the paternalistic feelings of the white planter class, and denying any distinctive African-American cultural heritage, such statements by Washington have not endeared him to modern historians. Viewed from another perspective, reference to the racially interwoven past can also be seen as implied criticism of later segregationist practice and dubious social science theory that stressed the natural and inevitable origins of racial separation.[13]

The Man Farthest Down (1911) gave Washington an alternative framework of analysis to reflect on U.S. culture and society. Written after a six-week tour of Europe, the book was ostensibly a sociological study. An investigation of the living conditions of the poorest laborers and peasants in Europe, the work was intended to highlight the comparatively favorable opportunities for advancement open to black Americans by dint of thrift and hard work.

Not surprisingly, publication of the book led to renewed, albeit familiar, attacks on Washington by his black American critics for being too accommodating to the racial sensitivities of southern whites. However, if predominantly conservative in tone, the work also contained hints of a more subversive message. Observations of ethnic prejudices in Europe, such as Magyar contempt for Romanians and Austrian distaste for Slovaks, tacitly invited Washington's readers to reflect on stereotyped prejudices against African Americans within the United States itself. The fact that he was able to highlight case studies of white Europeans living and working in conditions no better than, or even worse than, those experienced by African Americans was no less significant. Such findings challenged the then increasingly common notions of Anglo-Saxon superiority. They also made it harder to sustain the view that the poverty and deprivation suffered by African Americans were a direct result of black racial inferiority rather than other factors.[14]

An analysis of Booker T. Washington's thoughts and statements on racial injustice and segregation is complicated by the fact that he made a virtue out of inconsistency. Like other black American leaders before and after him, Washington said different things to different audiences, reserving his most outspoken remarks for listeners he gauged to be most sympathetic.

In an address before the Women's New England Club in Boston, on 27 January 1890, his sentiments and speaking style were very different from those of the Atlanta orator five years later. Although, predictably, outlining the merits of industrial education as practiced at Tuskegee, doubtless with the hope of encouraging some financial donations, Washington was also determined not to let his stress on black American opportunities overshadow their grievances. He highlighted the "iron claws" of debt peonage that impoverished "four-fifths" of black sharecroppers in the South. He denounced the poor quality of public education available to black children in the region, with each black child in Alabama receiving 81 cents from the state for his or her education that year compared to $15.00 per annum for each child in Massachusetts. Sixty percent of black children in the South had attended no school at all in the previous year, and at least 75 percent of southern blacks had not attained even the most basic standards of literacy.

Turning to "the wrongs growing out of prejudice," Washington condemned the denial of black voting rights and racial discrimination in employment, not only in the South but also in the North, where "let a Negro mechanic enter a northern factory as a labourer, and if the Negro remains, the factory will break up."

Continuing his theme, Washington spoke of the separate but unequal accommodations afforded to black passengers on southern railroads, and the denial of justice for blacks in the southern legal system, where "the Negro is completely at the mercy of the white man in the state courts." That was of course assuming that blacks were allowed to reach court, given the widespread practice of lynching in the South. This "barbarous mode of attempting to administer justice" usually began with an allegation of rape when in "the midst of excitement" there was "no time or disposition to inquire into the facts" and "some poor Negro" was "swung up to a tree and made to suffer for a crime which in five cases out of ten was committed, if committed at all, by someone else." Between 1865 and 1890 "at least ten thousand colored men in the South" had been "murdered by white men, and yet with perhaps a single exception, the record of no court shows that a single white man has ever been hanged for these murders."

The uncompromising nature of Washington's Boston address was influenced by the fact that he was speaking to a northern audience. Moreover, the event was a private meeting restricted to members of the woman's club. Reporting of the speech was strictly forbidden under the club rules.[15]

Although uncharacteristically forthright at Boston, because of the particular circumstances of the meeting, Washington appeared to qualify the conservatism of his 1895 Atlanta address on a number of occasions in his later career, and in more public fora. Speaking before an audience of 16,000 at the National Peace Jubilee in Chicago, on 16 October 1898, Washington reminded his listeners of African-American heroism on the battlefield in the service of the United States from the War of Independence, 1776–1783, to the recently concluded Spanish American War of 1898. The only victory that remained to be achieved was in the "blotting out of racial prejudices." This was particularly the case in the southern states, where such prejudices constituted "a cancer gnawing at the heart of the Republic, that shall one day prove as dangerous as an attack from an army without or within."

Applauded in Chicago, the speech was widely criticized in the southern white press. Opting for retreat as the best form of defense, Washington, at least in public, reverted to the views that he had previously espoused at Atlanta in 1895.[16]

Despite such a setback, the Chicago speech can be seen as a qualified victory for Washington, in that it had focused national public attention on the issues of racial discrimination and segregation. Paradoxically, the less often Washington spoke out in forthright terms against racial injustice, the more successful such condemnations were likely to be in attracting public attention, precisely because of their rarity value. This irony was not lost on Washington. Writing to Oswald Garrison Villard in 1904, on the issue of lynching, he admitted that it was "true I do not speak out every time a lynching occurs in the South," for "if I did my words would soon become so frequent and so common that the public press would give no attention to what I said." He therefore chose to ration his public indignation, "but when I think the proper season has come I never fail to speak out and rebuke the lynchers in every part of the country." From this perspective Washington's accommodationism, punctuated with occasional bolder statements, was part of a deliberate long-term strategy rather than a sign of inconsistency.[17]

Between 1911 and 1915 Washington did become more openly critical of Jim Crowism. If a conscious change of tactics, this shift may have been influenced by the rise of the National Association for the Advancement of Colored People (NAACP), founded in 1909. More outspoken than Washington on issues of racial injustice, the new organization began to win over the support of blacks and liberal whites who had previously backed the Tuskegee philosophy. Increasingly viewed as conservative and backward looking by the NAACP leadership, Washington needed to appear more dynamic and forthright to maintain his position as a race leader. On a personal level, Washington may also have become more disillusioned with the state of U.S. race relations following the Ulrich affair of 1911.

"Is the Negro Having a Fair Chance?," an article by Washington published in *The Century* magazine in November 1912, was one of his most important and most militant statements on racial segregation in his last years."A large part of our racial troubles in the United States," he noted, grew "out of some attempt to pass and execute a law that will make and keep one man superior to another, whether he is intrinsically superior or not."

The use of such explicit language was significant. In the 1896 *Plessy v. Ferguson* case the U.S. Supreme Court had rejected the claim that state segregation laws violated the rights of equal citizenship guaranteed to blacks, and all Americans, in the Fourteenth Amendment to the U.S. Constitution. This was because it was an "underlying fallacy" to assume that "enforced separation of the two races" stamped "the colored race with a badge of inferiority." Washington's choice of words put him at odds with the views of the Court and came close to suggesting that segregation laws were inherently unconstitutional. This impression was reinforced when he went on to remark that "No greater harm can be done to any group of people than to let them feel that a statutory enactment can keep them superior to anybody else." In the same vein the Tukegeean continued by noting that "No greater injury can be done to any youth than to let him feel that because he belongs to this or that race, or because of his color, he will be advanced in life regardless of his own merits or efforts."

Ironically, this argument was to bear a more than passing resemblance to the reasoning of the U.S. Supreme Court in the 1954 *Brown v. Board of*

Education decision that overturned the Plessy ruling. Expressing the unanimous opinion of the Court, then Chief Justice Earl Warren ruled segregation in education to be unconstitutional because it created an innate sense of inferiority in the minds of black children.

In 1912, having come close to making this very point, Washington confusingly went on to seemingly reject the logical conclusions of his own reasoning. In a later section of his article he assured his readers that it was not the existence of segregated facilities and accommodations that black Americans resented, but their unequal nature. On the railroads, for example, blacks paid the same fare as white passengers, but usually received inferior, dirty, and uncomfortable seating. Segregation was therefore wrong because it led to economic unfairness for black passengers and customers, rather than being unjust in terms of immutable moral principle.[18]

The contradictory nature of the thinking in his *The Century* article reflected an ambivalence in Washington's public and private persona. In his public statements, even before sympathetic audiences like the Women's New England Club in Boston, he principally attacked segregation on economic grounds. Defending the rights of black consumers against the practices of large business corporations was a line of argument most likely to appeal to white audiences during the Progressive era.

Condemning the unequal nature of segregated facilities, rather than attacking the principle of separation, had other advantages. There was little prospect of halting the spread of segregation given the depressing racial climate of the United States in the early years of the twentieth century. Criticisms of the gross inadequacies of the segregated accommodations provided for African Americans might, however, prompt some modest improvements in those facilities.

In the longer term the achievement of separate but less unequal amenities for blacks would increase the economic cost to private companies and state authorities of maintaining Jim Crow practices. This might ultimately lead consumers and taxpayers to question the principle of segregation itself. This type of thinking had attractions for Washington, who was always a firm believer in the philosophy of gradualism. As late as the 1930s and 1940s the NAACP Legal Defense Fund recognized the advantages of fighting for improvements in separate educational facilities for blacks over seeking any immediate end to segregation.

The private Washington was less patient. In what has been called his "secret life" Washington covertly sponsored antisegregation lawsuits and wrote, or encouraged, editorials and articles against segregation in black newspapers. A notable example of this double life came in 1906 with his successful behind the scenes campaign against the Warner-Foraker amendment to the Hepburn railroad bill in Congress. The amendment would have required equal facilities for white and black passengers, but by implication also allowed for the introduction of racial segregation on interstate transport.

Given Washington's publicly held views he should not have had any objection to such a measure. He might even have been expected to welcome it, given his oft-stated argument that it was not the principle of segregation that African Americans found unacceptable, but the unequal nature of the separate provisions that were made available. His actual response was very different. He covertly liaised with sympathetic influential contacts in Washington, D.C., to block the passage of the amendment. "During the session of the Congress I have had two colored and one white friend on guard at Washington, who have been very carefully looking into such amendments as were made to the rate bill," the Tuskegeean confided to Samuel Laing Williams, a trusted supporter in Chicago. "The white friend," Senator Henry W. Blair, "has access to the floor of the Senate" and "has kept out of the bill so far any legislation against us."[19]

Only in death did the public and private Washington become one. His last article, "My View of the Segregation Laws," published posthumously in the *New Republic* on 4 December 1915, was easily Washington's most outspoken statement against segregation. No longer concentrating his criticism on the practicalities of separate facilities, the Tuskegeean condemned Jim Crowism in principle. Segregation was "ill-advised" he concluded, on multiple counts. It was unjust. It invited other unjust measures. It created resentment among African Americans. It was inconsistent and it "widened the breach between the two races."[20]

The particular development that led to such anger in Washington had been the recent passage of segregation ordinances by some city and state authorities. In southern cities like Norfolk and Richmond in Virginia and Baltimore in Maryland, these measures introduced legally enforced residential segregation. In 1917, two years after Washington's death, continuing black opposition to such ordinances culminated in the first notable victory against the spread of racial segregation in the U.S. Supreme Court. In the case of *Buchanan v. Warley* the Court held that municipal ordinances requiring residential segregation were unconstitutional. Ironically, the opinion of the judges in the ruling echoed the kind of public reasoning that Washington had so often put forward. It was not that such measures infringed on black citizenship rights, they concluded, but the fact that they violated the property rights of householders to sell their homes to whomsoever they wished that made the ordinances unacceptable.

The contrast between the public and private persona of Washington was not the only source of inconsistency in his response to racial segregation. A pragmatist rather than an intellectual, Washington at times supported courses of action that were, by any strict exercise of logic, contradictory. In promoting black economic self-help, he urged African Americans to show race loyalty in their economic activities. They should consciously purchase goods and services from black shopkeepers and tradesmen rather than use white owned stores.

A similar faith in the possibility of racial solidarity in commerce helped to inspire the formation of the National Negro Business League (NNBL) in 1900. Specifically created with the idea of encouraging black economic enterprise, Washington hoped that in their local communities black tradesmen and professionals would form local leagues to exchange ideas and promote economic cooperation in a shared commitment to racial uplift.

Understandable as this aim may have been, it clearly ran counter to the arguments put forward by Washington in some of his public speeches and statements. In his 1895 Atlanta address Washington had urged blacks to strive for economic advancement precisely because racial loyalties and prejudices played no part in commerce. "Whatever other sins the South may be called to bear," when it came to "business, pure and simple," African Americans were "given a man's chance in the commercial world." Simply put, in commerce it was not race or color but the quality of service that mattered. Whatever their prejudices, whites would be prepared to buy goods and services from blacks who demonstrated their business worth.

In some instances, and under certain conditions, there was some validity in this argument. Tuskegee Institute, in particular, was an example of what could be achieved under favorable conditions. Situated in a remote rural location the produce and services made available by the institute benefited neighboring black and white communities alike.

When Tuskegee students first started making bricks they founded the only brickmaking yard in the county. "People who were engaged in building came to examine the bricks which the Tuskegee students made, and when they found they were good bricks wanted to buy them," recalled Washington's resident white ghostwriter Max Bennett Thrasher. "The school soon found that it could have a market for all the surplus product of the yard. As soon as it was possible to do so a brick-making machine was bought and set up." By 1901 the institute was "selling several hundred thousand bricks every year to be used in the surrounding country."[21]

In the 1870s Tuskegee, though formerly a prosperous town and a center for cotton sales, was in economic decline with a falling population. From the 1880s local white planters and merchants were keen to support the expansion of Tuskegee Institute to help revive the local economy.[22]

Elsewhere, and more generally, the situation was less encouraging. Rather than welcoming the development of thriving black businesses southern whites more often saw them as a threat to white supremacy. Successful black farmers and tradesmen, even if conservative in their politics and accommodationist in social behavior, were seen as being guilty of "insolence" because of their material prosperity. This was especially the case if they appeared to show signs of greater affluence than their white neighbors. The few African Americans who fell into this category risked having their crops destroyed and their shops burned, and being forced to leave their locality. In Mississippi, the driving of prosperous black tradesmen and farmers from their homes, a practice known as "whitecapping," was commonplace in the early 1890s and between 1902 and 1906. At times the fate could be even worse. For all the ritual allegations of sexual assault or rape, black lynch victims often first attracted white hostility because of their success in commerce or agriculture.[23]

Even the most exemplary of Tuskegee graduates were not secure from white vigilantes. In a Sunday evening talk at Tuskegee, in May 1900, Washington urged the assembled students to follow the example of Nelson Henry of Montgomery County, Alabama. A former student at Tuskegee, after graduation Henry had established a small farm and a school in the town of Ramer, Alabama. In 1902 the school closed after a visit by the nationally known female photographer Frances Benjamin Johnston. Johnston was an attractive white woman in her mid-thirties, and the episode was seen as an unforgivable violation of southern social and sexual taboos by local whites. Henry was driven from the town by an angry white mob and fortunate to escape death or serious injury.[24]

In the North, as well as the South, blacks suffered regular discrimination in employment. Factory owners were reluctant to hire black workers and, even when prepared to do so, found that this was unacceptable to white employees and trade unions that routinely excluded blacks from membership. Washington was well aware of the problem. Writing in 1899, he admitted that it was common for blacks to walk "the streets of a Northern city day after day seeking employment, only to find every door closed" against them "on account of . . . colour, except in menial service."[25]

In public he chose to deny the existence of such prejudice in the South. If, in private, he knew all too often this that was not the case, Washington's public position was less an act of hypocrisy than necessity. Black Americans were all too obviously denied equal opportunities in their civil, political, and social life in the South. This left economic advancement as the only means of racial uplift for Washington to encourage. If, even in this area, opportunity was severely limited, there was no alternative agenda for Washington to pursue other than to give up altogether in despair.

"If one gets in the habit of continually thinking and talking about race prejudice, he soon gets to the point where he is fit for little that is worth doing," Washington advised his daughter Portia in 1906. "In the northern part of the United States there are a number of colored people who make their lives miserable, because all their talk is about race prejudice."[26]

His positive and pragmatic mental outlook helps to explain Washington's separatist economic tendencies in the creation of the NNBL. Tacitly acknowledging the existence of racial prejudice in southern economic life, whatever his public statements to the contrary, Washington strived to achieve the most that was possible for African Americans under such conditions. If discrimination led to a loss of job opportunities for blacks in many trades and professions, Washington took the optimistic view that this would create openings in others, in what were seen as exclusively black occupations, such as Pullman car railroad porters. Similarly, if segregation excluded blacks from white-owned facilities this opened up new opportunities within a separate African-American economy. The "very fact that a negro cannot buy soda-water in a white drug store makes an opportunity for the colored drug store," he noted in 1912, "which often becomes a sort of social center for the colored population."[27]

Like many Americans of his day, Washington showed interest in the substantial growth in immigration to the United States from southern and eastern Europe between 1880 and 1914. He shared the concern of other African-American leaders about the possible impact of this development on the lives of black Americans. In the rapidly expanding industrial centers of the North immigrant workers took advantage of job opportunities that might otherwise have been open to blacks.

In the South, ever since the end of the Civil War in 1865, there had been periodic attempts by state agencies and private individuals to attract immigrant workers to replace black labor. The fact that these efforts had consistently ended in failure was only partially reassuring. Anxiety about the future of such schemes accounted for the xenophobic tone of some of Washington's remarks in his 1895 Atlanta address.

Typically, he also looked to draw positive lessons from the immigrant experience. Many immigrants arrived in the United States with little in the way of money or personal belongings. Like black Americans many of the newcomers suffered from the ethnic prejudices of native white Americans. Despite this, they generally succeeded in establishing themselves by developing semiautonomous ghetto enclaves in American cities. In this clannishness, Washington saw a model for black Americans to emulate.

Predictably, the rustic-minded Tuskegeean did not think in terms of black migration to the cities. Instead, he hoped that blacks might develop their own self-sufficient communities in a rural setting. The man was wise who "goes out into the country," he advised Tuskegee students in October 1906, "miles from any street car or soda fountain, and makes a kingdom for himself where he is master of all, and where he can say what shall take place and what shall not take place." Blacks might also establish their own townships, as some immigrant settlers had done. "If the settlement is started by the Poles, a Polander becomes the depot agent, a Polander becomes the telegraph operator," he told a Chicago meeting of the NNBL in 1912. "The first mayor is a Polander. The president of the first bank is a Pole. There is no segregation of the Poles in this city." Instead there was "freedom and a chance for unfettered and unlimited growth."[28]

In this vein Washington welcomed the establishment of all black towns, such as Mound Bayou in Mississippi, and Boley and Clearview in Oklahoma. The principal founder of Mound Bayou, Isaiah Montgomery, became one of Washington's strongest supporters in the Magnolia state.[29]

It is easy to be critical of Washington's aspirations for black economic self-sufficiency. The situation of blacks, some 90 percent of whom still lived in the South, mostly in rural locations, was different from that of European immigrants, who settled mainly in the expanding cities of the North. This urban growth was a sign of the rapid pace of industrialization in late nineteenth-century America. Agriculture was declining both in importance and profitability as a sector within the American economy. The rise of the Populist movement of the 1890s, and the relative poverty of southern and western farmers, even during the national prosperity of the 1920s, reflected this fact. In encouraging blacks to enter into farming and the creation of rural townships, Washington directed them into a way of life that was ending rather than a new beginning. Mound Bayou and Boley had both entered into irreversible decline by the time of Washington's death, largely because of these changing national economic conditions.[30]

If immigrants suffered from bigotry and discrimination, this was also distinct from the African-American experience. Second and third generations of immigrant families, Americanized in dress, speech, and even name, could hope to escape the burden of prejudice. For black Americans the color line ensured that persecution would be unrelenting across the generations.

Similarly, if segregation did help facilitate the creation of a separate black consumer market on which black businessmen could capitalize, this gain was more than offset by the many economic disadvantages of Jim Crowism. Segregation enabled employers to lower the wages of all workers, white and black. White workers often accepted poor contracts with companies in order to maintain an all white labor force. Black workers were forced to accept poor pay and conditions because job opportunities were so scarce for them. Black tradesmen who relied on a white client base lost out with the spread of segregation as jobs previously seen as black occupations were taken over by whites, such as barbershops, blacksmiths, and bakers.[31]

To condemn Washington for these shortcomings in his policies is, however, to overlook the very limited nature of the options that were available to him. Migration to the cities would not have offered any easy solution to the economic problems faced by black Americans. Washington's attempts to encourage black economic self-sufficiency represented the least worst option within the reality of an increasingly segregated society. A separate African-American economy was not Washington's preferred choice, for he was in principle opposed to racial separatism.

Booker T. Washington's public and private responses to racial segregation were often inconsistent and contradictory, and generally did not bring substantive gains. This is not surprising. Ultimately, such shortcomings were less a result of the failings of Washington himself, or his philosophy of racial uplift, than an inevitable consequence of the conditions in which he had to operate. Jim Crowism, in its very nature was often inconsistent and discriminatory against African Americans. Forced to work within the confines of a racially segregated society, it was a depressing fact that Washington's policies were at best often an exercise in damage limitation. Washington himself was only too well aware of the painful reality of the situation. "I feel the wrongs and appreciate the aspirations of the race just as keenly as any individual can," he wrote in 1903, "but it is the long patient road that we have got to travel; it is going to require hard work and dogged determination."[32]

CHAPTER 5

Realist or Reactionary?

Booker T. Washington
and the Great Migration

Addressing a racially mixed audience at the Atlanta Cotton Exposition in Georgia, on 18 September 1895, Booker T. Washington famously advised his fellow black Americans not to risk the uncertainties of "bettering their condition in a foreign land." Migration to the cities of the North, although not specifically mentioned in the speech, was, by implication, an equally unwise option. African Americans should instead cast down their buckets where they were, "cultivating friendly relations with the southern white man" who was "their next-door neighbor."[1]

Twenty years later, during a tour of Louisiana in April 1915, the Tuskegeean, as always a model of consistency, again advised blacks to profit "by the greater opportunities which they had in the South" and "stay on the farm, grow a variety of crops . . . keep away from the cities." Although Washington's sentiments have sometimes been perceived as reactionary prejudice, an examination of his specific objections to urban migration, and the most recent historical research on the Great Migration, 1915–25, arguably vindicates his views.[2]

The majority of modern historians have found Washington, with his conservative, accommodationist outlook, an unattractive figure. In respect to his opposition to the forces of urbanization and industrialization, even otherwise sympathetic commentators have acknowledged this as a failure of judgment. Washington's economic philosophy bordered on a "peasant conservatism" of "Uncle Tom in his own cabin." This outdated Jeffersonianism helped perpetuate the master-servant relationship between the races in the South. It overlooked the technological changes taking place in agriculture that would ultimately extinguish employment opportunities for black farm workers. Moreover, Washington was increasingly out of touch with the growing numbers of black southerners who were attracted by the opportunities and excitement of city life.[3]

Such lack of empathy and practical vision was the more striking given Washington's pride in his pragmatic outlook and his ability to tune in to the southern black psyche, in a way that his largely middle-class, radical northern black opponents found impossible.

A desire to please southern whites was doubtless one explanation for Washington's seeming urban myopia. Accommodationism was also comfortingly reinforced by the country boy prejudices ingrained by a childhood in the rural South. When formally attired for public occasions Washington gave the appearance of an uncomfortable, albeit prosperous, peasant who wore a brown derby instead of a top hat.[4]

Samuel Armstrong, the Principal of the Hampton Institute in Virginia, who became an almost surrogate father figure to the young Washington, himself had a distaste for urban life. Simply visiting New York City made him feel uncomfortable, "like an atom of no particular account."[5]

In conversation Booker T. Washington appeared to be like "some big-natured peasant," in contrast to the "very sharp and able . . . agitating Negroes of the North." Like some turn of the century Forrest Gump, Washington peppered his public utterances with simple rural imagery replete with deeper meaning and wisdom.[6]

Even in the few precious moments of leisure that a busy life could afford he found there was "nothing in a crowded city life that can approach the happiness and general good feeling which one may have in the country." More specifically, his preferred recreations were "hunting and horse-back-riding," and "to spend as many hours as I can in fishing with the old-time pole and line." Predictably, Washington "never had any use for, or success with, more modern 'new fangled' fishing apparatus."[7]

At times the Tuskegeean's rustic rhetoric could verge close on unconscious comic self-parody. In one of his customary Sunday evening talks to Tuskegee students, on 4 February 1900, Washington thus revealed that "one of the most interesting books" that he had "ever seen" was a work "describing the beautiful things which a person can find in a common mud-puddle in a common hole of water, such as you see on the roadside, during the summer time especially." It would be interesting to speculate as to the impact of this unusual disclosure on Washington's youthful charges. Many may well have agreed with him that they "would be surprised" at "how many really charming things one can find in a stagnant pool of water." As a man schooled in such simple pleasures it is easy to see why Washington's reactions to the more racy temptations of the city were, in the words of one biographer, akin to those "of a pious Scot thrown into the sins of eighteenth century London."[8]

If Booker T. Washington's bucolic character has been a source of gentle amusement to historians, such a rustic exterior also concealed a deeper, more profound, judgment. In short, the Tuskegeean's concerns over black urban life were based not simply on emotive bias, but, typically, on cold empirical logic. Washington was by no means ignorant of the daily realities of urban living.

The tentacles of the Tuskegee Machine extended well beyond southern climes. Leading benefactors of Tuskegee Institute included early giants of the industrial age, most famously Andrew Carnegie. The Tuskegeean had an effective controlling interest in much of the northern black press, including the New York *Age*, the Washington *Colored American*, the Boston *Colored Citizen*, and the Washington *Bee*.[9]

Charles W. Anderson, the leading black politician in New York City from 1890 to 1934, was one of Washington's most trusted lieutenants. Anderson kept the Tuskegeean regularly advised of developments in the city and ruthlessly persecuted any black New Yorkers who questioned the Tuskegee philosophy. In Chicago the black lawyer and confidante of Washington, Samuel Laing Williams, rendered equally faithful service.[10]

The passing of the years brought Washington increasing familiarity with urban life, as fund raising activities required him to spend some two-thirds of his time in the North. In 1910 he was an early influential supporter of the newly formed National Urban League (NUL) and, in 1914, recognizing the potential significance of the organization, he became a member of its governing board.[11]

Washington's judgment was also informed by recent historical experience. At the turn of the century most post-Civil War examples of black economic progress derived from agricultural initiatives rather than advancement through the new industries of the North. In particular, there were the black land cooperatives of the Sea Islands of South Carolina, set up during the Reconstruction period, and still showing signs of prosperity as late as World War I. Fifteen percent of black families in South Carolina had obtained their own homesteads from the Land Commission set up by the Republican state administration during Reconstruction. In the 1980s the direct descendents of some of these original settlers were still in possession of the same Land Commission tracts.[12]

At Davis Bend, Mississippi a multi-talented ex-slave, Benjamin Montgomery, established an all black community on the former lands of the Confederate President, Jefferson Davis, at the end of the Civil War. Montgomery's son, Isaiah, who became a close ally of Booker T. Washington, went on to found the all black township of Mound Bayou, Mississippi during the 1880s.[13]

In Georgia alone, blacks owned 1,400,000 acres of land, worth over $28,000,000 by 1906. In the South as a whole, there were some 1,100,000 black farmers in 1900. Of these, 359,000 were sharecroppers or hired hands, 552,401 were tenants or part owners, and 187,000 were full landowners in their own right. After prolonged postwar hardship, the price of cotton rose from seven cents a pound in the years 1890–1902 to 10.6 cents a pound during the period 1903–15, and 21.5 cents a pound between 1915 and 1925. In the light of such evidence of an encouraging economic upturn, it is not difficult to understand the basis of Washington's belief that, in time, many black tenants would be able to succeed in buying their own landholdings.[14]

The reality of the black historical experience between 1865 and 1915 seemed to lend support to his Jeffersonian vision of a future society of prosperous small black farmers. Washington was not alone in such a perspective. In the 1890s even the young W. E. B. Du Bois concluded that "the rush to cities, where the surroundings are unhealthful" had had a "bad effect" on black Americans.[15]

In the immediate years after 1915 future, rather than past events, were to assume the greater significance in determining the economic prospects of black Americans. A series of natural disasters, the most severe depredations of the cotton boll weevil, combined with rural economic recession, all but ended any prevailing sense of optimism in southern agriculture.

Similarly, a major expansion in northern industrial output stimulated by World War I was combined with an end to the previous tide of European immigration to the United States during the war years. In the following decade the National Origins Act of 1924 confirmed the legal restriction on the wartime changes in immigration patterns. In consequence, employment opportunities for blacks in the industrial conurbations of the North dramatically expanded in a way that Washington could never have envisaged.

For all the seismic alterations that took place in U.S. society between 1915 and 1925, the experience of newly urbanized blacks in these years of the Great Migration in many respects appeared to bear out the fears of city life that Washington had so consistently expressed in the years 1895–1915.

Work opportunities for urban blacks were always a source of concern for Washington. "In the South" there was "a job for every idle man," but "in the North, on the contrary," there were "frequently two or three idle men looking for every job." For blacks the prospects were particularly depressing, owing to racial prejudice, and because of "the competition with the foreign population with which they come in contact."[16]

Newly emerging labor unions further complicated the problems of the job market. The conservative Washington harbored serious doubts about the capacity of trade unions to enhance the pay and conditions of the workers they represented. His adolescent experience of an abortive miners strike in Malden, West Virginia, in 1874, reinforced this view. During the strike the workers "spent all that they had saved" only to "return to work in debt at the same wages" or "move to another mine at considerable expense." "In either case," the youthful educator concluded, "my observations convinced me that the miners were worse off at the end of a strike. Before the days of strikes in that section of the country, I knew miners who had considerable money in the bank, but as soon as the professional labour agitators got control, the savings of even the most thrifty ones began disappearing."[17]

The siren rhetoric of labor agitators was in fact often only a hypothetical danger for African Americans. Trade union leaders all too frequently shared the same prejudices as white employers, and refused to admit blacks as union members. "The labor unions, to whose interest it is to limit the supply of labour, have never been favourable to the employment of Negroes," Washington accurately noted in September 1907. "The fact that Negroes are frequently brought north as 'Strike breakers' helps to intensify the prejudice against them. The tendency of all this is to force the Negro down to the lowest rung of the industrial ladder and to make him, in short, a sort of industrial pariah."[18]

Unlike Italian, German, and other immigrants, blacks were poorly placed to cushion prejudice and discrimination with the possibility of employment in ethnic enterprises within their own community.

There were notable examples of successful black economic initiatives in the cities at the turn of the century. The Madame C. J. Walker chain of beauty parlors, built up in Harlem between 1904 and 1914, went on to develop outlets throughout the United States, and enabled its founder to enjoy a millionaire life-style.[19]

More typically, however, small businesses in the urban black ghettos of the North were white owned, as Washington recognized. "We must cease to have the reputation of a spending, thriftless and poverty stricken race," he advised black New Yorkers in September 1906. "We must profit by the example of the Italian and the German immigrant" who, although at first "unable to speak a word of our tongue," "work hard and . . . save," many "becoming bank presidents and directors and the controllers of great industrial enterprises."[20]

The end result of the employment disadvantages suffered by blacks in U.S. cities was that "with very rare exceptions, the Negro is a porter either in a bank or store or barbershop, or perhaps runs an elevator in a store." Black workers were, it seemed, permanently condemned to the role of errand boys or "odd job men," and "the white people, it seems, do not expect him to occupy any other position." This, and other fears expressed by Washington, mirror many of the conclusions reached by modern case studies of the Great Migration.[21]

The wartime industrial boom, combined with an end to white immigration from Europe, did help to create new job opportunities for blacks after 1915. In Cleveland, some 33 percent of employed black males worked in domestic or personal service prior to 1914, compared with only 22 percent in manufacturing. In 1920, 66 percent of employed black males in the city worked in industrial jobs, and just 12 percent worked in service occupations.[22]

In 1910, 51 percent of the male black workforce in Chicago and 37.4 percent in Pittsbergh were engaged in domestic or personal service. Ten years later these proportions had dropped to 28 percent and 29.1 percent, respectively. In contrast, the percentage of male black workers employed in trade and industry in Chicago more than doubled during the same decade. In Pittsburgh, 61.6 percent of black male workers were employed in industry by 1920, compared with 44.7 percent in 1910.[23]

Striking statistical advances did not, however, convey the full picture. The majority of newly created jobs were at the bottom end of the job market in the form of unskilled labor, often in appalling working conditions, and with little or no prospect of any career advancement. During times of temporary postwar recession even these modest positions failed to represent a secure source of employment, blacks being subject to the old discriminatory adage of being "the last hired and the first to be fired." During the 1920–1921 recession in the Pittsburgh steel industry thousands of black migrants returned to the South because they were unable to earn a living in the city.[24]

Gender discrimination in manufacturing work also meant that new employment opportunities were limited largely to men. The proportion of black women who relied on personal or domestic service for work barely changed in many northern cities between 1910 and 1920. In Pittsburgh, between 1910 and 1930, 90 percent of black working women were consistently engaged in domestic service, and a like situation prevailed in Cleveland. In 1910, 78 percent of black working women in Detroit and 66 percent in Chicago were in domestic or personal service. Ten years later the statistics were 79.1 percent and 64 percent, respectively.[25]

Racial tension within the burgeoning labor movement was another problem that persisted in the postwar years. The traditions of racial discrimination within unions continued to exclude blacks from membership. Where more enlightened labor leadership did exist black union membership still remained limited, because of the lack of union experience among recent black migrants coupled with the antiunion propaganda of employers. A union recruitment drive among black workers by the Stockyards Labor Council in Chicago, during 1919, thus failed because, as the Council Secretary ruefully admitted, "probably we do not understand the colored worker as we do ourselves." Stockyard employers took full advantage of this weakness, playing the race card to divide black and white workers during moments of tension in labor relations. Elsewhere, as in the 1919 steel strike and 1925–1928 coal strike in Pittsburgh, employers simply used nonunionized black labor to defeat union protests, leaving a poisonous legacy of racial enmity.[26]

Washington's justified anxiety over the lack of black economic initiatives in northern cities likewise remained a source of concern well after World War I. The scale of black migration from 1915 onward greatly expanded the market for black business, but too many of the traditional barriers to black commercial success remained. White prejudice, inadequate capital, inability to secure credit, competition from large white chain stores, and a lack of ethnic solidarity within black communities ensured the continued failure of most black economic initiatives. Less than 10 percent of the $39,000,000 spent by black Chicagoans in 1930 went to black shops or stores. Throughout the United States in 1939 there were fewer than 30,000 black retail stores, and these employing only a modest 43,000 staff.[27]

Insecurity in employment was only one of Washington's reservations about city life for blacks. Another anxiety was that if there were not enough ways for urban blacks to earn money, there were plenty of ways for them to spend it. In short, the material lures open to blacks, particularly those newly arrived from the country, were great. The delights in department store windows were so enticing that "the dollars almost jump out of your pockets as you go by on the sidewalk," Washington warned an audience of Harlem blacks. In the city the temptation was "to get a dress suit before we get a bank account," and "spend all that we get in for rent, food and dress" rather than "lay up a little for old age." The urban fleshpots of the North not only damaged the finances of blacks, siphoning off wages and savings that could otherwise be used to start a small business or family homestead, but also brought a moral decay in the character of African Americans. Alcohol abuse, gambling, and crime were all too prevalent in most northern cities.[28]

Blacks who avoided these particular evils might still succumb to the more general vice of an extravagant, self-indulgent life-style, well beyond their position in life. "Men working for rich men in the city," who smelt "the smoke of so many twenty-five cent cigars" would, after a while, come to feel as though they too "must smoke twenty-five cent cigars." Individuals with this outlook could be seen strolling on a Sunday afternoon replete with "high hat, imitation gold eye glasses, a showy walking stick, kid gloves, fancy boots and what not" and yet have scant other material possessions to their name.[29]

Washington's stereotyped images of city blacks, in high hats and kid gloves, doubtless owed some of its fanciful detail to his rustic bias. Nonetheless, the experience of black newcomers in the decade after 1915 revealed his views to have a legitimate foundation. "This city is too fast for me" wrote one Pittsburgh migrant in 1917, "they give you big money for what you do but they charge you big things for what you get."[30]

The practice in northern stores of allowing all customers, regardless of race, to try on clothes without first paying for them overly impressed southern migrants, making them easy targets for white salesmen. Confined by racial and economic barriers to slum ghetto areas, and with meager prospects for long-term advancement, migrants were also inclined to see little point in saving for deferred economic gratification. It seemed better to live for the moment, buying clothes, drinks, and meals out, to alleviate the drudgery of daily life.[31]

Ironically, in his turn of the century study of Philadelphia, Booker T. Washington's most perceptive critic, W. E. B. Du Bois, also bemoaned the "thoughtless and unreasonable expenditure" of urban blacks. "The crowds that line Lombard street on Sundays are dressed far beyond their means," he noted in a style of language more typical of the Tuskegeean:

> much money is wasted in extravagantly furnished parlours, dining-rooms, guest chambers and other visible parts of the homes. Thousands of dollars are annually wasted in excessive rents, in doubtful "societies" of all kinds, and in miscellaneous ornaments and gew-gaws. The Negro has much to learn of the Jew and Italian, as to living within his means and saving every penny from excessive and wasteful expenditures.[32]

High crime levels in northern black ghettos were equally worrying. In 1920s Harlem prostitution, illegal speakeasies, gambling rackets, and juvenile delinquency were all serious problems. According to police records in Detroit, during 1920, although African Americans made up only seven percent of the city population, they were responsible for 31 percent of all felonies, 18 percent of robberies, 75 percent of all breaking and entering, 70 percent of all burglaries of dwellings, and 47 percent of all murders. Even allowing for racial bias in police statistics, crime levels in the black ghettos of the North were clearly well above average, as members of those communities themselves acknowledged. One migrant to Cleveland, Ohio, found the city "crowded with the lowest Negroes you ever meet . . . all kinds of loffers, gamblers and pockit pickers." It was unsafe to walk the streets at night and "you are libble to get kill at eny time."[33]

Overcrowded and unsatisfactory urban living conditions were a further source of concern highlighted by Washington. Prohibitively high rents, he concluded, forced blacks to accept poor, unsanitary accommodation. Consequently, illness and death rates among blacks in the North were much higher than in the South. Morality and family life were also placed under threat, he argued, as families were forced to take in lodgers to help pay the rent. Ghetto families were the more vulnerable because of the social isolation of city life, without the extended communal and kinship networks that existed in southern black society. Washington's observations on family living conditions, like his other comments on black life in the cities of the North, were vindicated by the experience of the Great Migration.[34]

Housing conditions for blacks in Pittsburgh during and after World War I were so overcrowded that there were often three to four residents per room, and this was among the more fortunate. Other migrants ended up living in railroad cars, boathouses, and makeshift shelters built in ravines and hollows. In Detroit, the housing shortage for black migrants in 1920 was so great that gambling clubs turned pool tables into makeshift beds overnight.

Those able to obtain more conventional sleeping quarters were often scarcely better off. Social work reports recorded cases of black housing in which rain poured in through the ceiling and where the walls and floor were so damp that the beds had to be placed in the middle of the room to keep them dry. In other urban centers, the quality of residential accommodation, which varied from city to city, may have been better. Nonetheless, with depressing uniformity, blacks in the urban North paid higher than average rents, and were forced to live in the least desirable quarters of the city in substandard accommodation.[35]

Poor and unsanitary living conditions inevitably resulted in health problems. The mortality rate for blacks in Harlem during the years 1923–1927 was 42 percent higher than for the rest of the city, despite the fact that some two-thirds of black New Yorkers were in the 15–44 year age group. High levels of infant mortality and deaths from consumption and pneumonia were among the worst killers in New York, as was the case in other northern cities.[36]

Superstition and ignorance of basic hygiene among newly arrived southern migrants exacerbated the problems of infection and disease. Washington's oft repeated moralizing strictures on the importance of cleanliness, and the civilizing influence of carbolic soap and the toothbrush, tend to make him appear a risible, even ludicrous, figure to modern eyes. The standards of hygiene that prevailed among many southern blacks at the turn of the century serve as a reminder that such sermonizing was not altogether misplaced. Even the sophisticated Du Bois was moved to urge the preaching of the "gospel of soap and water."[37]

The image of Washington as a conservative accommodationist, who did little to resist the tides of racism and segregation that engulfed black American society at the turn of the century, is, to a degree, deserved. The stereotype of Washington as an outmoded rustic reactionary is arguably less justified. The Tuskegeean, it is true, did have some of the prejudices of

a country boy against city life. However, his overall perception and understanding of the urban environment were the product of more profound
insight. His innumerable visits to, and many contacts in, the cities of the
North afforded him a close knowledge of the metropolitan landscape. The
black migration to the cities that occurred in the decade after his death further confirmed the fact that his reservations about urban black migration
were well founded.

The experience of the Great Migration gave added weight to
Washington's philosophy in other respects. The Tuskegeean's claim that his
northern black critics were middle class professionals, out of touch with
the mass of southern blacks, was given greater credence by the reaction of
old settlers in the North to the new migrants. Class divisions in northern
black communities intensified after 1915. Newcomers were less welcome
and were looked down on as ignorant country bumpkins. Editorials in the
northern black press often outdid even the speeches of Booker T.
Washington in their level of sanctimonious moralizing directed at newly
arrived immigrants. The radical Du Bois appeared to perceive black
migrants less as racial brethren than as some kind of pathological social
problem.[38]

In 1895 Washington's claim that it was in the South that "the Negro is
given a man's chance in the commercial world" sounded uncomfortably
like the pleadings of some perpetual Pollyanna, unwilling to face up to an
unpleasant reality. Thirty years later, this criticism may still have been
valid, but the rising levels of white hostility, segregation, and discrimination encountered by black migrants in the North demonstrated that racism
was a complex and endemic evil, not simply a sectional problem. Blacks
may not have had a fair chance in the commercial world in the South, but
they would not be able to gain a fair chance anywhere else in the United
States.[39]

On the subject of political rights, Washington adopted the by modern
standards unfashionable view that blacks should rather concentrate first
on economic self-help and advancement. During Reconstruction, he
believed that African Americans had been given voting rights too early.
Consequently, instead of using the ballot to effect an improvement in their
own situation, they had been used by unscrupulous whites, and became an
electoral shuttlecock between the political parties.

It is difficult to entirely agree with such logic. Even the most modest
political voice via the ballot box was still better than none at all.
Nonetheless, the Great Migration did vindicate Washington to the extent
that voting rights were shown to be far from a universal panacea for the
ills suffered by blacks in American society. African Americans may have
had free access to the ballot box in the cities of the North, but its use
resulted in only modest improvements to their condition.[40]

In 1920s Chicago, the geographical division of electoral wards, and the reliance of Republican mayor William "Big Bill" Thompson on the black vote, probably gave African Americans more political power in the municipality than in any other city in the United States. Even in Chicago, however, the gains for the black community through the political process remained limited. The black share of jobs through the spoils system was largely confined to the lowest levels—porters, office boys, and janitors—areas of employment that had been traditionally allocated to blacks anyway. Virtually nothing was done to improve the problems of poor housing and woefully inadequate public services that confronted most blacks in the city.[41]

All else notwithstanding, migration to the cities of the North clearly held out many advantages to southern blacks. Wages in the North were relatively high. Educational opportunities were better, as were social relations between the races. Compared to the South, where schooling for blacks was often all but nonexistent, and African Americans could be lynched for even the most minor infringement of social norms, almost any change was likely to be an improvement. Washington himself admitted as much on occasion.[42]

Nonetheless, migration also had a downside. If wages were high, working conditions were grim, and employment was insecure. Even after the impact of wartime industrialization, a significant proportion of black men in northern cities still relied on personal or domestic service for work. The large majority of black women usually had little alternative, and many black families were dependent on female income to meet the high urban living costs. These factors taken together, it may not be an exaggeration to suggest that even after World War I, jobs in domestic and personal service, of the type associated with the Tuskegee philosophy, continued to be as important for many northern black families as the much vaunted new opportunities in industry and manufacturing.

Black landownership in the South fell from over 15 million acres in 1910 to less than 10 million acres by 1930. Similarly, of over 200 black banks in the United States in 1900, most of which were in the South, less than 20 remained by 1930. Economic recession in agriculture, and the depredations of the cotton boll weevil, were clearly major causes of such downturns. Urban migration may have been an added factor. One recent commentator has gone so far as to suggest that northern migration, between 1915 and 1930, may have drained off the most youthful, dynamic elements of southern black society and retarded the development of effective civil rights leadership in the region by two or three decades.[43]

It is easy to view black migration to the cities between 1915 and 1930 as an inevitable, and positive, process of modernization. The migration certainly aided the development of industrial capitalism, providing northern manufacturers with a cheap workforce at a time when the supply of labor from European immigration was largely curtailed.

In the long term, African Americans themselves may have benefited from the move to the North. In the period up until World War II, however, the impact of the Great Migration on black society was more mixed. Several modern case studies of individual cities, weighing the advantages and disadvantages of migration, have come close to concluding that the experience was no more than a zero sum game for black Americans. In the light of such research, the words used by Booker T. Washington, in a speech as long ago as 1906, appear thoroughly up to date. "Some may think that the problems with which we are grappling will be better solved by inducing millions of our people to leave the south for residence in the north," he noted, "I warn you that instead of being a solution it will but add to the complications of the problem."

CHAPTER 6

The Realist and the Dreamer?

Booker T. Washington and W. E. B. Du Bois

"I understand that Dr. Booker T. Washington stands for the 'Hog and Hominy Policy' of dollars, dollars, all the time," noted an observer from the British Isles on 22 April 1910, whereas "Dr. Du Bois stands for the intellectual and ethical policy of free and equal manhood and womanhood."[1]

This perception of Washington and Du Bois as personifying competing opposites in an ideological struggle within black American society is one that was generally endorsed by contemporary commentators within the United States and by later historians. Samuel R. Spencer, a biographer of Washington in the 1950s, reflected that the Tuskegeean "was a practical realist, interested primarily in attaining tangible goals." In contrast, Du Bois "was a romantic, willing and eager to fight for principle even if the battle cost him his life." Du Bois as an academic and intellectual "liked to deal with ideas, while Washington preferred men and things."[2]

It is understandable that the two men should be portrayed in such terms. A century after its first publication W. E. B. Du Bois's essay "Of Mr. Booker T. Washington and Others" in *The Souls of Black Folk* (1903) remains the classic critique of the Tuskegee philosophy. The founding of the Niagara movement in July 1905 by Du Bois and other like-minded African-American intellectuals represented the first concerted, organized black opposition to Washington. Implicitly rejecting the Tuskegee emphasis on industrial education, the demands of the movement included a call for education to be made open to talent at all levels, regardless of race. Whereas Washington focused on economic advancement and accommodationist interracial diplomacy, Niagara members stressed the need for black civil and political rights to be achieved through "constant protest." In a thinly disguised attack on Washington's control of black newspapers and journals through the workings of the Tuskegee Machine, they stressed the need for freedom of speech and criticism and a free and unsubsidized press.[3]

Between 1909 and 1915, as the most prominent black member in the NAACP, and the editor of the NAACP journal the *Crisis*, Du Bois was the leading African-American critic of Washington. When, in 1910, Washington visited England, and gave an address to the Anti-Slavery Society in London that stressed the improving nature of race relations in the United States, it was predictably Du Bois who penned a rebuttal, "An Appeal to England and Europe." "If Mr. Booker T. Washington, or any other person, is giving the impression abroad that the Negro problem in America is in process of satisfactory solution, he is giving an impression which is not true," Du Bois tersely noted. Washington's "large financial responsibilities," and his consequent dependence on "the rich charitable public," meant that he was "compelled to tell, not the whole truth" but only "that part of it which certain powerful interests in America wish to appear as truth." Despite the "pleasant pictures" evoked by Washington's address, race relations in the United States was one of "the gravest of American problems."[4]

The intensity and bitterness of Washington's response to Du Bois's criticisms of him between 1905 and 1915 confirm the view that the Tuskegeean himself perceived Du Bois as his most dangerous and implacable enemy within the African American community. He infiltrated the Niagara movement with spies and sought to dissuade potential recruits from joining it. Black newspapers and journals under the control or influence of the Tuskegee Machine published hostile reports on the new organization, or, perhaps even worse, sought to ensure that it received no press coverage at all.[5]

By August 1906 Washington was able to note with satisfaction that the policy pursued by the New York *Age* had helped to drive "the Niagara people to the point where they can see that they cannot afford any more to let the public understand that their organization is opposing me." Having "accomplished this much" the increasingly confident Tuskegeean believed that "the next policy to pursue" was "to ignore the whole organization as much as possible. Without the use of my name, it is impossible for them to keep themselves before the public very long."[6]

In 1909 the inclusion of Du Bois within the NAACP effectively ensured Washington's hostility to the Association, despite the best assurances of one of its leading founders, Oswald Garrison Villard, that there was "not the slightest intention of tying up this movement with either of the two factions in the Negro race." It was "not to be either a Washington movement or a Du Bois movement."[7]

In his increasingly bitter differences with Du Bois the concept of impartial neutrality was an idea that the Tuskegeean was unable to accept.

Du Bois was "a big dunce" who "was puffed up with insane vanity and jealousy" that deprived him "of common sense." Du Bois was engaged in a personal vendetta to destroy the reputation of Washington and tear down all that his painstaking work at Tuskegee had accomplished. In such a contest there was no scope for mediation or compromise. Any individual or organization that was not for Washington was effectively against him. It is unthinkable to imagine that Washington could ever have contemplated an interracial marriage, but in other respects the Tuskegeean clearly viewed Du Bois as an Iago to his Othello. The Niagara founder was a jealous and small-minded individual set on ruining the life and work of a greater and nobler man.[8]

Washington's emotive hostility toward Du Bois reflected the fact that the ideological differences between the two men were reinforced by their contrasting backgrounds and personality. Washington was born a "slave among slaves." His childhood home was a 14–foot by 16–foot log cabin with an earth floor and without glass in the windows. Du Bois was "born by a golden river and in the shadow of two great hills." As a child he could "never remember being cold or hungry." His home was "quaint, with clapboards running up and down, neatly trimmed." It had "five rooms, a tiny porch, a rosy front yard, and unbelievably delicious strawberries in the rear."[9]

Even allowing for poetic license by Du Bois his early life was clearly privileged in comparison to that of Washington. After a New England schooling he went on to complete his education at the all black Fisk University in Tennessee and later at Harvard and the University of Berlin. Washington had little in the way of formal schooling until he enrolled on a course of industrial education at Hampton Institute in Virginia around the age of 16. After completing his three year course of study at the institute he later spent a year at a Baptist Theological Seminary in Washington, D.C., but otherwise had no form of higher education.

The contrasting experiences of Washington and Du Bois in their formative years gave them a fundamentally different outlook on life. This fact was graphically highlighted by their conflicting responses to a similar experience shared by the two men during their student days.

At Hampton, Washington helped finance his studies by part-time employment as a janitor. On graduating from the institute he secured a summer job as a waiter in a Connecticut hotel. His initial inexperience led to him being demoted to a dish-carrier but, accustomed to adversity, Washington refused to be discouraged. He "determined to learn the business of waiting" and did so with such enthusiasm that "within a few weeks" he was restored to his former position. In later life Washington saw his time as a waiter as a positive experience that had helped teach him the value of humility, patience, and hard work. This message was reaffirmed by the fact that in his subsequent career as an educator and race leader he had "the satisfaction of being a guest in this hotel" on several occasions.[10]

Du Bois, in common with college students of his day and ever since, also sought summer vacation employment between graduating from Fisk and enrolling at Harvard. Like Washington, he took as a position a waiter, at a hotel in Minnesota. At first all seemed well, the young Du Bois being impressed by the "flamboyant architecture, the great verandas, rich furniture, and richer dresses." Disillusion soon set in. It was not the work itself, which "was easy but insipid," but "the dishonesty and deception, the flattery and cajolery, the unnatural assumption that worker and diner had no common humanity. It was uncanny. It was inherently and fundamentally wrong."

A particularly unpleasant memory was that of "one fat hog, feeding at a heavily gilded trough" who, unable to find the waiter assigned to him, beckoned to Du Bois. "It was not his voice, for his mouth was too full. It was his way, his air, his assumption. Thus Caesar ordered his legionaries or Cleopatra her slaves. Dogs recognized the gesture. I did not," recalled Du Bois. In contrast to Washington, Du Bois did not find his experience as a waiter a lesson in the dignity of labor. Instead it left him convinced of the need to disown "menial service for me and my people." Domestic service was a "hateful badge of slavery and mediaevalism." On walking out of the hotel, "and out of menial service forever," he "felt as though in a field of flowers" his "nose had been held unpleasantly long to the worms and manure at their roots."[11]

In adult life the differences in personality between Washington and Du Bois were striking, even down to their dress and demeanor. Washington "had the appearance of a sturdy farmer in his Sunday best," whereas "Du Bois, with his well trimmed goatee, looked like a Spanish aristocrat." Even before their public rift the two men seemed uncomfortable in each other's presence. When interviewed by Washington for a teaching post at Tuskegee, in 1902, Du Bois found the Tuskegean "not an easy person to know. He was wary and silent. He never expressed himself frankly or clearly until he knew exactly to whom he was talking and just what their wishes and desires were. He did not know me, and I think he was suspicious." Du Bois himself had the opposite tendencies. He "was quick, fast-speaking and voluble" and at the end of their conversation "had done practically all the talking." Emerging ill at ease from their meeting, Du Bois's second interview went even worse when he resolved to say equally little himself, resulting in what can only be imagined as prolonged and uncomfortable silences. So unlike in character, it would seem that the two men found even the act of talking to each other an uphill task.[12]

Ironically, the few traits that Washington and Du Bois did have in common made it all the harder for them to overcome their differences in philosophy. Both men found it difficult to accept criticism and seemed unable to work together with other independent, strong-minded individuals.

The intellectually gifted Du Bois lacked patience when it came to taking account of the views of those he regarded as his mental inferiors. Even with people he respected, and who shared his general philosophy, relations were not easy. Despite admiring William Monroe Trotter "in many ways" Du Bois admitted in January 1914 that he still had "difficulty in working with him." Du Bois's working relationship with leading members of the NAACP was also stormy. "People yield to you for the reason that parents yield to spoilt children in company, for fear of creating a scene," Joel E. Spingarn, the NAACP Board Chairman wrote to Du Bois in October 1914. Others "were less willing than you to wreck our cause before the colored world."[13]

Washington had similar failings. He was inclined to view disagreement as a personal attack on himself rather than as constructive criticism. Staff at Tuskegee were expected to obey his instructions without question at all times. Dissent, even if well intentioned or carefully reasoned, was likely to earn his displeasure, often culminating in the resignation or dismissal of the individual concerned. Washington "enjoyed his power and meant to keep it," observed the NAACP founder Mary White Ovington. In consequence, he "was surrounded with followers, not equals. A stream of young teachers entered Tuskegee one year and a swift-running rill left it the next."[14]

The ideological differences between Washington and Du Bois have been well documented. Although not opposed to industrial schooling altogether, Du Bois believed that the emphasis placed by Washington on such training neglected the importance of higher education. A college-educated elite, or "Talented Tenth," of African Americans was needed to provide leadership for black Americans in their search for racial uplift.[15]

Industrial education itself also had some suspect qualities. It risked consigning blacks to second-class citizenship as a perpetual servant class. It prepared them for a life of domestic service, "the most poorly paid and disadvantageous branch of human industry."[16]

The other main emphasis in industrial education, the training of blacks as artisans and small farmers, was equally misguided, such occupations bringing "the least return" and being increasingly marginalized within a modern industrial society. "As a result, technology advanced more rapidly than Hampton or Tuskegee could adjust their curricula. The opportunities for artisans to be successful small businessmen grew slimmer even for white Americans, while the whole relation of labor to capital became less a matter of technical skill than of basic organization and aim." Although in the years 1905–1915 Du Bois and others "did not foresee exactly the kind of change that was coming," they "were convinced that the Negro could succeed in industry and life only if he had intelligent leadership and far-reaching ideals."[17]

Du Bois's other major concern was that Washington, in his efforts to win over white support, paid insufficient attention to the need for vigorous agitation in defense of black civil and political rights. This was a fatal error for, "stripped of political power and emasculated by caste;" blacks "could never gain sufficient economic strength to take their place as modern men." Moreover, in advising blacks to give up the immediate pursuit of full civil and political rights, Washington's actions were inconsistent and at worse insincere. This was because the Tuskegean himself was all too eager to use his influential political and philanthropic white contacts to exert a controlling influence on the distribution of patronage in the black community. In short, Washington sought political power for himself while counseling other blacks to forego it.[18]

Although real and substantive differences of opinion existed between Washington and Du Bois it should not be overlooked that they also shared many ideas in common. The Tuskegean may have stressed the need for industrial schooling but he did also recognize the importance of higher education.

Washington sent his own children to college and his daughter, Portia, was so named because of her father's fondness for the character of that name in Shakespeare's *The Merchant of Venice*. In 1906 Washington paid for her to go to Germany to study the piano under Professor Martin Krauser, a former pupil of Liszt. He hired a special tutor to help his son, Booker, Jr., learn Latin. By December 1907 Portia had made sufficient progress in her musical tuition for Washington to buy her, and her new husband, Sidney Pittman, a piano as a Christmas present.[19]

When the Tuskegean urged less fortunate black Americans to focus their efforts on industrial training it was because this was what was most appropriate for their immediate needs. "I am not seeking to confine the Negro race to industrial education nor make them hewers of wood and drawers of water," Washington complained in 1912. Instead, he was rather "trying to do the same thing for the Negro which is done for all races of the world, and that is to make the masses of them first of all industrious, skillful, and frugal." This would "enable them to combine brains with hard work to the extent that their services will be wanted in the communities where they live, and thus prevent them from becoming a burden and a menace."[20]

In his speeches and public writings Washington often mocked the stereotyped image of "an educated Negro," who with "a high hat, imitation gold eye-glasses, a showy walking-stick, kid gloves, fancy boots and what not" distained hard work for a living and preferred to "live by his wits." It is understandable that such rhetoric often gave the impression that Washington was opposed to college education in principle. This was not the case. What concerned the Tuskegean was that blacks who achieved a higher education might acquire values and attitudes that would prevent them from returning to their families and communities as constructive members of society. Worse, they might instill in less educated blacks a contempt for manual labor that for many represented their only hope of economic advancement.[21]

Such reservations did not prevent Washington from recognizing the advantages of higher education for blacks who could benefit from it. "In all my writings I have emphasized the necessity for college and professionally trained men and women as well as those with industrial education," he advised Oswald Garrison Villard in 1904. "The fact is that at Tuskegee we employ more college graduates and university graduates than is true of any similar institution in the world. Just as in Massachusetts they have the Institute of Technology and the Simmons Industrial School; so in the South there should be the Atlanta University, the Tuskegee Institute and others. There is a place for all of the institutions to do their work." The Tuskegeean "did not believe in placing any limitation upon the mental development of the black man." If he wanted the mass of Southern blacks to concentrate first on securing "an economic foundation" this was because "it would add to the opportunity of future generations to secure the very highest training."[22]

Washington's words may, in part, have been chosen to win the sympathy of an important liberal white benefactor. At the same time they were not without sincerity, as was borne out by the fact that at times Washington himself funded poor, but able, blacks to enable them to achieve a college or university education. Writing in October 1906, he was even prepared to admit that Tuskegee Institute itself needed to devote more time to academic subjects. There was a danger that "the physical work, including the mechanical part of our plant," was "absorbing too much of our income and time," he acknowledged, and would give this problem "immediate attention." He had "already reorganized our course of training so that we are spending more time in strictly academic work."[23]

In respect to civil and political rights Washington did not remain silent. "In all cases where a state has made an attempt to take from our people the political franchise I have spoken out frankly and directly," he observed in 1904. He had made it clear "to the people in that state" the "injustice of not making the same conditions for one race as for the other."[24]

If Washington did not speak out as often and as bluntly as his critics would have liked this was because he felt such a course of action would have been counterproductive, serving only to alienate white opinion. Instead he thought that patience and indirect behind the scenes maneuvering were more likely to get results. It is arguable that Washington may have been mistaken in this belief, but if so his argument with Du Bois was over tactics not objectives. The two men were in agreement that it was important for blacks to enjoy full civil and political rights. Where they differed was on how this could best be achieved.[25]

Even if it is assumed that Du Bois was right, and that Washington's conservative approach was misguided, the practical consequences of this were arguably limited. Washington did not surrender black civil and political rights in the South because this process was well underway long before the emergence of the Tuskegeean as a national race leader. "You and I both know that before Frederick Douglass died the Negro had lost practically all political control and power in the South," Washington pointed out to Oswald Garrison Villard. This occurred at a time when Washington "was a mere boy attending school at Hampton." Well before his "name was known outside of Tuskegee the southern states, leading off with Mississippi and South Carolina, began to pass new constitutions disfranchising the colored people."[26]

If Washington's aims and ideas were often misrepresented, the same was also true of Du Bois. The economic and political radicalism of Du Bois's thinking during the last third of his life, after 1930, concealed the fact that in his earlier years his views were often deeply conservative. In 1900 Du Bois's reverence for voting rights did not extend to a belief in universal suffrage. Like Washington he supported educational and property qualifications for voters so long as these were applied impartially to blacks and whites alike. If anything the Tuskegeean was the more liberal of the two men, for his belief in voting restrictions derived from the "peculiar conditions" that existed in the South following the emancipation of blacks from slavery, which justified "the protection of the ballot in many of the states, for a while at least." "As a rule" however, he was in favor of "universal free suffrage."[27]

Du Bois was equally conservative in his social and economic philosophy at the turn of the century. In February 1901 he attended a two-day farming conference at Tuskegee Institute and wrote a glowing account of the event for *Harpers Weekly*. In a 1902 publication, *The Negro Artisan*, he praised "Trades Schools" as "a means of imparting skill to Negroes, and manual training as a means of general education." Such initiatives, "especially in the last ten years," had been "of inestimable benefit to the freedmen's sons." The following year he taught as a visiting lecturer at the Tuskegee Institute summer school.[28]

In an 1899 address "The Problem of Negro Crime," at the Emancipation Celebration of the Colored Citizens of Atlanta, Du Bois's words were so conservative in tone that Washington could easily have penned them. Blaming blacks themselves for their high crime rates, rather than social and racial injustice, Du Bois identified what he saw as the solutions to the problem. Black parents should make sure that their homes were "reformed, purified and made places for the proper training of children." It was not enough to provide "food and fire and furniture" or "clothes and money and fun." Parents must also enforce "order and cleanliness and discipline" as well as "obedience and reverence," "regularity and punctuality, and truthfulness and honesty." If black homes were "dirty and ugly and unpleasant" they would send "dirty, ugly and hateful children into the world." If they were "gay and careless and wasteful" they would "add to the spendthrifts and idlers on our streets." "Throughout the land" the worse black homes were "poverty stricken, dirty and immoral," while many of the best homes were "nests of extravagance and indiscipline."

Undaunted by any thought that his moralizing words might have a dampening effect on the festivities, Du Bois continued in a rebuking vein. African Americans needed to learn the value of hard work, for there was "no disgrace on earth equal to the disgrace of idleness." Conveniently forgetting his experiences as a waiter in Minnesota, he noted that there was "no work so low and menial and despised as not to be infinitely preferred to idleness." It was natural for parents to want their children to rise in the world, but all such hopes would be ruined if they should let their children "once learn the lesson of idleness—once get used to loafing about waiting for something to turn up—to sitting in the parlour pouting and lounging because the particular kind of work wanted is not at hand." Instead, children should be put to work, "let them plow, sew, cut wood, scrub or wash dishes, anything so they learn what God meant when he said, 'By the sweat of thy face shalt thou eat bread.'"[29]

Given such views it was not surprising that Du Bois and Washington enjoyed a cordial, even amicable, personal relationship in the years 1894–1903. In 1894 Du Bois applied for a teaching job at Tuskegee and would have taken up the resulting offer of employment from Washington had he not by then accepted a position at Wilberforce University, an African Methodist Episcopal Church school in Ohio.[30]

In 1895 Du Bois sent Washington a telegram of congratulations on the Atlanta Cotton Exposition Address, praising the oration as words "fitly spoken" and "the basis of a real settlement between whites and blacks in the South." In 1900 it was Du Bois who gave Washington the inspiration for the creation of the National Negro Business League and provided him with a list of useful contacts among black businessmen to help launch the organization.[31]

On his part the Tuskegeean reciprocated such support by quoting approvingly from the speeches and writings of Du Bois in his own public statements. Washington's regard for Du Bois in these years was such that in October 1899 he made him a renewed offer of employment at Tuskegee at a salary of $1,400 a year, and, in the winter of 1902, was still seeking to recruit him into the teaching staff at the institute. As late as the summer of 1903, several months after the publication of his critical essay "Of Mr.

Booker T. Washington and Others" in *The Souls of Black Folk*, Du Bois was still afforded the honor of being a dinner guest at Washington's home, "The Oaks," at Tuskegee.[32]

In the years 1904–1915 the personal relationship between Washington and Du Bois was irrevocably soured. The ideological differences between the two men also widened as Du Bois modified the conservatism of some of his earlier views. At the same time he still retained some elements of his previous thought.

In July 1918 the publication of his "Close Ranks" editorial in the NAACP journal *Crisis* can be seen as marking a reemergence of his earlier accommodationism in response to war-time conditions. In Washingtonian language he urged black Americans to forget their "special grievances" and "close our ranks shoulder to shoulder with our own white fellow citizens and the allied nations that are fighting for democracy."[33]

The resulting denunciation of Du Bois by the black socialist and labor leader Philip Randolph as a "hand-picked, me-too-boss, hat-in hand sycophant, lick spittling Negro," was certainly the kind of personal abuse to which the Tuskegeean had become accustomed. Randolph himself saw the parallel, concluding that the editorial would "rank in shame and reeking disgrace with the Atlanta Compromise."[34]

In the 1920s, Du Bois's support for the Pan African Congress movement highlighted some of his differences with Washington. Du Bois's involvement reflected his race consciousness, his spiritual attachment to Africa, and his sense of internationalism. These were all qualities that were at best only partially developed in the Tuskegeean.

Nonetheless, the Congress movement was not inconsistent with the philosophy of Washington, who had been involved in the planning of the first Pan African Congress, held in London in 1900. Significantly, the four Pan African Congresses convened between 1919 and 1927 were held in Europe and the United States, rather than in Africa. The movement sought to improve the lives of black Africans, and to secure their political independence, in cooperation with the colonial powers of the day. Recognizing the need for pragmatism and compromise, the Congresses can be seen as a logical postwar development of Washington's earlier attempts to work with imperial authorities to better conditions in Africa.[35]

Between 1904 and 1915 significant ideological differences did develop between Washington and Du Bois. This polarity was reflected in Du Bois's 1915 obituary on Washington in the *Crisis*. As is customary in such pieces Du Bois began by praising the positive qualities and achievements of his subject. Washington "was the greatest Negro leader since Frederick Douglass, and the most distinguished man, white or black, who has come out of the South since the Civil War." Black Americans could "generously and with deep earnestness lay on the grave of Booker T. Washington testimony of" their "thankfulness" for his role in "the accumulation of Negro land and property, his establishment of Tuskegee and spreading of industrial education and his compelling of the white South to at least think of the Negro as a possible man."

If the good that Washington had done should be remembered rather than interred with his bones, Du Bois was, however, equally keen to ensure that the evils he had committed were not forgotten either. There could "be no doubt of Mr. Washington's mistakes and shortcomings," but, just to make sure, Du Bois provided his readers with a sobering catalogue of them. Washington "never adequately grasped the growing bond of politics and industry; he did not understand the deeper foundations of human training and his basis of better understanding between white and black was founded on caste."

Saving the worst for last, Du Bois, "in stern justice" laid "on the soul of this man, a heavy responsibility for the consummation of Negro disfranchisement, the decline of the Negro college and public school and the firmer establishment of color caste in this land." If the most distinguished of all Southerners since the Civil War could have such grievous faults, Du Bois's readers might have been forgiven for wondering what must have been the even more dreadful failings of all the others.[36]

Du Bois's heavy judgments against Washington in 1915 notwithstanding, the origins of the feud between the two men in 1903–1904 stemmed more from personal differences than disagreement over policy. "I was greatly disturbed at this time, not because I was in absolute disagreement to the things that Mr. Washington was advocating," Du Bois later acknowledged. It was rather that "above all" he "resented the practical buying up of the Negro press and choking off of even mild and reasonable opposition to Mr. Washington in both the Negro press and the white." In 1910 Du Bois declared that it was "not now a fight between advocates of the higher education and the industrial education, but it is a fight against an attempt to deliver the whole Negro race into the hands of one boss." Washington was "a man who buys and bulldozes his way up in the esteem of the world." He had "suppressed and hammered," the "Negro intelligentsia" "into conformity."[37]

In short, the activities of the Tuskegee Machine were Du Bois's prime source of concern. In the first years of the twentieth century Washington's influence with white philanthropists was so great that "almost no Negro institution could collect funds without" his "recommendation or acquiescence." His privileged access to two Republican Presidents, Theodore Roosevelt, 1901–1909, and William Howard Taft, 1909–1913, enabled Washington to become a "political dictator of the Negro race," with the distribution of almost all federal government patronage in the black community subject to his approval. Added to this the Tuskegeean enjoyed widespread influence among state Governors and officials, particularly in the South. The result of this network of contacts was that "few political appointments" of blacks "were made anywhere in the in the United States without his consent. Even the careers of rising young colored men were very often determined by his advice and certainly his opposition was fatal."[38]

In the case of Du Bois the sense of injustice created by this situation was reinforced by bitter personal experience. The Harvard scholar saw himself as one of the "rising young colored men" whose career was blighted by the Tuskegee Machine. The first sign of the malign influence of Tuskegee against him came in 1900 when Du Bois applied for the post of Superintendent of Negro Schools in Washington, D.C. The position offered twice the salary Du Bois was then receiving at Atlanta University in Georgia. Moreover, his wife, Nina, was unhappy in Atlanta and anxious for a move elsewhere. Du Bois secured a letter of recommendation from Washington in support of his application that increased his hopes and expectations of success.[39]

At this point events took a curious turn. On 11 March 1900 Washington wrote to Du Bois advising him not to use the testimonial that he had provided. Supposedly, this was because Washington had just received a letter from one of the Educational Commissioners in the District of Columbia asking him to recommend a suitable candidate for the vacancy. The Tuskegeean assured Du Bois that he had replied by presenting a powerful case on his behalf. Under such circumstances it would strengthen Du Bois's application if he did not present the written reference that Washington had given him. To do so would make Du Bois seem overeager and appear "to be in the position of seeking the position."[40]

Duly heeding the Tuskegeean's advice Du Bois was then chagrined to find his application unsuccessful. Over time he became convinced that the setback was a result of more than just bad fortune or strong competition for the job. "The Tuskegee Machine was definitely against me," he concluded. A "prominent colored official took the matter straight to President Theodore Roosevelt and emphasized the 'danger' of my appointment."[41]

If Du Bois's suspicions were correct Washington's motives for such action remain unclear. It is possible that he received advice from contacts in Georgia or Washington, D.C. that suggested Du Bois was a less than committed supporter of the Tuskegee philosophy. Alternatively Washington may have been hoping to recruit Du Bois to the teaching staff at Tuskegee. By the early months of 1902 Du Bois became convinced that pressure was being put upon him to give up his employment at Atlanta University and accept a position at Tuskegee Institute. Later in the year he was invited to a private meeting at the home of William Baldwin in Long Island, New York. A railroad magnate and leading backer of Washington, Baldwin advised Du Bois that his "place was at Tuskegee; that Tuskegee was not yet a good school, and needed the kind of development that" he "had been trained to promote." This attempt at persuasion was unsuccessful in the case of the independent minded Du Bois who was left even more suspicious of Washington.[42]

In any event, the final break between the two men came in January 1904 following the failure of the Carnegie Hall Conference in New York City. Planned and organized jointly by Washington and Du Bois, the event was supposed to be a secret meeting between Washington and his growing numbers of more radical critics within the black community. Du Bois, who was seemingly sincere in his intentions, was dismayed to find that the Conference was so manipulated by the Tuskegeean as to become less a forum for genuine discussion than a "Booker T. Washington ratification meeting." Leading white philanthropists, including the main sponsor of the event, the industrialist Andrew Carnegie, lectured those present on the virtues of Washington's program and the dire consequences that would result from departing from it. [43]

A "Committee of Twelve," set up at the end of the Conference to continue the debates that had been initiated, was packed by Washington with his own supporters. One of the minority opposition members on the Committee, Du Bois became increasingly frustrated as his proposals were regularly voted down. By the end of the year his anger was such that he insisted that "under no circumstances whatsoever" was his name "to be used in connection with the so-called 'Committee of Twelve,'" nor did he wish to receive "any further communication concerning it."[44]

By this time Du Bois had "began to feel the strength and implacability of the Tuskegee Machine." Black newspapers regularly published "jibes and innuendoes" at his expense. The methods of the Machine, "the distribution of advertising and favors, the sending out of special correspondence, veiled and open attacks upon recalcitrants, the narrowing of opportunities for employment and promotion," seemed to him "monstrous and dishonest" and he "resented it."[45]

In the months and years that followed it suited both Du Bois and Washington to stress their differences in policy rather than personality or tactics. Emphasizing the "clear blue water" that lay between their respective programs enabled Du Bois to act more effectively as a rallying point for radical black opposition to Tuskegee.

On the part of Washington it benefited him to contrast his own pragmatic moderation with Du Bois's unrealistic militancy when it came to courting the backing of wealthy and powerful white benefactors. Du Bois believed in "making 'demands' and asserting 'grievances,'" whereas Washington believed that "we will secure more quickly and have in our possession more permanently the rights which we should possess through the more slow but sure channel of development along all commercial and

industrial lines in connection with education, morality and religion." The
"successful Negro operating a bank" was more powerful "in securing
respect and justice for the race than a hundred men making mere abstract
speeches or abstract demands for justice." Simply put, Du Bois's superficial appeal to some blacks was because he was "in the position of a doctor
offering a sick child candy or medicine. The average child will take the
candy because it pleases him for the minute and refuses the medicine
which will permanently cure his ills."[46]

Long after Washington's death it remained common practice for biographers and commentators to stress the differences of principle between
Washington and Du Bois. The radical views held by Du Bois in the last
years of his life obscured the extent of his earlier conservatism. In the
changed climate of the 1950s and the 1960s it was easy to see Du Bois as
providing an attractive, radical, alternative to the unappealing conservatism of the Tuskegeean.

There was also a tendency to make Washington a scapegoat for the
troubles suffered by black Americans earlier in the century. Washington
himself had understood this temptation. It was "but natural that in the
midst of the wrongs and many obstacles surrounding our people that they
should grow impatient and feel that some individual is responsible for
their untoward condition," he had observed in 1903. Similarly, it was a part
of human nature to hope that "some individual" could "by the wave of his
hand remove all present difficulties." In comparing and contrasting the
respective positions of Washington and Du Bois the desire became parent
to the thought.[47]

Whatever their divergences in outlook the ultimate objectives of
Washington and Du Bois were the same, to secure economic, civil, and
political equality for African Americans in U.S. society. In developing a
strategy to achieve these goals the disagreements between the two men
were ones of emphasis and degree rather than differences of kind. Close
contemporaries of each believed as much and lamented the fact that they
did not work with, rather than against, each other.

In 1905 Professor Albert Bushell Hart, who had supervised Du Bois
for his Ph. D. thesis on "The Suppression of the African Slave Trade to the
United States of America, 1638–1870," wrote to his former student to
make this point. "I am rather troubled to find that a great many people
suppose that you head a kind of opposition to Booker T. Washington's
ideas," he noted. Yet, as far as Bushell could see, there was "no innate lack
of harmony between your purposes in life and his. You take a certain thing
which must be done, viz. the higher education of those who can profit by
it, he takes another end of the same problem." It was to be expected that
"each of you thinks that his interest is the more important," but "I do not
see how either excludes the other."[48]

In 1913 Seth Low, a Tuskegee Trustee, wrote to Oswald Garrison Villard along similar lines. "From my own observation Dr. Washington does not seem to me to lack any courage; but his philosophy of the situation is radically different from your own," he admitted. At the same time Low believed there was "room and need for both philosophies. To borrow a military figure your own is a frontal attack; Dr Washington's is a flank movement."[49]

Ultimately, even Washington himself was able to recognize that his own views and those of Du Bois were not incompatible. "The fact is, all of us are aiming at the same thing; we may be pursueing [sic] different methods, trying to reach the same goal by different roads and there is no necessity quarreling," he observed in 1904. In respect to his black critics the Tuskegeean believed that "if you would suggest pretty strongly to these people that they could help more by friendly and sympathetic cooperation than by mere abuse that it would help them." The mere "heaping abuse on individuals" would achieve "very little in bringing about a change as a rule." It was a sad irony that even more than Du Bois, Washington himself was psychologically incapable of heeding such good advice.[50]

CHAPTER 7

The Wizard and the Goat

Booker T. Washington, Ralph W. Tyler,
and the National Negro Business League

The National Negro Business League (NNBL), founded in the summer of 1900, was a key component in Booker T. Washington's program for racial advancement. Designed to promote black economic self-help, and to spread the Tuskegee philosophy, it was envisaged that the League would create local chapters of small businessmen in African-American communities throughout the United States with the aim of exchanging ideas and increasing entrepreneurial drive. The League was also central in the communications network of the Tuskegee Machine, enabling Washington to keep a careful eye on developments in black society through intelligence provided by regional League members and officials.[1]

Publicly, the League appeared to constitute an unqualified success for the Tuskegee educator. The 300 delegates who attended the first convention of the League, in Boston in 1900, had grown to 3,000 when the organization's annual convention again met in the city in August 1915. In 1915 there were over 600 local leagues in 36 states throughout the nation, and even a League chapter in West Africa.

Washington himself, not surprisingly, filled the office of League President from 1900 to 1915. However, a no less important position within the League hierarchy was the office of National Organizer, a role taken on by a succession of Washington's supporters, including Fred R. Moore, Charles R. Moore, and A. Holsey. It was the National Organizer who had prime responsibility for League fundraising and promoting the League's endeavors. In this capacity he or she was expected to regularly visit and monitor the work of existing League chapters, as well as establishing new local branches.[2]

Unfortunately, documentation on the League's activities, both at Tuskegee University and in the Booker T. Washington Papers in the

Library of Congress, is far from complete. Records and letters of local Leagues are all but nonexistent. Some of the best material that survives relates to the period from May 1913 to August 1914, when the position of National Organizer of the League was occupied by Ralph Waldo Tyler. Tyler's correspondence and reports during these months provide valuable information on the work of the League and grass roots African-American society in general. Moreover, the personal and working relationship between Tyler and Washington provides interesting insight into the Tuskegeean's character and style of leadership.

A one-time barber, Tyler enjoyed a successful career well before his professional association with Washington. Born in Columbus, Ohio, he worked for the white newspaper the Columbus *Evening Dispatch* from 1884 to 1900, rising to the position of Assistant Manager. Having won the confidence of the paper's proprietor, Robert Wolfe, Tyler moved on to work as a reporter on another Wolfe publication, the Ohio *State Journal*, from 1901 to 1904.

Tyler's evident talent, and skill at self-promotion, was reflected in the fact that from 1907 to 1913, during the Roosevelt and Taft administrations, he held the post of Navy Auditor in the Treasury Department in Washington, D.C., at a time when the number of African Americans in federal government employment was being sharply reduced. His enduring tenure derived from the fact that Tyler enjoyed the personal confidence of President Taft, having played a supporting role in the 1908 Presidential election by distributing Republican funds to black newspapers in the Midwest to ensure their support.

In *The Booker T. Washington Papers* Louis Harlan and his editorial team go so far as to suggest that Tyler's influence during the Taft administration may have been equal to, or even greater than, that of Booker T. Washington himself. This overstates the case. In his two volume biography of Washington Harlan more prudently describes Tyler as a "lower echelon lieutenant" in the Tuskegee Machine. Nonetheless, during his residence in Washington, D.C., Tyler was still a notable figure in the city's black community, most especially through his political connections and ventures into journalism. In the last two years of Taft's Presidency, when Washington took a less active role in political events, Tyler played a leading, albeit unsuccessful, role in trying to persuade the President to adopt a more enlightened attitude on racial issues.[3]

Long before his days in government service Tyler had been a qualified supporter of Washington's policies. In September 1895, he wrote to the Tuskegee educator to express his admiration for Washington's "magnificent address" at the Atlanta Cotton Exposition, adding "would that we had a Booker T. Washington in every hamlet and city; then our race would surely push on along the road of real substantial advancement." In 1905,

Tyler felt confident enough to write to Washington to request his support in seeking a Diplomatic Service post under the administration of Theodore Roosevelt. Although this ambition was not fulfilled, Washington's influence may have been a factor in Tyler's subsequent appointment to the Treasury Department in 1907.

The closeness of Washington's links with Tyler in these years is attested to by the fact that it was Tyler who drafted the infamous 1907 "Brownsville Ghouls" editorial, attacking Washington's militant black critics for their conduct in the wake of the 1906 Brownsville affair. Following a racial incident in Brownsville, Texas, President Roosevelt had summarily discharged three companies of black troops, some of whom had reputedly been involved in the affray. Despite public protestations by northern black radicals, and private solicitation by Washington himself, Roosevelt refused to reverse his decision. The "Ghouls" editorial accused the black radicals of seeking to make political capital out of the misfortunes of the black soldiers.[4]

For all his professed loyalty to the Tuskegee philosophy Tyler's support could never be taken for granted. At heart he was an independent, a trimmer who sought to advance his own career interests by whatever means were available. To this end he was careful to maintain contacts with Washington's opponents in the black community and never became a prisoner of the Tuskegee Machine.

The election of Woodrow Wilson, in 1912, which finally signaled the end of Tyler's career in government administration, provided Washington with an opportunity to bring Tyler more firmly into the Tuskegee camp, by way of an offer of employment in the by then vacant post of National Organizer for the Business League. The recruitment of Tyler afforded Washington the prospect of a valuable new ally, at a time when the influence of the Tuskegee Machine was being challenged by the growth of the NAACP. Moreover, Tyler's proven administrative and journalistic skills would provide much needed rejuvenation to the League's internal organization.

The importance attached by the Tuskegeean to the appointment was indicated by the fact that when Tyler initially declined the position, on grounds of inadequate salary, Washington felt moved to significantly increase the amount of remuneration on offer. This was despite the weak financial position of the League. "It may be that we shall have to pay him a larger salary than we have paid any other organizers," Washington confided in a letter to the Tuskegee benefactor S. C. Napier, but "the right man in this position could, in my opinion, make the League self-sustaining, and I believe Mr Tyler is the right man, and a larger salary for him than we have hitherto paid, in my opinion, would be money well spent."[5]

His financial conditions met, Tyler relented and agreed to take up the post of National Organizer for the League in May 1913, at a salary of $135.00

per month pus traveling expenses. Displaying the eagerness of a new employee, Tyler spent his first three weeks in the post at Tuskegee, familiarizing himself with the work of the League and its records, writing correspondence, and entering into personal consultation with Washington.[6]

Whatever initial enthusiasm Tyler may have had for his new job soon gave way to frustration. One of his first tasks was to write to the officers of local Business Leagues, to compile information on their current membership and activities, and to arrange for himself to go on the road to visit League branches. Having posted his correspondence off he waited in vain for the anticipated replies.

One problem may have been the limitations of southern postal services. Writing to Booker T. Washington in September 1913, on the subject of "your complaints against some of the officers in not promptly answering communications received from Hon. Ralph W. Tyler, National Organizer," J. E. Bush, of Little Rock, Arkansas, protested his innocence. "I have to say in justification of myself that I plead not guilty," he noted, "for the reason that I have never received a communication from Mr Tyler."[7]

Washington appeared to favor an alternative explanation. "In your great anxiety to succeed I fear you will have to exercise a little patience, especially during the month of September," he advised Tyler on 24 September 1913:

> Long experience has convinced me that it is practically impossible to do business in this country, either North or South, in September. I myself just now am on the Mobile Bay fishing. I find that to attempt to do business is simply throwing away my time and strength in September. I tried sometime ago to get the people in our section of Alabama to come to hear President Roosevelt speak at Tuskegee in the fall of the year when they were picking cotton. They refused to do so. It is practically impossible to do much in the South in the way of definite constructive work until December or after Christmas. . . . People are either away from home or are returning from their vacations and are unsettled."[8]

It soon became apparent that the problem was more deep-seated than temporary seasonal factors. Communications difficulties persisted not only into the New Year but also well into the following spring. "In all of your work you will have to bear in mind that many of our men are not in the habit of answering letters promptly," Washington cautioned Tyler in a piece of advice that was perhaps a more realistic, if more gloomy, appraisal of the situation. "The writing of a letter is an irksome and tremendous task to them. That is one of the things that the League wants to teach them, the importance of answering business communications promptly."[9]

Given the evident frustrations of paperwork, Tyler initially may have seen the opportunity of going out into the field, visiting local Leagues in person, as a welcome source of relief. Unfortunately, any romantic thoughts about life on the road were quickly dispelled by the brutal and uncomfortable reality, during Tyler's first major public tour, through the South Atlantic states during June and July 1913.

The quality of board and lodging on offer was far removed from the standards to which Tyler had become accustomed in Washington, D.C. At Greenville, South Carolina, "I had to put up with 'catch-can,'" he complained to Washington's Personal Secretary, Emmett J. Scott. "I had a room that gave me the creeps, and board which almost forced me to be a herbiferous animal." Things did not improve. "This traveling around, getting my meals irregularly and getting all kinds of meals from good to vile, has put a crimp in my abdomen," he again complained on 13 July. "I fear, if it keeps up I will either have to order a new stomach or a pine-box plush covered, with silver mountings. . . . this has been the hardest work I have ever done."[10]

A second public speaking and promotional tour, centered on the Deep South, from October to December 1913, was no better. Traveling on public transport, particularly in rural districts, was arduous and time consuming. "Traveling in Okla(homa) is tough," Tyler wrote to Scott on 24 November. "Many has been the time that I have started in the morning to make a town perhaps a hundred miles away and not yet get there until seven in the evening—going the whole day without a bite to eat." By 19 December the daily attrition of this regime was taking its toll. "You cannot imagine how tired I am. Three months—almost three on the road has greatly fatigued me," Tyler wrote Scott from Memphis, Tennessee. "Traveled all night last night from Jackson (Mississippi) . . . sitting up – only got snatches of sleep. . . . Have lost so much sleep feel I could sleep for a week without waking." Physically worn out, but still determined, Tyler finally arrived back home in Washington, D.C., at 2.00 AM on Christmas day, "just tired out, and banged up with a nasty cold."[11]

Given his comfortable civil service background, it is possible that Tyler was protesting too much. However, similar horror stories by Charles H. Moore, a previous National Organizer for the League, reinforce the impression that, in the main, Tyler's complaints were justified. The manifest inadequacies of Jim Crow facilities added to Tyler's discomfort. Despite legislative provisions that required segregated accommodations to be "equal in all points of comforts and conveniences" Tyler found barely any railroads running through the South that complied with the law. Typically, the carriage set aside for blacks "was a wooden affair and attached immediately behind the baggage car." It was "a vantage point for all the engine smoke and cinders [sic] and a dangerous point in case of wreck."[12]

The receptions that awaited Tyler at the various stopping off places on his southern tour did little to revive his spirits. On occasion, things went well. At St. Louis, Missouri, he addressed an audience of nearly 1,000 people on 2 November 1913, and attended a banquet held in his honor by local businessmen two nights later. By 21 November he had moved on to Muskogee, Oklahoma, and "held a most splendid meeting." T. J. Elliott, the local League President, reported to Emmett J. Scott that the event

> was attended by hundreds of our citizens who were delighted with the talk, which was very inspiring, and I am sure will mean much to us in our effort to stir up general enthusiasm in our city and state. In company with different men of our local League he visited several nearby towns and left them fairly ablaze. We only wish that he could be with us for a full month.[13]

Even the insomniac train journey through Mississippi, in late December, may have seemed worthwhile given that the Magnolia state's League organization was among the most successful in the entire country.[14]

Unfortunately, such uplifting experiences were the exception, not the rule. The ongoing communications problems meant that Tyler often arrived at venues to find that no preparation had been made for his visit.[15] At the other extreme, the reception could be all too warm, as Tyler found himself in the position of a reluctant arbiter in local rivalries, disputes, and jealousies.[16]

Most serious of all, it became apparent that many supposed local League organizations existed only on paper. "The apathy I find to League work everywhere is amazing," Tyler noted on 13 July 1913. "Few of them have had a meeting for a year, many have not held a meeting for two years. Some are skeletons, and some are barely that." In almost every region the story was the same. At Louisville, Kentucky, the local League was "dormant, not having held a meeting for many months." A like situation existed in Greensville, South Carolina, and Danville and Lynchburg in Virginia. The state of affairs was no better in the North. "My trips to all cities north of the Ohio river has convinced me that before any attempt is made to organize new Leagues the old chartered Leagues, all of which are either dead or dying, must first be revived," Tyler informed Washington on 12 July 1913:

> In no northern city that I have visited outside of Wilmington, Del, Atlantic City, NJ, and Philadelphia has the local League met in one or two years. My visits to date have also shown the necessity of revising your list of names of people to whom to write. In many areas the people written to are inactive members or persons whose influence is nil.

Have also found that many Leagues were organized without rather than with business men as members and officers.

In Cumberland, Maryland, the League President was "a waiter in a second rate hotel" who was "ripe for retirement even as a waiter." Another branch President, Spencer Lewis, was "simply a laborer," and in Wheeling, West Virginia, the League was run by a schoolteacher. In a number of chapters the local "saloon keeper" was a prominent member, a fact that deterred other businessmen from joining.[17]

Albeit unwelcome, this report revealed little that was surprising or new to Washington. Fred Moore, one of Tyler's predecessors as National Organizer, had noted as far back as 1906 that of the then 320 recorded League chapters only 175 were active, and that each of these needed to be visited every year by the National Organizer to remain so.

Even in Washington's adopted home state of Alabama there were difficulties in arousing sufficient interest in the League's work. "It was imperative that more interest be shown by Alabama and the individuals thereof," J. G. Cook, the State Organizer for Georgia, warned in July 1906. If not the state might not be able to "present a proper showing" at the League's annual convention in Atlanta in August.[18]

The long-standing deficiencies in League organization were at best a challenging legacy inherited by Tyler. The situation was made worse by the ambitious financial expectations that Washington imposed upon his new National Organizer. The finances of the League had always been in a fragile state of repair, and were further strained by the size of Tyler's salary. To justify this outlay, Washington expected Tyler to solicit regular financial contributions in his visits to local Leagues. Given the difficulties in just securing a turnout at many of the meetings this was clearly an unrealistic objective.

"Getting money out of these people is like hunting for a needle in a haystack," the less than gruntled Tyler reported in July 1913. Appeals for "contributions to the League" were akin to "pulling teeth to get a pittance." Even active League chapters balked at making donations to League coffers, feeling that the costs of entertaining Tyler during his visit were more than sufficient. "On my trips I found getting contributions for the League was very hard," Tyler reflected in June 1914. "At some places nothing was contributed, at others the contribution was most niggardly, and at but few places did the contributions cover the actual expenses reported much less the amount I advanced out of my own pocket without turning in record of same."[19]

If Tyler's testimony is believed this last issue was a particular source of personal grievance. In the absence of adequate funds it appears that he was often obliged to use his own income to help meet the costs of travel and board. Given the weak fiscal resources of the League he then felt uncomfortable about claiming these expenses back at a later date, and more than once waived the money owed to him.

To add to his problems the difficulties in maintaining regular postal contact with Tyler when he was on the road meant that even his normal salary checks were not always received on time. Tyler also became convinced that the League's Financial Secretary, Charles H. Anderson, resident in Florida, was dilatory in dispatching these payments. This further complaint was thus regularly added to his already long list of grievances in communications to Tuskegee.[20]

All things taken into account, it was no surprise that Tyler completed his first year in office feeling less than encouraged. "I don't know of anything in which I have worked harder than on this League work," he wrote on 12 June 1914, "and yet not be satisfied with the results, financially as well as in enthusiasm on the part of various localities."[21]

Tyler was not alone in having doubts about his continued employment as National Organizer. In the spring of 1913 Booker T. Washington had enthusiastically head hunted Tyler for the League, in the belief that he was recruiting a valuable ally, and that Tyler's administrative skill could help turn around the League's organizational shortcomings. The Tuskegeean was soon to have serious misgivings about both these assumptions.

The administrative failings of local Leagues may have caused Tyler much angst but, by the spring of 1914, doubts also began to arise as to his own competence. On 4 April 1914 John Dickerson, the local League President in Jacksonville, Florida, complained to Washington that Tyler had failed to honor a program of events that had been agreed on during a visit to the city. Tyler was "a poor representative of the National Organization," Dickerson concluded that "the impression made in Florida by him is like that of an apprentice among Proffessional [sic] Business men."

Worse was to follow. The next month A. N. Johnson of Nashville, Tennessee, one of the "strongest helpers in connection with the Business League movement," sent a similar complaint to Tuskegee. Johnson, as League President in Nashville, was aggrieved that Tyler had failed to attend a full program and reception that had been organized for him in the city from 7–9 May. To add to the embarrassment, over 3,000 handbills had been printed and distributed in advance to publicize the proceedings.[22]

It was not just Tyler's timekeeping, but also his whole personality that seemed to be a problem, making him "a weight to the Business League." In the role of "a press agent," Tyler was "pretty good," R. W. Thompson, President of the National Negro Press Association, noted to Emmett J. Scott in September 1914, but that was only part of the job. What was needed was an individual who could "reach down and pick up the humblest factor in race progress and make him worth something to the organization." Tyler had a "temperamental unfitness" for this kind of work. "He felt above the masses, talked above them, associated above them and they felt the frost that he generated."[23]

Another concern was the financial cost of Tyler's employment, made more acute by his lack of success in fundraising. In a visit to Mississippi, from 3–22 December 1913, Tyler amassed only $71.85 in contributions from local Leagues, well short of his own basic monthly salary of $135.00. Moreover, this was a good month as his fundraising endeavors went, and from a state in which the League's organization was particularly strong. It became clear that Washington's early hopes that Tyler's employment could be self-financing, with the National Organizer's salary being met from the cash contributions he collected, were not realistic.

On the contrary, Tyler was becoming a major liability in cash terms. From 4 August 1913 to 3 January 1914 his salary and expenses amounted to $605.00. In the 12 months from 2 August 1913 to 1 August 1914 he cost the League a total of $2,200.00. This represented the "bulk of the expenses" of the League for this period, a fact that did not escape the attention of the League's leading officers and financial auditors. "I think more effective work can be done and at much less expense," Charles H. Brooks advised Washington from Philadelphia. J. E. Bush of Little Rock, Arkansas, was more blunt. "I regard Mr Tyler as a very valuable man," he noted, but "he is too expensive for the orgainization" [sic], particularly "when you remember that every cent that we handle is either a free and a gracious gift or we must beg for it."[24]

Serious as the League's financial problems may have been, Washington was experiencing even more pressing concerns in his working relationship with Tyler by early 1914. Tyler had a justified reputation for being a man of strong and frank views. He did not tolerate those he perceived to be fools gladly, and was not reticent about letting all and sundry know it. This bluntness quickly drew him into conflict with some of Washington's most trusted lieutenants.

Samuel Laing Williams, one of Washington's closest and most influential supporters in Chicago, was one of Tyler's early targets. When Williams was dismissed from his employment in the Attorney General's Office in Chicago, following the election of Woodrow Wilson as President of the United States in 1912, Tyler was quick to comment. Williams was "simply a liability," he forthrightly, but injudiciously, told Washington. Williams was "a man of ability, but . . . short on energy and practicality." Charles H. Anderson, the Financial Secretary of the Business League, was another, and frequent, source of ire because of what Tyler believed to be Anderson's excessive delays in processing his salary and expenses checks.[25]

In-house tensions, disruptive enough on their own, were often made worse by Tyler's tendency to go public with his grievances. Prior to taking up his employment with the League, Tyler had sought to develop a journalistic career for himself. He continued with this aspiration during his office as National Organizer, and was a frequent columnist for black newspapers and journals in New York City and Washington, D.C. Leading figures in the Tuskegee Machine suffered the indignity of being regularly pilloried in print in Tyler's articles. So serious was the problem that R. W. Thompson advised Emmett J. Scott to keep Tyler busy on the road in the service of the League as a means of limiting his journalistic efforts. Tyler's "presence in Washington" was "detrimental to the Tuskegee interests and productive of turmoil in every relation of life here. The stuff sent to the New York *News* and *Amsterdam News* is vile. Keep him out of town."[26]

The "vile stuff" in question included a number of scurrilous articles attacking one of Washington's closest supporters, Charles W. Anderson, who was one of the most powerful and influential black leaders in New York City. In pieces for the *Amsterdam News* Tyler questioned Anderson's race loyalty, and portrayed him as sacrificing the interests of the African-American community in order to seek government office for himself. The enraged Anderson sent a succession of complaints to Tuskegee, denouncing Tyler variously as a "scoundrel," a "dirty assassin," and "a garfish-mouthed ex-barber" who needed reminding that "his barber days are over," and that "he must lay aside his razor." "Dante has described several kinds of hells," Anderson wrote to Washington on 22 January 1914, "but I do not think he described one with punishments severe enough for a reptile like this."[27]

The continuing financial and organizational problems of the League, combined with Tyler's journalistic forays, brought Washington's relations with Tyler to a crisis point by the start of 1914. Hoping for an early New Year resolution of his difficulties, Washington's initial response was, typically, to seek a way out through a combination of a renewed commitment to hard work and greater thrift, combined with backstage diplomacy.

In respect to the League, Washington concluded that Tyler's field trips simply needed better preplanning and preparation. Washington himself undertook to write personal letters of support and encouragement to black community leaders in the districts to be visited by Tyler. Tyler for his part should be more economical in the extent of his travels. "I feel more and more convinced that it will be best for you, and all of us, for you not to try to cover so much territory, that is not do so much traveling," Washington suggested to Tyler on 28 November 1913. "Of course when you speak to a local audience you reach perhaps from three to five hundred people in many cases more, but when you use your pen, you will be speaking to perhaps two or three hundred thousand."[28]

The unfortunate fact that it was precisely Tyler's unrestrained use of the pen that had created so many other problems was a different matter that required other remedies. Washington's first action was to send letters of reassurance to the victims of Tyler's writings, and to encourage them in the belief that such attacks would soon cease.[29]

Dealing with the author of the attacks, Tyler himself, the sensitivity of the problem, combined with Washington's preference for diplomatic language, made the Tuskegeean's initial correspondence subtle to the point of being obscure. "I wonder if you realize that certain parties in New York claim that you are the author of certain letters sent out from Washington to a New York paper," he wrote to Tyler on 29 September 1913. Moreover, "the paper to whom these letters were sent give out your name regularly to certain other parties in New York as the author of these letters."

When such circuitous correspondence proved ineffective, Washington was obliged to resort to a more direct mode of communication, namely a face-to-face interview with Tyler. Finally, by February 1914, both Emmett J. Scott and Washington were forwarding on to Tyler the letters of criticism that had been received at Tuskegee from Anderson and others about Tyler's newspaper articles.[30]

In the event, none of Washington's retrenchment schemes proved effective. The financial position of the League did not improve. Tyler's journalistic outbursts showed no sign of abatement. If anything they may have intensified, for, when his attention was drawn to the criticisms made of his writings, Tyler, rather than being chastened, seemed to perceive himself as the victim of malicious foes. "I was a staunch friend" of Charles W. Anderson, "reposed every confidence in him," Tyler wrote to Emmett J. Scott on 21 January 1914, but "I have a different opinion of him now, and have excellent reasons for it." The point of no return came on 17 February 1914 when Anderson wrote to Tuskegee formally resigning from the Business League "because of that scoundrel Tyler."[31]

Anderson's action placed Washington in an unenviable position. Anderson enjoyed considerable influence within the African-American community in New York. The loss of his good will would have seriously undermined the efforts of the Tuskegee Machine in the city.

Unfortunately, the only obvious action to prevent this, the immediate dismissal of Tyler, was scarcely more palatable. Tyler carried much status in the black community of Washington, D.C. Moreover, the nation's capital was a center of activity for the expanding NAACP, the organization most feared by Washington as a threat to his own power. "The NAACP is growing fast, and it has all but blanketed this community here," Tyler had warned Emmett J Scott as recently as 4 January. "The fact is we have, and are losing ground, and the enemy is gaining." The possibility of a dismissed and embittered Tyler joining the swelling NAACP ranks could not be viewed with equanimity.[32]

Trapped in an impossible situation, Washington pragmatically opted for a course of damage limitation. Turning the financial difficulties of the

League to his advantage, he wrote to Tyler on 26 June 1914, advising him that "the League Treasury was empty." Although falling short of an actual notice of dismissal, on this occasion Tyler was in no doubt as to the meaning of Washington's words. "The advice that the Treasury is empty suggests that I can expect no further salary," he replied on 29 June, "and the natural inference that my services must end."[33]

The state of League finances may have been a genuine consideration in Washington's action. The League was short of income, and lack of finances resulted in an abrupt end to employment for at least two other National Organizers of the League, Fred Moore in August 1906 and Charles H. Moore in August 1910.[34]

Perhaps more revealing of Washington's motives, however, was a letter he wrote to Charles W. Anderson on 20 February, advising that "I have directed Mr. Scott not to accept your resignation but to leave the matter in my hands for a few weeks." He further reassured the New Yorker that "I think you will find conditions will change. We cannot afford to accept your resignation."[35]

In the event, Washington's carefully laid plans for easing Tyler out of the employment of the League almost foundered at the last moment. At the annual convention of the League at Muskogee, Oklahoma, in August 1914, Tyler arrived early and met with members of the League Executive Committee, who asked him if he "would not serve again," and how "he felt about continuing the work." Tyler himself noted to Washington, on 26 August, that he was on the point of giving a favorable reply when "on your putting in appearance I was given to understand that the Treasury was insufficient; that an organizer could not be employed that the work must be done at Tuskegee." This intervention reinforces the impression that Washington's own agenda, rather than just financial need, lay behind Tyler's termination of contract.[36]

In the aftermath of Tyler's departure, harmony was once more restored within the Tuskegee Machine. Tyler himself was, understandably, embittered, and was soon reported to be denouncing the League as "a fake and a humbug," and declaring it to be "on its last legs." More worrying still was his declared intention to start a paper in Columbus, Ohio that would be "a radical of radicals and stand up straight for all the rights of the Negro."[37]

The actual form of employment secured by Tyler proved to be of a different, but still intriguing, nature. Within a month he was marketing a product by the name of Varni-Shine, "the Gloss Producing Marvel." A new preparation, it was claimed by its makers to be "superior to anything on the market," for use on "furniture, pianos, automobiles, painted and varnished finishes, on metal and interior woodwork." It reputedly not only cleaned, but also polished and preserved, "with surprising and gratifying results." Such was Tyler's sense of new found optimism, that he even wrote to Emmett J. Scott, on 10 October 1914, in the hope that Tuskegee Institute might become a source of custom for Varni-Shine.[38]

The fact that Tyler was still in communication with Tuskegee confirmed that for all his dissatisfaction, he was still on speaking terms with Washington. Writing to Tyler on 2 September 1914, Washington felt able to record that "while you will not be in the service of the League any longer it will be a great satisfaction to know that you are still on friendly terms." Further reassurance was provided with the suggestion that if "at any time I can be of service to you, please be kind enough to let me know." This final comment was later to take on unexpected significance.[39]

In January 1915, Tyler, now resident in Ohio, had evidently become disillusioned with the "Gloss Producing Marvel," and sought employment within the Office of the State Governor. Taking Washington up on his earlier promise, he duly asked the Tuskegeean to write to Governor Willis on his behalf.

Washington clearly had no desire to offend, yet, at the same time, may well have preferred not to associate himself too closely with the volatile Tyler. Treading a fine diplomatic line, Washington advised Tyler that it would be inappropriate for him to write to the Governor directly since Willis was not a personal acquaintance. Instead, he forwarded a general testimonial for Tyler to use as he saw fit:

> To whom it may concern:—
> This is to state that I have known Hon. Ralph W. Tyler for a number of years. He held the position of Auditor of the Navy Department under both Mr Roosevelt and Mr Taft, and gave eminent satisfaction while performing the duties of this important position. Aside for this, he has extraordinary ability as a newspaper man, and stands high in character and general intelligence. He knows the condition and needs of the colored people and has great influence with them. Any favor shown Mr Tyler will be much appreciated.

The careful understatement of this testimonial, and potential veiled meaning to the phrase "extraordinary ability as a newspaper man," may not have escaped Tyler, who was notably less than pleased on receiving it.[40]

Viewed from a historical perspective, Tyler's correspondence relating to his employment as National Organizer of the National Negro Business League in 1913–1914 is of double value as primary source material. In the first instance there are his eyewitness accounts of the grass roots organization of the League. Ever the skilled propagandist, Booker T. Washington was careful to ensure that the public image of the League was one of unqualified success. Visits by Washington to local League chapters were carefully chosen and orchestrated well in advance. Similarly, much effort was put into the preparations for the annual convention of the League, in August each year, to ensure a good attendance and smoothly run proceedings.

Perhaps impressed by such careful stage management, Virginia Lantz Denton, a 1990s commentator, has described the League as "a strong business network with hundreds of local leagues across the nation." The success of the organization "was measured by increasing numbers of black businesses, public recognition, racial pride, cooperation and success, as well as increased wealth." Tyler's reports all too painfully demonstrate that this perception and the actual reality were starkly at odds.[41]

In 1903–1904 Booker T. Washington identified six criteria that had to be met if local leagues were to be effective. These included regular meetings, with an hour set aside for "thorough discussion of business methods at each meeting." Branch officials had to be "active and efficient" and should ensure the involvement of "all reputable business and professional men." More generally, "all persons who believe in giving support to their own" should be urged to join. League members had to be willing to give a portion of their time "to the betterment and improvement" of the local black community. A clear majority of local Leagues failed to meet most, if not all, of these objectives. Worse still, by 1913–1914 at least half of all League chapters were moribund organizations that existed only on paper.[42]

A second source of interest lies in Tyler's personal and working relationship with Washington himself. Washington's so-called "secret life," carefully concealed civil rights campaigning, the covert persecution of perceived enemies, and the rewarding of allies, has been well catalogued.[43]

Tyler was an influential maverick who defied such easy classification. The manner in which Washington sought to channel the energies of this volatile and semidetached supporter provides useful insights into the Wizard of Tuskegee's Machiavellian skills in man management. "I was played for a sucker. In return for fealty and sacrifice, I had the pleasure of serving as the goat," Tyler noted of his experience. He has "been used as the goat right along," he concluded, tacitly recognizing the extent to which he had been made use of in the wider interests of the Tuskegee Machine. "Whenever there were chestnuts to be pulled out of the fire, the task was assigned to me. Whenever anyone was left to stand and take the cussing I was the one to unflinchingly take the cussing . . . to save others," he bemoaned. "Whenever it was expected to make a goat, I was made the goat. . . . Goat, that's been my role ever since being in Washington, in order that the interests of presumed friends might be conserved, and in order that presumed friends might be protected from criticism."[44]

Even at this late stage, it would appear that it was the "presumed friends," rather than Booker T. Washington himself, who were the principal source of Tyler's resentment. After Washington's death, in November

1915, Tyler continued to remain on good terms with the Tuskegeean's representative on earth, Emmett J. Scott. When Scott became Special Assistant to the Secretary of War, in October 1917, Tyler's journalistic abilities were once more called into use, as a war correspondent in France reporting on the activities of black troops. Washington's skills in interpersonal diplomacy had, perhaps, achieved one last triumph from beyond the grave.[45]

CHAPTER 8

The Sorcerer and
the Apprentice

Booker T. Washington and
Marcus Garvey

During the period 1895–1925 Booker T. Washington and Marcus Garvey
were the best known and most influential black spokespersons in the
United States. If the Wizard of Tuskegee was the dominant figure in
African-American society between 1895 and 1915, Garvey enjoyed an
equal, if not greater, ascendancy from 1917 to 1925. The careers of the two
men were also highly controversial. Other black American leaders of his
day were sharply critical of Washington, and many of these, most notably
W. E. B. Du Bois, went on to oppose the policies and ideas of Garvey during the 1920s with even greater vehemence.

At times this hostility became personalized and offensive, reflecting
the highly charged emotions that the two men could arouse. Writing in
1902, William Monroe Trotter denounced Washington for possessing features that "were harsh in the extreme," with "vast leonine jaws," and "mas-
tiff-like rows of teeth," that "were set clinched together like a vice." Any
onlooker would be left "uneasy and restless during the night" if he or she
failed "to report to the police such a man" before retiring to bed. Similarly,
in 1923, the usually more restrained Du Bois derided Garvey as "a little fat
black man, ugly but with intelligent eyes and a big head." The following
year an editorial by Du Bois in the NAACP journal *Crisis* was entitled
simply "Marcus Garvey: Lunatic or Traitor."[1]

It may have been some consolation to Washington and Garvey that
hurtful insults were a tacit acknowledgment of their importance. Had each
not possessed status and influence their appearance would not have been
deemed worthy of comment. A less philosophical, but perhaps more satisfying, source of comfort was that the two men were more than capable of
employing even more wounding comments and actions against their
detractors.

Apart from their importance, and unflattering partisan accounts of their outward appearance, Washington and Garvey at first sight shared little in common. Washington was deferential to white opinion and sought the integration of African Americans into U.S. society. Garvey was frequently inflammatory in his public statements, argued for racial separatism, and envisaged the return of black Americans to an independent African homeland.

Despite such differences Garvey admired Washington for his achievements and found the Tuskegeean's ideas a source of inspiration in developing his own philosophy. Chancing upon a copy of Washington's *Up From Slavery* in 1912, while living in London, was, by Garvey's own testimony, a defining moment in his career. It was then that his "doom" of "being a race leader" became apparent to him, and led him to question the world around him. "Where is the black man's Government?" Garvey pondered. "Where is his King and his kingdom? Where is his President, his country, and his ambassador, his army, his navy, his men of big affairs?" Unable to find any such examples of black achievement, Garvey concluded that it was his destiny to "help to make them."[2]

Undoubtedly dramatic, the factual accuracy of Garvey's recollection is, perhaps, less certain. It is unlikely that the Tuskegeean could ever have envisaged, still less intended, that his autobiography would have provoked such thoughts in the minds of his readers. Furthermore, Garvey may have been aware of Washington long before his reading of *Up From Slavery*. Industrial education was a subject of discussion during Garvey's childhood days in Jamaica. The anticolonial politician and journalist, Dr. Robert Love, was a qualified supporter of the Tuskegee philosophy on the island in the early years of the twentieth century. Later, in London, Garvey's interest in Washington may initially have been stimulated by reports on Tuskegee in issues of the *African Times and Orient Review*, a monthly magazine edited by the Egyptian writer Duse Mohamed Ali.[3]

Whatever the source of inspiration, on his return to the West Indies, in the summer of 1914, Garvey was committed to establishing a "Tuskegee in Jamaica." To this end he launched the Universal Negro Improvement Association (UNIA) in August that year. In addition to holding weekly musical and literary meetings, the stated aims of the new organization included the creation of "educational and industrial training colleges for the purpose of the further education and culture of our boys and girls"; reclaiming the "fallen and degraded"; assisting the needy; and rescuing "the fallen women of the island from the pit of infamy and vice." The conservative nature of Garvey's ideas at this time was indicated by the fact that early UNIA resolutions included affirmations of loyalty toward the British Crown.[4]

Despite such undertakings Garvey found it difficult to raise money for UNIA projects, a problem that led him into an extended correspondence with Washington at Tuskegee between September 1914 and October 1915. In later years Garvey liked to give the impression that this exchange attested to a shared vision, mutual respect, and emerging friendship between the two men. In reality, Washington's replies to Garvey's unsolicited letters were polite rather than warm, and understandably noncommittal.

Washington wished Garvey well in his activities, and volunteered to send copies of the *Tuskegee Student* in return for those of the UNIA paper the *Negro World*, but carefully avoided any offer of funds. In April 1915 he welcomed the news of a tour of the United States by Garvey that would include a visit to Tuskegee, promising that everyone at the institute would make his stay "as pleasant and as profitable as we can." If the use of such language hinted at possible financial help the death of Washington in November ensured that any such hopes Garvey might have entertained failed to achieve fruition.[5]

During 1916 Garvey maintained contact with Tuskegee. He wrote to Emmett J. Scott about his impending trip to the United States, and sent Robert R. Moton, Washington's successor as Principal of Tuskegee, lengthy letters of advice on a visit by Moton to Jamaica in early spring. At this time Garvey continued to support Washington's philosophy. On 22 November 1915 the UNIA in Jamaica held a memorial meeting to commemorate the life and work of the Tuskegeean, with an oration by Garvey himself that lasted for more than an hour. He took care to inform Scott of the event on UNIA notepaper that included an uplifting quotation of Washington's in the letterhead, "One cannot hold another down in the ditch without staying down in the ditch with him; in helping the man who is down to rise, the man who is up is freeing himself from a burden that would else drag him down."[6]

It is possible to see such actions as part of a calculated effort by Garvey to further his career as a race leader. Little known, even in Jamaica, it was beneficial to Garvey to link his ideas with those of the famous Tuskegeean. Moton and Scott were potentially valuable contacts for UNIA fundraising efforts in America. At the same time, Garvey's enthusiasm for all things Tuskegee was also a reflection of his genuinely held views.

In the early 1920s, at the height of his fame and success, Garvey continued to give fulsome praise to Washington's contribution to racial uplift. At the annual UNIA convention in New York City in August 1922, he described Washington as "a great man and a great educator, probably the greatest in the American continent" as "he made himself out of nothing," and "because he was a creator and not an imitator." He informed delegates that in September the Booker T. Washington University, a UNIA institution, would be opened in Harlem. Although short lived, because of the UNIA's growing financial and legal problems, the University was envisaged by Garvey as a major initiative. It was his intention that all future UNIA leaders would be trained at the University. It was also to offer courses in agriculture and commerce, and to send trained experts "throughout the world" to educate "our people in the art and science of fruit raising, agriculture and business administration and efficiency."[7]

In late October and early November 1923, Garvey and his wife, Amy Ashwood, visited Tuskegee in what amounted to almost a pilgrimage to Washington's memory. In an address to students at the institute Garvey praised Washington as "the greatest man in America—yea, the greatest man in the Western world." At the end of the visit he made a $50.00 donation to the institution with the promise to Principal Moton that "you may count on me as one of your annual supporters."[8]

In 1924 the Wizard of Tuskegee was again honored when the *SS Goethals*, one of the flagships of the Black Star Line, was renamed the *SS Booker T. Washington*. Purchased for $100,000, and requiring the expenditure of a further $25,000 in reconditioning costs, the vessel was ultimately sold for only $25,000 in April 1926 to help pay the debts of the shipping line.[9]

In the last years of his life, in England during the 1930s, Garvey continued to venerate Washington, at a time when there was no longer any obvious financial or career advantage in doing so. A June 1935 editorial in the *Black Man*, a journal published by Garvey in London, lauded the Tuskegeean as "an outstanding genius," whose "memory can never fade in American history." Washington was "the greatest Negro of the century" and for centuries to come "his place will be very high in Negro achievements."[10]

Despite Garvey's reverence for Washington he was unable to win enthusiastic support from leading members of the Tuskegee Machine. However, he did remain on amicable terms with Washington's successor, Moton. In addition to allowing Garvey to address Tuskegee students in 1923, the institute's new Principal wrote an article for the 1921 Christmas edition of the *Negro World*.[11]

Such cordiality reflected the fact that Garvey was popular with students at Tuskegee. It was also Moton's policy to stay on good terms with other race leaders wherever possible. This even-handedness in itself precluded him from active involvement in the Garvey movement. Conservative in temperament and ideas, Moton was, in any case, an unlikely recruit for the UNIA. He was always careful never to become too closely associated with Garvey.[12]

Garvey himself recalled that on his arrival in the United States in 1916 he "went to see Dr. Moton, but I was too insignificant for him to notice." In 1920 Moton was alleged to have turned down a payment of $10,000 to attend the UNIA annual convention in New York and be nominated as "leader of the American negroes" in the UNIA. He also failed to respond to a request to address the August 1922 UNIA convention.[13]

Garvey recognized that there were important differences between Moton's thinking and his own. At the UNIA convention in New York in August 1921 he informed delegates that "Du Bois and Moton are no more; we buried them in 1914. The New Negro demands a leadership that refuses to beg but demands a change." He publicly disapproved of a visit by Moton to Glasgow, in September and October 1922, to address the Scottish Churches Missionary Congress on the subject of "Africa in Transformation." Stopping short of openly impugning Moton's motives for the trip, Garvey argued that the Tuskegee Principal would unwittingly be used by the Congress to persuade Africans to accept white Christian missionaries and European colonial administration.[14]

"Dr. Moton's ideas on the Negro question are not the same as those of Garvey," noted Henri Jasper, a senior Belgian diplomat in Washington, D.C. Garvey "wishes Negro emancipation with the exclusion of white participation, whilst Dr. Moton thinks that it is impossible for Negroes to make progress in civilization without white help." Similarly, within the United States, the reliance of Tuskegee on white philanthropy led Garvey to fear that the work of the institute would be used to promote white rather than black interests. In August 1922 Charles Hallaert, the Belgian Vice Consul in New York City, went so far as to describe Moton as Garvey's "most dangerous enemy," a "very intelligent man" who was "especially well known in the South."[15]

Garvey's differences with Emmett J. Scott were even more pronounced and, over time, increasingly less polite. After an exchange of letters, Scott first met Garvey when the Jamaican finally visited Tuskegee in 1916. The reception given to the UNIA leader was polite but offered little in the way of practical encouragement, particularly in respect to Garvey's fundraising mission.[16]

In the years that followed Scott became increasingly hostile in his outlook as he came to know Garvey's personality and ideas more fully. In December 1918, when serving as Special Assistant to the Secretary of War, he confided to the U.S. Military Intelligence Division that Garvey was of "the agitator type," a "soap box orator" who could "cause a certain amount of mischief" around New York, but was "not a man around whom any serious movements can be prompted." The UNIA was no more than a "paper organization" that offered little to attract the support of African Americans, other than "the growing unrest of Darker peoples who are groping their way and wondering how they are coming out of the present situation."[17]

The remarkable growth of the UNIA, and Garvey's widespread popularity among African Americans in the early 1920s, did nothing to alter

Scott's negative opinion of the movement, despite continuing efforts by the Jamaican to win his backing. At the UNIA annual convention in New York City, in August 1922, Garvey honored Scott by making him a Knight Commander of the Nile in his newly created black nobility. The bestowal of this title, as was doubtless intended, led both contemporaries, and some later historians, to conclude that Scott was a Garvey sympathizer.[18]

The reality was very different. Scott wrote to Garvey in advance of the convention declining the offer of any decoration and he did not attend the award ceremony. In the immediate aftermath of the event his anger at what had transpired prompted Scott to send a telegram to a leading black newspaper, the New York *Age*, to make public his refusal to accept the UNIA ennoblement. The *Age* duly published the communication. In a private letter the next month Scott denounced "Garvey's foolish schemes" and "the many efforts that were made to inveigle me into an association" with his organization.[19]

Scott's choice of the *Age* to make his public disavowal reflected the fact it was a newspaper that had consistently supported the work of Tuskegee. The editor of the *Age*, Frederick Moore, had originally purchased the paper in 1907 with financial help from Booker T. Washington. During the 1920s, Moore's distaste for Garvey surpassed that of even Scott. In August 1920 the *Age* denounced the Jamaican as "a mountebank, a money grabber and a discredited but cunning schemer." The UNIA would "amount to nothing" and "Garvey at its head" was "a huge joke" if it were not for the fact that he was "hoaxing a lot of good hardworking negroes."[20]

The black journalist Timothy Thomas Fortune, who had owned the *Age* before Moore, was the only one of Washington's leading associates to openly support Garvey. From October 1923 to 26 January 1924 he served as assistant managing editor on the UNIA newspaper the *Negro World*. Garvey himself retained the position of managing editor, but was forced to give up the post in February 1924 because of his imprisonment for fraud. In Garvey's absence Fortune assumed full editorial duties on the paper, a position that he retained until his death in June 1928, dictating the last editorials from a hospital bed.[21]

On learning of Fortune's passing Garvey, by then freed from jail and resident in London, wrote to the journalist's son to convey his condolences. He assured Frederick Fortune that his father had been "a very good friend and one who did his best to help" in the work of the UNIA. Garvey would "ever remember him for his painstaking effort to promote the best interests of the Negro race."[22]

Garvey's kind words, as is customary with obituaries, did not reveal the full truth about his relationship with the elder Fortune. In August 1925, during his incarceration in the Atlanta Penitentiary, he claimed to have "never had much confidence" in Fortune. He believed that Fortune had abused his editorial position to publish articles in the *Negro World* that "gave expression more to his own personal feelings than to the opinions and program" of the UNIA. Garvey appointed his wife, Amy Ashwood, as Executive Secretary and Director of Policy on the paper to curb Fortune's influence. On 28 October 1926 Fortune officially resigned his post on the *Negro World* because of the restrictions placed on his editorial authority.[23]

In any event, Fortune stayed on in his duties, despite the fact that Garvey had advised acceptance of his departure. This continued incumbency doubtless reflected a change of heart on the part of either or both of the two men. Practical considerations may also have played a part. The UNIA's continued financial problems meant that by 1926 it was common for staff on the *Negro World* to work for weeks, if not months, before being paid. Under such conditions it would not have been easy to find a suitable and willing replacement as editor.[24]

On his part, Fortune lacked alternative job options. Poor health, poverty, and his well-known addiction to alcohol meant that he had little choice but to continue working for the *Negro World*. These desperate personal circumstances were an important factor in his securing employment with the paper in the first place. Impressed by Fortune's past reputation as a journalist, and his association with Washington, Garvey was one of the few newspaper proprietors prepared to offer him permanent full-time work. In ideological terms Fortune's disagreements over the editorial policy of the *Negro World*, and the fact that he did not take out membership in the UNIA, support the view that he was never a whole-hearted convert to the Garvey movement.[25]

The indifference of senior members of the Tuskegee Machine toward Garvey in the years 1916–1918 can be explained by the fact that he was then little known and that they underestimated his potential as a race leader. By the early 1920s indifference turned to hostility, not just because Garvey was successful, but also because his ideas had become more radical. Moving beyond his original aim of creating a Tuskegee in Jamaica, he aspired to leadership of a worldwide movement that called for racial separation and the creation of an independent black African state.

Given the far-reaching changes in his thinking, the constancy of Garvey's admiration for Booker T. Washington requires some explanation. One factor was that Garvey saw parallels between Washington's career and his own. Born a slave, the Tuskegeean overcame childhood poverty and racial discrimination to become a "self-made man." In his public statements on Washington, Garvey often emphasized this fact. Washington's autobiography, *Up From Slavery*, which so impressed Garvey, had the qualities of a moral fable, relating the rise of the Tuskegeean from humble beginnings to fame by dint of ability and hard work alone.

Even in his early twenties Garvey felt that he too was similarly destined for greatness. If never a slave himself he had slave ancestors. His early life had not been privileged. He was the youngest of 11 children, and his father had "died poor." He left school at 14 years of age and, like Washington, never completed any form of higher education. Between 1881 and 1915 Washington built Tuskegee from nothing and turned it into an internationally acclaimed educational institution. In his own career Garvey founded the UNIA and transformed it from an unknown organization into a worldwide movement that, at its height, had more than one million members in the United States alone.[26]

In the 1920s many of the individual race leaders and civil rights organizations that denounced Garvey had also opposed Washington. In defying these critics, most notably Du Bois and the NAACP, Garvey often gave the impression that he was taking part in a struggle that had began under Washington, and that he was now continuing on the Tuskegeean's behalf.

In his public addresses and published writings Garvey frequently used praise for Washington as an oratorical or literary ploy to ridicule Du Bois. Scornful comparisons of the respective achievements of the two men lauded Washington as "honest, ambitious and true to his race," whereas Du Bois was "a narrow selfish opportunist who at no time ever loved his race, but only himself." Washington had been a powerful and creative force for good, but Du Bois was "an iconoclast" who liked "to smash anything not originated by himself and by his white associates." He was "a destroyer" who "attempted to tear down the great genius of Tuskegee because he was not properly trained in the ways of the world to handle such men."[27]

The use of such emotionally charged language reflected the fact that like Washington, Garvey was by temperament inclined to see any opposition to him in personalized terms. He perceived critics of the UNIA not as being motivated by genuine differences of opinion, but as small-minded men who were jealous of the organization's success and out to destroy him as an individual.

The insulting comments that regularly appeared in print about Garvey's physical appearance made such a response understandable. The "Garvey Must Go" campaign, initiated in 1923 by other black leaders to secure Garvey's deportation, reinforced these feelings of persecution, as did the exultation of some of his rivals at Garvey's conviction and imprisonment for fraud in 1925.

At the same time, Garvey was naturally prone to paranoid suspicion. Even within the UNIA he found it difficult to tolerate dissenting opinion. A contributory factor in the mismanagement problems of the organization was Garvey's inclination to surround himself with compliant individuals who could be relied on to agree with his ideas rather than point out objections to them. Advisors who showed more spine were seen as having devious motives. Differences over the editorial policy of the *Negro World* in 1926 were thus attributed by Garvey to an attempt by Fortune to "undermine my program, no doubt for the good of the group that . . . has been fighting me through the NAACP."[28]

An unpleasant corollary of Garvey's suspicious instincts was that it encouraged him to be vindictive toward any individuals who he, rightly or wrongly, perceived as enemies. This retribution was not always limited to ridiculing speeches or mocking articles in the *Negro World*. In 1923 the black trade union leader Asa Philip Randolph received a severed hand through the post with the warning that he himself may suffer such mutilation if he did not cease his opposition to Garvey. Ostensibly sent by the Ku Klux Klan, it was no less possible that the grisly package came from UNIA members or supporters. On 1 January 1923 James Eason, a former leading UNIA official who had later criticized the organization, was assassinated by Garvey supporters. After the event Garvey made known his approval of the killing, and may even have been involved in planning the murder.[29]

If less extreme in conduct, Booker T. Washington had taken equal satisfaction in vicious reprisals against his own critics. Through the covert initiatives of the Tuskegee Machine his opponents were subjected to vilification in the press, malicious lawsuits, and loss of employment. Garvey took pride in the fact that he shared Washington's humble beginnings and status as a "self-made" man. When a mature race leader in his own right Garvey, in common with Washington, also suffered the psychological insecurities and intolerance of criticism that such a background can engender.

In policy terms the aspect of Washington's program that most attracted Garvey was the Tuskegeean's emphasis on economic self-help. "After a people have established successfully a firm industrial foundation they naturally turn to politics and society," Garvey noted in 1924, "but not first to society and politics, because the two latter cannot exist without the former."[30]

Like Washington, Garvey at times seemed to view economic advancement as a universal remedy that would resolve the wider problems faced by blacks in American society. "The Negro is ignored today simply because he has kept himself backward," Garvey asserted in 1915. If "he were to try to raise himself to a higher state in the civilized cosmos, all the other races would be glad to meet him on the plane of equality and comradeship." At the 1922 UNIA annual convention he argued that even lynching would "be stopped only through industrialism and acquiring a high standing in the realms of finance by the Negro on his own initiative." This would enable African Americans to command "the respect and serious consideration of the world."[31]

Thoughts of this sort sometimes led Garvey to blame African Americans themselves, rather than the racial injustices of American society, for the disadvantages they encountered. In moralizing tones, reminiscent of Washington himself, Garvey contrasted the thrift of European immigrants with the extravagance of black Americans. "Negroes love luxuries," he noted disapprovingly. "We bought silk shirts at $10 apiece, and $15 apiece. We bought shoes at $30 and $25 a pair. We bought ladies dresses at $100 a suit; we bought the most expensive hats, silk socks at $3 a pair, at $2 a pair, and $1.50 a pair, and we took automobile rides and paid $24 for a Sunday afternoon ride." In such fashion "we spent every nickel of what we received."[32]

An added attraction of Washington's economic self-help initiatives for Garvey was the fact that they contained elements of black separatist thinking that accorded with Garvey's own emerging philosophy in the 1920s. In the context of the National Negro Business League (NNBL) Washington encouraged African Americans to unite in all black business ventures and purchase goods from black shops and stores rather than from white competitors. He supported the creation of all black farming communities and African-American townships like Mound Bayou in Mississippi and Boley in Oklahoma. Garvey's own economic initiatives, like the Black Star Line and Negro Factories Corporation, seemed a logical continuation of the Washington program.[33]

Moreover, Washington, like Garvey, had rejected the idea of black involvement in the emerging American labor movement. Early experience in adolescence convinced Washington that trade unions were a negative influence on black workers. In his years as a mature race leader Washington's dependence on financial donations from industrial magnates, like Andrew Carnegie, to meet the ever-growing running costs of Tuskegee Institute reinforced his opposition to organized labor.[34]

Another consideration was the fact that trade unions were invariably white run and frequently excluded blacks from membership or subjected them to segregated, inferior treatment. Under such conditions there was little to attract blacks to the cause of organized labor. Worse, in seeking union membership they would lose one of their main attractions to employers, as a source of strike-breaking labor during periods of industrial conflict.[35]

In the case of Garvey his philosophical objection to interracial cooperation in the American labor movement was reinforced by similar factors. Like Washington, Garvey's first personal experiences of organized labor were not encouraging. A printing strike in Kingston, Jamaica, in which he had participated, had ended in failure. Garvey, along with other striking workers, was sacked by the employers in way of retribution. During the 1920s Garvey's attempts to seek an accommodation with the Ku Klux Klan, an organization not renowned for its trade union sympathies, provided a further motive for him to be hostile to black involvement in union activity.

In contrast to the strong agricultural bias in Washington's economic initiatives the principal businesses of the Garvey movement, the Negro Factories Corporation and the Black Star Line, were essentially urban based. Despite this Garvey was able to empathize with the Tuskegeean's rustic perspective. In Jamaica Garvey had spent the first 16 years of his life in the country districts of the island, his family moving to the capital, Kingston, only in 1903. Garvey's mother Sarah never managed to adjust to city life and died the following year. Garvey himself was often mocked for his rustic ways. In 1915 he was one of the lead speakers in a UNIA debate in Kingston on the subject "Rural or City Life, which helps more in the development of the State?" Predictably Garvey was a strong advocate for the agricultural case.[36]

Although in later life Garvey opted for urban living the country values of his early life still, in part, remained. Addressing a UNIA meeting in New York City in February 1921, he informed his audience that he had learned important lessons from observing farmers at their work. "I saw that if the farmer planted corn, he got corn; I saw that if he plowed under the soil in the fall, put in fertilizers, put in the seed and then cultivated it, he got results."[37]

The best known and most influential UNIA chapters during the 1920s were located in northern cities, like New York and Chicago. At the same time a clear majority of UNIA branches, nearly 400 in total, were located in the predominantly rural South. In 1926 there were 74 UNIA chapters in Louisiana and 44 in Mississippi, compared with 23 in Illinois and 16 in New York. An important factor in the UNIA's success below the Mason-Dixie line was that southern blacks perceived Garvey as the successor to Booker T. Washington, the previous dominant race leader in the region.[38]

Despite some similarities in their thinking, and Garvey's veneration of Washington as a role model, there were still important differences between the two men. In June 1922 Garvey met with leaders of the Ku Klux Klan in Atlanta, Georgia, in what he claimed to be a summit between a proud black man and race-conscious whites. Washington, understandably, always viewed the "Invisible Empire," as the Klan was commonly known, with distaste. Writing in 1901, he saw it as a sign of improving racial conditions that "Today there are no such organizations in the South, and that such ever existed is almost forgotten by both races." Moreover, there "were few places in the South . . . where public sentiment would permit such organizations to exist."[39]

The overly optimistic Tuskegeean did not live to see the full extent of the Klan revival between 1915 and 1925, but it is difficult to believe that he could ever have approved of Garvey's clandestine assignation with the organization. During the last year of his life Washington actively campaigned against the film *Birth of a Nation*, in part because of its romanticized portrayal of the Klan during the Reconstruction era.

In some respects, however, Garvey's initiative was a continuation, rather than a betrayal, of Washington's philosophy. During his own time as a race leader, from 1895 to 1915, the Tuskegeean had regularly courted the approval of the planter class as the dominant political, social, and economic group in the South. By the early 1920s the continued ascendancy of the planter class was less certain. The phenomenal rise of the Ku Klux Klan in the years after World War I made it appear likely that the "Invisible Empire" would become a decisive political and social force in the region. Behind his militant rhetoric, Garvey's attempted Klan diplomacy was an accommodationist maneuver to win over Klan approval for the expansion of the UNIA in the southern states. Albeit unpalatable, Garvey's action can, in some respects, be viewed as no more than an updated version of Washington's own efforts as an interracial diplomat.[40]

Garvey and Washington also differed on their views on race relations in an international context. At times the Tuskegeean could be highly critical of the excesses of European imperialism in Africa, most notably in the Belgian Congo. In 1904 this concern led him to accept the position of Vice President in the Congo Reform Association, an organization that campaigned for more enlightened administration in the region. More generally, however, Washington supported the prevailing popular notion of the "White Man's Burden." He perceived the native tribes of Africa as being in a backward state of civilization and believed that enlightened colonial administration represented their best hope of advancement. He publicly praised the repressive German imperial rule in West Africa and graduates from Tuskegee cooperated with the German authorities in Togo to develop cotton-growing programs. Tuskegee students also participated in similar projects in Nigeria and the Sudan.[41]

Further evidence of Washington's interest in Africa came in 1912 when he played a major role in securing an international loan from the United States for the independent black African republic of Liberia. In April of the same year he organized an "International Conference on the Negro" at Tuskegee to discuss how the teaching methods employed at the institute might be applied in Africa, the Caribbean, and South America. Delegates from 21 countries attended, most particularly from "the sections of the world where the Negro is most thickly settled and where the race question is more or less acute."[42]

If Washington sought to export the Tuskegee philosophy to Africa he was, however, always strongly opposed to the idea that black Americans themselves should settle in the Dark Continent. In his first autobiography, *The Story of My Life and Work* (1900), he concluded that there was "little, if any, hope of our people being able to better their condition by emigrating to Africa. This was because "Africa is almost completely divided up among various European nations, leaving almost no hope for self-government." The one exception was "in the little republic of Liberia," which was "notably unhealthy and undesirable from almost every point of view."[43]

In later years Washington, if anything, became even more convinced of the correctness of his views. Joseph Booth, who wrote to the Tuskegeean in October 1913 suggesting the resettlement of black Americans in South Africa, saw his ideas curtly dismissed. "I am certain that all Negroes in America have a sentimental interest in Africa and many of them would gladly go out to Africa as missionaries," Washington tactfully began his reply. However, "the Negroes of America regard this country as their home and are convinced that they are better off here than they would be in any other part of the world." Consequently, "they have no desire to emigrate." On this occasion the pith preceded the postscript. With untypical sharpness the Tuskegeean went on to observe that "For my part I cannot help feeling that any funds that were raised to assist Negro emigration to Africa might be better used in sending back home the class of white people in South Africa who are making most of the trouble."[44]

Washington's views on black American emigration to Africa clearly placed him at odds with Garvey's vision of creating an independent black African republic founded by UNIA members. At the same time, in the early years of the twentieth century Washington's work at Tuskegee made him a source of inspiration to a number of black nationalist leaders in Africa. Pixley Ka Isaka Seme, the political organizer of the African National Congress (ANC), visited Tuskegee in 1903, and corresponded with Washington over several years. John Langalibalele Dube, a Zulu educator and the first President of the ANC, was an admirer of Washington and visited Tuskegee in May 1897. He saw industrial education as practiced at the all black institute as a model for the advancement of the Zulu population in South Africa. Known as the "Booker T. Washington of South Africa," Dube went on to found the Bantu Business League (BBL) in 1932. Based on the principles of Washington's National Negro Business League in the United States, the BBL aimed to promote business activity among the Bantu people of Natal.[45]

Washington's autobiography, *Up From Slavery* (1901), was translated into a number of African languages and European missionary schools often made the book a set text for their pupils. Tuskegee Institute not only provided an example of practical self-help for black Africans but also appeared to be a rare example of successful independent black endeavor. This feeling was reinforced by periodic demonstrations of black consciousness by Washington when he declared himself proud of his color and race.[46]

In any event the conservative Washington's sense of black pride was always underdeveloped. The independence of Tuskegee was undermined by its reliance on white capital. Garvey's perception of this weakness was an important factor in his efforts to establish genuinely autonomous black businesses and ultimately an independent black African state.[47]

Beyond a certain point a difference in degree becomes a difference in kind, and it is clear that Garvey's ambitious nationalistic vision transcended any separatist tendencies in Washington's program. At the same time his planned African republic was not altogether inconsistent with the Tuskegeean's thoughts and values. Despite the claims of his critics to the contrary, Garvey did not envisage that all black Americans would join in a "Back to Africa" movement. "It did not take all the white people of Europe to come over to America to lay the foundation of the great republic," a *Negro World* editorial explained in 1926. Consequently, "It does not mean that all Negroes must leave America and the West Indies and go to Africa to build up a government." Possibly Garvey only envisaged that as few as 100,000 black Americans would move to his new African state. He did not think in terms of any mass exodus of black Americans of the type that Washington so deplored.[48]

In his perspectives of native black Africans, Garvey could be equally dismissive of tribal culture as Washington. The founding aims of the UNIA in 1915 had included "the civilizing of the backward tribes of Africa," a task that was necessary as "the people of Africa were still in darkness." Garvey hoped that in time his new organization would be able to send "technical missionaries" to Africa to educate and instruct the native populations there. This was also one of his objectives in founding the UNIA's Booker T. Washington University in 1922.[49]

At the annual UNIA convention in New York City, in August 1920, Garvey insisted that a native-born African could not be elected as President of the planned new UNIA republic in that continent. Objecting to this proviso an African delegate, not unreasonably, put the case that an African would better understand African society and tribal chiefs who would resent an outsider. Unwilling to debate the issue, Garvey ruled the speaker "out of order, told him to shut up, sit down and be quiet, thereby carrying out his own ruling." Two days later Garvey himself was elected by the convention as Provisional President of the republic with an annual salary of $12,000 plus expenses.[50]

Given such attitudes toward native black Africans it is not unreasonable to believe that if Garvey had succeeded in founding an independent black African state, the majority of the leading political and military posts in the new republic would have been filled by a select group of UNIA officials from the United States. Arguably, the type of benign European imperialism encouraged by Washington would simply have been replaced by a neocolonial administration made up of black Americans. Expressing this fear, an NAACP press release of 10 August 1923 warned that social life in the planned "Republic of Africa" would be dominated by Garvey's UNIA nobility, the "Knights and Ladies of Ethiopia, Knight Commanders of the Nile, Dukes of Uganda, 'Sir' this and 'Sir' that."[51]

For all the important differences between the two men Booker T. Washington and Marcus Garvey shared more than a mutual belief in economic self-help. In respect to personality both men rose to high status from humble rural beginnings and were authoritarian and intolerant in temperament. Each powerful orators in their own right, they possessed a common ability to empathize with the life experiences of their listeners, and sought to encourage positive practical initiatives rather than debate points of principle. Such qualities, in part, explained their ability to win over the support of ordinary black Americans when their northern black intellectual critics noticeably failed to attract any mass following.[52]

In terms of policy, Garvey's black nationalism went much further than any of the programs developed by Washington. At the same time the Tuskegeean's idea clearly contained some elements of separatist thought. Conversely, if Washington was at heart an integrationist and Garvey a black nationalist, the Jamaican did not support separation under any circumstances. He welcomed autonomous black initiatives for the purpose of racial uplift. He opposed segregation imposed by whites with the objective of permanently restricting blacks to a position of political, social and economic inferiority in American life. To this end UNIA meetings and editorials in the *Negro World* regularly attacked legally enforced segregation and other forms of racial discrimination.[53]

Had he lived longer Washington would surely have opposed many of Garvey's thoughts and actions. Garvey himself was well aware of the important differences between the Tuskegeean's policies and his own. In explaining this divide the Jamaican claimed that the changed international conditions brought about by World War I and its aftermath required the development of fresh, more dynamic ideas. Within the United States the impact of the Great Migration of 1915 to 1925 and a new mood of assertiveness among black Americans meant that the cautious conservatism associated with Tuskegee was out of date.

Ironically, some 20 years earlier, Washington had himself used similar arguments to explain the differences in thinking between himself and Frederick Douglass. He reasoned that the issues and policies affecting black Americans in the middle of the nineteenth century were no longer relevant to their needs and conditions in the first decade of the twentieth century. In articulating this point of view Washington, like Garvey after him, tacitly acknowledged the simple truism that the programs of leading individuals in history, however influential they might be, are ultimately shaped more by the conditions of the society in which they live than by their own ideas.

CHAPTER 9

Booker T. Washington and African-American Autobiography

Booker T. Washington's principal autobiography, *Up From Slavery*, is a key primary source for any historian seeking to understand his life and career. The book embodies the image of himself that Washington wished to present to the American public. For many readers *Up From Slavery* constitutes their first introduction to Washington's philosophy and work.

Originally published in serial form in *Outlook*, a respected magazine with a circulation in excess of 100,000 copies, in 17 installments between 3 November 1900 and 23 February 1901, *Up From Slavery* was first printed in book form in March 1901 by Doubleday, Page and Company of New York. The work was an immediate critical and commercial success. Reviewers praised Washington's simple, direct written style and the uplifting moral tone of the book.[1]

By September 1901 the journal the *World's Work* ranked *Up From Slavery* as the fifteenth most popular book in the United States as calculated by returns from librarians. The same month book dealers reported the work as being sixteenth on the bestseller list. In April 1902 a poll of librarians in New York State undertaken by the New York State Library placed *Up From Slavery* as equal second in a list of the 50 most important books published within the last year for use in a village library. Receiving 102 votes Washington's autobiography was surpassed only by Winston Churchill's historical novel *The Crisis*, which achieved 108 nominations.[2]

Writing to a sympathetic correspondent in February 1902 Washington professed himself "very greatly surprised" at the widespread attention his original *Outlook* articles had received. "I had no idea before I began writing that they would arouse one hundredth part of the interest they have aroused. They seem to be read by all classes and conditions of people." The following month Walter Hines Page of Doubleday, Page and Company confirmed the success of Washington's work in book form.[3]

Letters of support sent to Washington by enthused readers provided further evidence of the popularity of the autobiography. In January 1902 George Eastman, inventor of the Kodak camera, was sufficiently moved by the work to send Washington a $5,000 donation for Tuskegee Institute. Nearly 12 years later, in December 1913, the institute benefited from a like gift from the estate of a Col. W. G. Robinson of Oswego, New York, who had first read *Up From Slavery* at the time when he had drawn up his will some years earlier. Such largesse if gratifying, came from a likely sympathetic source given Robinson's background as a cavalry commander in the Union army during the Civil War. Perhaps less predictable was a letter Washington received in the same month from P. C. Jackson, a Confederate veteran from Macon County, Alabama. With Christmas approaching Jackson sought two copies of *Up From Slavery* to give as gifts to neighboring black farmers to "inspire and impel them to keep on in the road of Justice right and usefulness like yourself."[4]

The commercial success of *Up From Slavery* was geographically widespread as well as enduring over time. In 1902 the first foreign language version of the book appeared when it was translated into Spanish for sale in Cuba. A German edition, published by Dietrich Reimer of Berlin, soon followed, and by November 1904 editions in Arabic, Chinese, Dutch, Finnish, French, Malayan, Norwegian, Polish, Russian, and Zulu were all pending or already in print. By 1915 Emmett J. Scott speculated that the work had probably been translated into more languages than any other book written in America, with the possible exception of Harriet Beecher Stowe's abolitionist novel *Uncle Tom's Cabin* (1851).[5]

Linguistic differences understandably led to some minor difficulties, as in the case of the translator for the German edition who was bemused at Washington's use of the phrase "Grape Vine Telegraph." Overall, however, the message of the book seemed to have universal appeal. Readers from all over the world showed interest in Washington's life and his story of racial uplift.[6]

The appeal of the work transcended class as well as national boundaries. In September 1902 Robert Elliott Speer, Secretary of the Presbyterian Board of Foreign Missions, informed Washington that *Up From Slavery* was being used by missionaries in China and Japan to provide inspiration and instruction. Six months earlier Prince Henry of Prussia wrote to the Tuskegeean of how deeply the book had touched and interested him. In October 1904 Washington personally mailed a copy of the work to Randall Davidson, the Archbishop of Canterbury in England, in fulfillment of a promise made at a meeting with the churchman at the Waldorf-Astoria Hotel.[7]

Within the United States the American Publishing House for the Blind printed a Braille edition of *Up From Slavery* in 1903. The continued popularity of the book in America was such that by 1914–1915 there was discussion of a Hollywood film of Washington's life. By October 1915 negotiations were sufficiently advanced for Emmett J. Scott to secure cinematic rights for the project from Doubleday, Page and Company. The venture lost impetus following the unexpected death of Washington the following month and Scott turned his attentions to the making of an alternative film *Birth of a Race*. Released in 1919 it was a commercial and artistic failure.[8]

One hundred years after the first publication of *Up From Slavery* there was still no mainstream Hollywood film version of Washington's life. The reputation of Washington himself had also suffered. Nationally and internationally acclaimed as a role model for self-help and racial uplift during his own lifetime, since the 1960s the Tuskegee educator has more generally been seen as overly conservative and too accommodating to the views of southern whites. In ideological terms industrial education and the late nineteenth-century mantra of self-help, which Washington's life and career so graphically personified, have long since lost the capacity to command universal support.

Despite these changing perceptions Washington's autobiography enjoyed commercial success throughout the twentieth century. Between 1901 and 2001 public demand for *Up From Slavery* was sufficient to ensure that the book remained constantly in print with sales overseas as well as in the United States. In the 1980s and the 1990s the work was printed by a major publishing house, Penguin Books, perhaps an indication that the appeal of the autobiography was not confined to academics and specialist researchers.[9]

This enduring popularity can be attributed to a number of factors. Writing in 1901 one early reader predicted to Washington that the book would last "not only for its own merits, as fascinating reading" but also because his "career began in the most interesting and complicated period of our nation's history, when it was casting out slavery," and he was "one of the most important factors in the working out the problem of reconstruction."[10]

In a wider perspective autobiography is a form of literary expression that has consistently had a timeless and universal appeal. This is perhaps particularly the case in a "rags to riches" life story of the type that was embodied in the career of Booker T. Washington. Mary Mackie, one of Washington's former teachers at Hampton Institute in Virginia, noted that his life read "like a romance." "It is like a fairy tale to think of a man who does not know even when he was born with any certainty, or who was his father, and to read how he finally came to take afternoon tea with the Queen of England and dinner with the President of the United States," wrote another southern white correspondent in 1902. "One recalls his child-hood's stories of Aladdin and others, who rose to fame and fortune."[11]

Perhaps for this reason *My Larger Education*, published as a sequel to *Up From Slavery* in 1911, failed to match the impact of the earlier work and has since been largely neglected. Focusing more on the career of the mature Washington the book lacked dramatic incident. Co-authored by Washington, Emmett J. Scott, and the white ghostwriter Robert Park, it also gave the impression of having been written by a committee. Piecemeal and disjointed it did not have the flowing qualities of autobiographical narrative.[12]

Washington's first autobiography, *The Story of My Life and Work*, has also been generally ignored by later generations of readers. First appear-ing in late May 1900, the book was printed by the comparatively obscure publishing house J. L. Nichols and Company, a small firm that specialized in subscription and door-to-door sales. The principal market for the com-pany's publications was in the South, and its readership was generally less educated than the more cosmopolitan and middle-class audiences targeted by *Up From Slavery*. Washington himself was clearly aware of this. Writing to Nichols and Company in 1901 he justified the publication of *Up From Slavery*, only nine months after the appearance of *The Story of My Life Work*, on the grounds that a "book to be effective is very much like an address; if it is prepared for one audience and then delivered to another it becomes non-effective and non-interesting." The initial publication of *Up From Slavery* in *Outlook* would thus not harm sales of the earlier book because the magazine sold mainly to northern and eastern readers.[13]

In the 1890s Nichols and Company had a successful track record of marketing books for a black readership, a factor that almost certainly influenced Washington in agreeing to publish his first autobiography with the firm. This consideration also had an impact on the presentation and content of the book. In comparison to *Up From Slavery*, *The Story of My Life and Work* placed greater emphasis on encouraging black self-help. A whole chapter in the book was given over to an account of the first Negro Farmers Conference held at Tuskegee Institute in 1892. Significantly this section was omitted in *Up From Slavery*.[14]

The written style of *The Story of My Life and Work* was also more basic and less polished than in the later work. In part this may have reflected Washington's awareness of the limited education possessed by most southern black readers. Always keen to portray himself as the cham-pion of ordinary African Americans the Tuskegean could at times be con-descending and patronizing about the constituency he claimed to repre-sent. Writing in April 1911 he advised one forthcoming speaker at Tuskegee Institute to "bear in mind that your audience will be composed for the most part, practically of hard working farmers, men and women of our race." The content of his address should thus reflect this accordingly.

"The lower down the fodder is put, the more of it the animals will get, and digest it accordingly."[15]

A less calculated, and perhaps more compelling, reason for the literary limitations of *The Story of My Life and Work* was the fact that the book was mostly penned by a black ghostwriter, Edgar Webber.

A demanding public life taken up with the day-to-day administration of Tuskegee Institute, lectures, addresses, and after dinner speeches, and fundraising in the North, meant that many of the numerous books and articles supposedly authored by Washington were actually ghost-written. After 1900, however, he was careful to ensure that his surrogate scribes had proven writing ability.

Max Bennett Thrasher, a white sympathizer from Vermont, and Washington's principal "ghost" between 1901 and 1903, was an experienced teacher, administrator and journalist. He had worked as a reporter on the Boston *Journal* from 1895 to 1897, wrote numerous magazine articles, and, in 1900, had a book published on Washington and Tuskegee Institute in his own right, *Tuskegee: Its Story and Its Work*.[16]

Following Thrasher's death from peritonitis in 1903, Washington turned to the northern white writer Robert Park as his principal source of literary inspiration. A social reformer with editing experience on a Boston newspaper, Park was also in possession of a doctorate and had teaching experience in the Philosophy Department at Harvard. His services were regularly employed by Washington until 1914 when Park resigned his position at Tuskegee to become a Professor of Sociology at the University of Chicago.[17]

In comparison to his distinguished successors, Edgar Webber was largely unknown at the time of his involvement with *The Story of My Life and Work*. Washington first met Webber in 1895 when, as President of the Fisk University Lecture Bureau, Webber invited the Tuskegeean to give a lecture to Fisk students. A graduate of Le Moyne Institute and Howard University Law School, as well as Fisk, Webber already had four years teaching experience at Central Tennessee College when commissioned by Washington to ghost *The Story of My Life and Work* in 1898. He had also worked as a journalist on both black and white newspapers in Nashville and Memphis, Tennessee.

Despite such credentials Webber's selection for such an important task was a risky choice. Washington knew relatively little of his background and character. Moreover, born in 1870 Webber, at only 27 years of age, was also young and inexperienced. It was not surprising that he soon ran into problems with his commission.[18]

Although based at Tuskegee for the project Webber found it difficult to gain sufficient access to Washington because of the Principal's many, and more pressing, commitments. In consequence he was forced to rely heavily on press cuttings and transcripts of Washington's speeches for the information that he needed. The budding writer was himself less than diligent. He shirked his academic and administrative duties at Tuskegee making him unpopular with other staff at the institute. His literary output was painfully slow and when he completed the book manuscript toward the end of 1899 the work was full of stylistic and grammatical errors.[19]

Still preoccupied with other work Washington left the task of proofreading to his longstanding and trusted acquaintance Thomas Fortune. A talented writer, and editor of the leading black newspaper the New York *Age*, Fortune was in theory an ideal choice for the task. In practice he was himself too busy to give the work the attention that it needed and initially failed to detect many of the inadequacies in the manuscript.

It was not until he received the typeset proofs from the publishers that Fortune realized his mistake. At this stage Nichols and Company were unwilling to incorporate the copious corrections belatedly made by Fortune, and declined to send him the proofs for the last two chapters altogether because his suggested revisions to earlier sections had been so extensive. When the book was finally published, in May 1900, a lot of flaws remained. Even when a revised second edition of the work appeared in 1900 many of the changes sought by Fortune were still not incorporated because of the refusal of Nichols and Company to incur the extra expense that extensive type resetting would have involved.[20]

Washington's own misgivings about *The Story of My Life and Work* were reflected in a noticeable loss of warmth in his relations with Webber. In the revised edition of the work a picture of Webber with Thomas Fortune and Emmett J. Scott entitled "A Trio of Brilliant Colored Americans," was pointedly removed. The portraits of Fortune and Scott remained but the likeness of Webber was replaced by one of Samuel Laing Williams, a Chicago lawyer and loyal supporter of Tuskegee and its work. Webber's name was similarly removed from the index of the book.[21]

The decision of Washington to commit himself to the publication of his second autobiography, *Up From Slavery*, at the same time as a second edition of *The Story of My Life and Work* was still in progress requires some explanation.

In financial terms Washington's contract for *Up From Slavery* clearly represented an improvement on that for the earlier work. Doubleday, Page and Company was a more prestigious publishing house. It was likely that they would advertise the book more effectively and achieve higher sales. Moreover, the firm was prepared to offer Washington a more generous share of the profits. His deal with Doubleday gave him 10 percent royalties for the first 2,500 copies sold, 12.5 percent for the next 2,500, and 15 percent thereafter. In contrast Nichols and Company provided a return of six percent, a figure subsequently lowered to just four percent.[22]

If welcome, it is however unlikely that book royalties were a central factor in Washington's decision to write a second autobiography. The practical Tuskegeean would have been well aware that even a successful work of nonfiction was unlikely to match the dramatic sales figures that could be achieved by a popular novel. Ironically, in 1902 the bestselling book published by Doubleday and Page was *The Leopard's Spots*, a lurid and deeply racist fictional work by the conservative white southerner Thomas Dixon. *Up From Slavery*, if selling well, was notably further down Doubleday's list of successes. Fortunately for Washington there is no evidence to suggest that he ever envisaged book sales as a major source of income.[23]

Aesthetic considerations are, at first sight, a more credible factor to explain the publication of *Up From Slavery*. It was potentially embarrassing for Washington, a leading educator, to be associated with *The Story of My Life and Work*, which, even in revised form, still contained many stylistic flaws. Worse there was the danger that white racial extremists might highlight the failings of the book as proof of the limited educational abilities of even the most able of African Americans. Such arguments notwithstanding it is difficult to see a concern for literary standards as the prime motivation for Washington's second autobiography. An eloquent orator, the Tuskegeean was always notably less inspiring as a writer. Simply put, *Up From Slavery*, if more polished than *The Story of My Life and Work*, was not without its own stylistic weaknesses.

Washington's prime concern as an author was with factual detail rather than literary elegance. Corresponding with Lyman Abbott, of Doubleday, Page and Company, about his writing technique in *Up From Slavery* he noted that his general concern was to give priority to "facts and incidents and to hang the generalizations on to these facts." This was because most readers were "more interested in an interesting fact than in a generalization based on that fact" and he had thus "sought not to use too many generalizations and when they are used to have them well sugarcoated with some interesting incident."[24]

The commercial success of *Up From Slavery* makes it difficult to disagree with such logic in marketing terms. From a purely literary perspective the end product was less satisfactory. The accolades of praise bestowed on *Up From Slavery* following its initial publication owed much to the approval of reviewers for the moral tone of the book rather than the quality of its prose. A review of the work by the distinguished literary figure William Dean Howells, for the *North American Review* in August 1901, was a prime example. Entitled "An Exemplary Citizen" the piece was a tribute to the work of Washington the man rather than a critique of the autobiography in its own right.[25]

A more modern review, by a less enthused commentator, found the prose style of *Up From Slavery* unappealing, bordering on "pure inertia."

Washington wrote "as if language were matter rather than energy." The events about which he wrote were thus "not so much dramatized as deadened into matter with which to make the narrative." Even allowing for changes in literary fashion the style of *Up From Slavery* can be criticized as leaden and overly repetitive, a consideration tacitly acknowledged by Lyman Abbott in 1901 who urged Washington to greater "compactness" in the draft manuscript.[26]

Booker T. Washington's most authoritative modern biographer, Louis Harlan, has suggested that *Up From Slavery* had a much greater personal input from the Tuskegean than *The Story of My Life and Work*. Able to devote more time to the project Washington dictated sections of the new work to Max Thrasher while traveling by train. He wrote chapters from Thrasher's notes in his own hand and provided outlines for some segments of the book for Thrasher to develop into continuous prose. Consequently, Harlan concluded that *Up From Slavery* was much more consciously the product of Washington's mind and personality than his earlier autobiography.[27]

It is possible that this claim is overstated. Despite significant differences between *Up From Slavery* and *The Story of My Life and Work*, many passages in the two books show striking similarities. The parallels are sufficiently close and numerous for a subsequent commentator to have suggested that the later book was essentially a revision of the earlier autobiography rather than a freshly written work of Washington's own making. A desire to stamp his own persona on the book thus serves only as a partial explanation for Washington's decision to write *Up From Slavery*.[28]

Arguably the most telling reason for the Tuskegean's desire to publish a second autobiography was the fact that, as Washington realized, the two books were intended for different audiences. *The Story of My Life and Work* was, in the main, sold to southern black farmers and laborers. *Up From Slavery* was aimed at educated northern and southern whites. This consideration necessitated not just a correction of stylistic and grammatical errors in the later book, but also a reworking of the moral themes of the work if it was to have the impact for which Washington hoped.

One of the most striking, if unsurprising, differences between the two autobiographies was thus that *Up From Slavery* was notably more generous and forgiving of southern whites for racial injustice past and present.

In *The Story of My Life and Work* Washington recalled that the experience of slavery that had left the greatest impact on him was watching his uncle stripped naked, tied to a tree, and whipped with a cowhide. The incident, he assured his readers, had made such an impression on his "boyish heart" that "I shall carry it with me to my grave." Significantly, Washington chose not to carry forward this recollection into *Up From Slavery* where the anecdote was deleted. If a formative event in the development of

Washington as a person, the memory was best omitted lest it prove embarrassing or offensive for white readers.[29]

Similarly, recalling his parents, in *The Story of My Life and Work* Washington confined himself to the bald statement that the only thing he knew of his father "with any degree of certainty" was that "he was a white man." In *Up From Slavery* this was amended to the observation that in respect to "my father I know even less than of my mother. I do not even know his name." He had "heard reports to the effect that he was a white man who lived on one of the near-by plantations," but, if so, Washington did "not find especial fault with him." He was only "another unfortunate victim" of the institution of slavery "which the nation unhappily had engrafted upon it at that time."[30]

Reinforcing the message, the Tuskegeean reassured his readers later in the same chapter that "I have long since ceased to cherish any spirit of bitterness against the Southern white people on account of the enslavement of my race," a sentiment that moreover reflected the feelings of ex-slaves in general. The "cruel wrongs" of the institution notwithstanding, "the black man got nearly as much out of slavery as the white man did." Blacks "who themselves or whose ancestors went through the school of American slavery" had experienced many benefits. They were "in a stronger and more hopeful condition, materially, intellectually, morally and religiously" than others of their race "in any other portion of the globe." Predictably, Washington had not found it apposite to include these uplifting thoughts in *The Story of My Life and Work*.[31]

Washington's efforts to appease his white readers in *Up From Slavery* were inevitably linked to his hopes of securing financial donations from philanthropic benefactors for Tuskegee and black education in general. This agenda also helps to explain other differences between his two autobiographies. The stress on black self-help in *The Story of My Life and Work* was clearly included to benefit the book's black purchasers, and was of less direct interest for white readers. At the same time the omission of such sections from *Up From Slavery* may also have derived from a subtler motive. To attract white largesse it was desirable to portray blacks as victims, unable to save themselves without outside help. Examples of blacks effecting their own uplift therefore needed to be carefully rationed less they prove counterproductive in fundraising terms.[32]

The image Washington sought to project of himself in both of his autobiographies was understandably a positive one. Predictably neither work revealed any details of what Harlan has dubbed Washington's "secret life" that included covert challenges to segregation and sabotaging the efforts of his black critics.

In *Up From Slavery* the Tuskegeean also skillfully repackaged the narration of his life history to create an impression of unbroken achievement, and a seamless transition from poverty to international acclaim and material success. *The Story of My Life and Work*, over which Washington exercised less tight control, tended to be both more detailed and more forthright about his early life and career ambitions.

Readers were thus made aware that in 1878 Washington had studied for a year at Wayland Seminary in Washington, D.C., and that he had aspired to become a lawyer before opting for teaching as his chosen profession. The less informative *Up From Slavery* made only a brief reference to the Tuskegeean's decision "to spend some months in study at Washington D.C.," and omitted mention of his abortive legal career altogether.[33]

Apart from a desire for greater brevity there are other likely explanations for this editing. The revelation that in his youth Washington had entertained a variety of career options would undermine the idea that he had always felt a calling to be an educator. Mention of the fact that he had started, and then abandoned, training in other vocations might also be less than positive. Such admissions might tarnish Washington's public image as a man of iron resolution who always saw any task through to its conclusion and surmounted any problems through hard work and moral fortitude.

An added embarrassment was the suggestion that Washington may have contemplated a career in the ministry. In his public addresses after 1895 Washington often entertained white audiences with jokes at the expense of black clergymen, suggesting that they had been attracted to their employment by a desire to escape manual labor rather than a sense of divine mission. The Tuskegee educator might thus have been reluctant to acknowledge that he himself, albeit briefly, had considered becoming a man of the cloth. Pointedly, in *Up From Slavery* he went out of his way to deny that he had ever felt such a calling.[34]

There is at least some evidence that Washington resorted to fabrication, as well as omission, to achieve the literary impact he desired in *Up From Slavery*. One incident recalled by Washington in the book was how, as a slave child, he was once a week given the task of taking corn to the nearest mill, three miles away, to be ground into flour. It was a responsibility that he "always dreaded." During the journey the heavy sack of corn would inevitably become lopsided and eventually fall off the horse. Too young to reload the sack the tearful Washington often had to wait for hours for some kindly passer-by to assist him. He then faced a long and lonely journey home at night through the woods, which frightened him, and the prospect of a "severe scolding or a flogging" as punishment for his lateness. A touching tale, the story doubtless won over the sympathy of many readers for the childhood hardships faced by the Tuskegeean. If so this concern may have been misdirected since it was not Booker T. Washington but his brother John who was most likely given the burden of the mill trip.[35]

In another anecdote Washington recalled how, arriving at Hampton Institute in 1872, his "entrance examination" had taken the form of an instruction from one of the teachers to sweep out one of the classrooms. Never too proud to engage in manual labor, Washington applied himself to the task with such vigor that his enrollment became a mere formality. An uplifting tale, the story was only spoiled by the fact that when reading it in 1901, Mary Mackie, the tutor concerned, was unable to recall ever setting Washington such a task.[36]

Given the care and attention Washington devoted to the marketing of his self-image a surprising aspect of both his autobiographies is the lack of detail they give about his personal life. The two books provided Washington with an obvious opportunity to portray himself as a loving husband and father. In addition to endearing himself to his readers, images of an idyllic home environment would have provided an effective counter to racial extremists who denied the capacity of African Americans to experience higher parental and family feelings.

Despite such considerations Washington's three wives and children barely feature in either *The Story of My Life and Work* or *Up From Slavery*. Although Washington did dedicate *Up From Slavery* to his last wife, Margaret Murray, she is afforded only one substantive mention in the text of the book. Moreover, the language in this brief section is cold and unemotional. Washington laconically informed his readers that during "1893 I was married to Mrs. Margaret James Murray, a native of Mississippi, and a graduate of Fisk University, in Nashville, Tenn., who had come to Tuskegee several years before." Discussion of the role of Murray in Washington's life was limited almost exclusively to details of her professional duties at Tuskegee and work in the surrounding black community.[37]

Fannie N. Smith, Washington's first wife, was given even shorter shrift. Readers were made aware of the Tuskegeean's marriage to her in 1882, the fact that she came from Malden, West Virginia, and was a graduate of Hampton Institute. Other than this the only information offered up about her was that following "earnest and constant work in the interests of the school" she "passed away in May 1884" leaving one child, Portia.[38]

Olivia Davidson, Washington's second wife, fared a little better, meriting seven entries in the index of *Up From Slavery*. However, as with Margaret Murray, these related almost entirely to her duties at Tuskegee. Davidson's death, in 1889, like that of Fannie N. Smith, was reported as barely more than a piece of useful factual information, with no insight into Washington's sense of loss at the bereavement.[39]

Washington was equally unforthcoming in respect to his three children, Portia, Booker Jr., or Baker as he was known, and Ernest Davidson. The only joys and responsibilities of parenthood he chose to reveal in *Up From Slavery* was the less than surprising fact that he read them bedtime stories, and that the family liked to walk in the countryside on a Sunday afternoon. Other references served only to highlight the dedication of the young Washingtons to the Tuskegee ideal, with Portia working as a teacher at the institute, Baker training as a brick mason, and Ernest aspiring to be a physician.[40]

Deficient in personal warmth by modern standards, Washington's lack of information on his family life in *Up From Slavery* reflected the different conventions of late nineteenth-century autobiography. Other factors also played their part. Significantly, Washington's publishers consistently urged him to reveal more about himself in his writings. Lawrence Abbott and Robert Townsend of *Outlook* magazine requested more of "the personal element," whilst Lyman Abbott of Doubleday and Page wanted greater detail on the "pictorial side of your life" from the Tuskegeean, "the experiences through which you have passed" and "the incidents which you have seen."[41]

Washington's reticence to expand on these themes was ultimately a product of his own psychological make up. The demands of public life, and the constant need to weigh his every thought and action, made Washington's persona cold, unemotional, and devoid of spontaneity. He found it difficult, if not impossible, to develop close friendships and unconditional loving relationships because these would involve exposing his deepest feelings and emotions, which he always strived to repress.

Washington's work colleagues consistently sensed a distance in their daily contact with him. Staff members at Tuskegee Institute were loyal to Washington because they respected him and lived in apprehension of him. Few, if any, appeared to experience feelings of genuine warmth and affection for their employer. "I'll venture to say that there are not more than two or three of your teachers who sympathize with you as they would if you were a little more sociable," a former Tuskegee staff member advised Washington in 1890. Employees at the institute would be more committed to their work if they felt that Washington "had an interest in them beyond their drudgery in the schoolroom." He needed to "come out of" himself and "enter into the lives of those about" him.[42]

Washington viewed even his closest and most long-standing associates as expendable if their welfare appeared to conflict with the interests of Tuskegee. In April 1907 he insisted on the resignation of the Reverend Edgar Penney after flimsy and unsubstantiated allegations of sexual impropriety against the minister. Penney's protestations of innocence, and more than 15 years faithful service at the institute, counted for nothing against Washington's determination to maintain Tuskegee's spotless image. Later the same year the Tuskegeean was equally clinical in his dealings with Thomas Fortune. Taking advantage of the New Yorker's ill health and financial problems, Washington covertly purchased a controlling inter-

est in Fortune's newspaper, *The Age*, to obtain an added propaganda out-
let for the Tuskegee Machine.[43]

Ultimately Washington subordinated even his immediate family to his
public career. The voluminous Booker T. Washington Papers in the Library
of Congress, revealing in so many ways, contain no intimate correspondence between Washington and his wives. In their daily memos and letters
each of his three spouses found it easier to refer to him as Doctor or Mister
rather than use a less formal term of endearment.[44]

When writing of his personal life in *Up From Slavery* Washington's
words only served to reveal how much of the private man was given up to
the career of the public servant. Games he cared little for, having "never
seen a game of football," and not knowing "one card from another." When
reading he favored newspapers or instructive biographies of great men,
but had no time for fiction. Public affairs separated him from his family for
"so much of the time" that he envied "the individual whose lifework is so
laid that he can spend his evenings at home." Those persons who enjoyed
"this rare privilege" did not always "appreciate it as they should." If
Washington ruthlessly persecuted his northern black critics for what he
perceived as the greater good of Tuskegee, he was no less willing to sacrifice his own personal happiness in the same cause.[45]

In the United States, as in many other countries, autobiographies
occupy an important and special place in the nation's literary heritage.
Historically, the American autobiographical tradition is often seen as dat-
ing back to Benjamin Franklin, whose eighteenth-century writings related
his rise from humble beginnings to national and international acclaim by
dint of hard work and single-minded perseverance. Booker T. Washington's
autobiographical accounts of his own life are clearly consistent with this
mode of writing, a factor that in part explains their success.[46]

In conjunction with the *Narrative of the Life of Frederick Douglass*
(1845), *Up From Slavery* has been seen as providing the foundations of a
distinctive African American form of the U.S. autobiographical tradition.
In the early twentieth century the lives of the two men easily constituted
the bestknown examples of self-made black Americans. In his autobiographical writings, as in his role as a race leader, Washington was aware of
the position that he shared with Douglass. Significantly, a photograph of
Douglass was included at the front of the first edition of *The Story of My
Life and Work*, a publishing decision that effectively invited readers to
compare the lives of the two men. No less interesting was the fact that in
the second edition of the book the likeness of Douglass was replaced with
a picture of Washington himself next to Prince Henry of Austria. The reasons for this change are uncertain, though topicality or an early attempt by
Washington to distance himself from his great predecessor are perhaps the
most likely explanations.[47]

In *Up From Slavery* Washington again made efforts to link himself with Douglass. He recalled how in 1899, a year before writing the work, he had read a life of Douglass while on board ship from Southampton to America. During his stay in Britain he had met many distinguished individuals who had "known and honoured" the late Douglass, and who, by unspoken implication, afforded Washington himself the same respect and status. Another incident in the book recalled a conversation between Douglass and Washington during a train journey, suggesting a closeness between the two men and that the encounter was a meeting of two equal minds.[48]

Washington shared Douglass's slave origins and the first paragraph of *Up From Slavery* gives the impression of being a conscious echo of the beginning of Douglass's *Narrative*. In his opening words Douglass informed his readers that "I was born in Tuckahoe, near Hillsborough, and about twelve miles from Easton, in Talbot county, Maryland. I have no accurate knowledge of my age, never having seen any authentic record containing it." Fifty-six years later, Washington began his own autobiography with the observation "I was born a slave on a plantation in Franklin County, Virginia. I am not quite sure of the exact place or exact date of my birth, but at any rate I suspect I must have been born somewhere and at some time." The intended humor in this statement may have been a conscious echo of Harriet Beecher Stowe's abolitionist novel, *Uncle Tom's Cabin* (1851). In this work the slave child Topsy, when asked about her ancestry, replied "Never was born" and that she "never had no father nor mother, nor nothin.'"[49]

Traditionally the first words of any book are often seen as the most difficult to write. In *Up From Slavery* Washington faced the different problem of how to continue. Douglass's *Narrative* had been a great success in its day, selling some 30,000 copies in Britain and America by 1850. By 1900, however, white Americans had long since lost interest in the injustices of slavery. The commercial fate of the last of Douglass's three autobiographies, *Life and Times of Frederick Douglass*, provided hard evidence of this fact. First published in 1881 and later in a revised updated form in 1893, sales of both editions of the book had been deeply disappointing with a combined total of around 800 copies sold between 1881 and 1894. Learning from this experience Washington judiciously chose to devote only 22 of 319 pages in *Up From Slavery* to his memories of slave life.[50]

Douglass's *Narrative* and Washington's *Up From Slavery* had some obvious similarities. Each work told the success story of a former slave who had achieved greatness through determination, self-sacrifice, and self-help. In other respects, however, the moral lessons that could be drawn from the two books were profoundly different. In his *Narrative* Douglass had triumphed through a constant refusal to accept injustice. Final vindication of this resolve was demonstrated by securing his own liberation from slavery. In *Up From Slavery* Washington stressed the virtues of patience, thrift, and hard work with proof of his triumph being provided by the accolades heaped on him by white America in the wake of the 1895 Atlanta Cotton Exposition. Douglass found fulfillment by defying southern whites, Washington by courting their approval.[51]

In the second half of the twentieth century *The Autobiography of Malcolm X* constitutes arguably the most influential and bestknown work in the African-American autobiographical tradition established by Douglass and Washington. Although Washington and Malcolm X were in many ways diametric opposites in character and outlook, there are also notable similarities in the style and some of the themes of *Up From Slavery* and Malcolm X's *Autobiography*. Both books are essentially black success stories as the subjects of each rise from impoverished beginnings to international recognition and acclaim.

In a manner typical of rags to riches autobiographies each work begins by highlighting the deprived background of the two men to maximize the sense of contrast with their later achievement. The family of the young Malcolm Little, and future Malcolm X, were so poor that they "would eat the hole out of a doughnut." Born a slave, Washington could justifiably claim that his life "had its beginning in the midst of the most miserable, desolate, and discouraging surroundings."[52]

In contrast, the final two chapters of *Up From Slavery*, "Europe" and "Last Words," narrated Washington's grand tour of Europe in 1899 and cited the accolades he had received from the good and the great in both Europe and the United States. Use of this testimony provided final and irrefutable proof of Washington's triumph over his beginnings. From a slave boy to an internationally admired race leader and educator who took tea with Queen Victoria, his personal victory was now complete.[53]

In *The Autobiography of Malcolm X* the penultimate chapter, "El-Haji Malik E-Shabazz" constitutes a similar apologia. Recounting the lavish hospitality of Prince Faisal, "the absolute ruler of Arabia," and the receptions laid on for him by intellectuals and state officials in Ghana and Nigeria, Malcolm X effectively demonstrated the enormous gulf between his childhood and the status he enjoyed in the last months of his life. Even the modest observation that he was often mistaken in the Middle East for Cassius Clay served to invite the reader to reflect that Malcolm X was the only African American able to command the same international recognition that was enjoyed by the World Heavyweight Boxing Champion. If the Saudi public conflated the two men it was because a local newspaper had recently "printed a photograph of Cassius and me together at the United Nations."[54]

At appropriate junctures in their journey to self-fulfillment Washington and Malcolm X further encouraged their readers to reflect on the transformation that has taken place. In *Up From Slavery* Washington thus recalled how, while a student at Hampton Institute in Virginia, he had worked during the summer vacation as a waiter and dish carrier at a hotel in Connecticut. The recollection then provided Washington with an opportunity to note how more recently he had "had the satisfaction of being a guest in this hotel several times."[55]

Employing a similar use of contrast *The Autobiography of Malcolm X* recounted a speaking engagement by the Black Muslim leader at the Harvard Law School. During the course of his address Malcolm X "happened to glance through a window" and realized that he "was looking in the direction of the apartment house" that he had used as a hideout in his former life as a burglar.[56]

In respect to the means by which Washington and Malcolm X had effected their personal transformation a recurring theme in both autobiographies is the emphasis on the puritan virtues of self-sacrifice and hard work. Typically the moral lessons intended are conveyed in parable-like stories involving incidents in the life of the two men.

In *The Autobiography of Malcolm X* the redemption of the book's subject begins when he is introduced to the Nation of Islam and strives to improve his education. Borrowing works from the prison library he copied, in longhand, the pages of an entire dictionary. His hunger for books became so voracious that following "lights out" at 10.00 PM he continued to read by the glow of light from the outside corridor, taking only three or four hours sleep per night. At Tuskegee Institute living and working conditions were no less severe with staff and students rising at 5.00 AM to a packed daily timetable of activities that concluded only at 9.30 PM.[57]

Like Washington, Malcolm X was inclined to view material success rather than spiritual happiness as a measurement of individual fulfillment. Recalling his one time association with West Indian Archie, a runner for a Harlem numbers racket, he thus reflected that in a less racist society Archie's "exceptional mathematical talents might have been better used." Material deprivation, rather than psychic damage, was seemingly the prime evil of racism. Similarly, one of the most painful experiences for Malcolm X during his youth occurred when a white teacher informed Malcolm that his aspirations to be a lawyer would be in vain because he was black.[58]

Not all commentators have endorsed the view of the historian Harold Cruse that the Black Power movement of the 1960s was a form of militant Booker T-ism. This notwithstanding, a comparison of *Up From Slavery* and *The Autobiography of Malcolm X* would seem to suggest that such an observation is not entirely without foundation.[59]

CHAPTER 10

Booker T. Washington and African-American History

A Historiographical Perspective

The Reconstruction era, 1865–1877, has received extensive coverage from historians. The first concerted academic study of the period, in the 1880s and the 1890s, coincided with the professionalization of the study of history in the United States. Full-time salaried historians were employed in American universities and colleges to carry out teaching and research. The writing of history by gentleman amateurs became largely a thing of the past.

From 1886 to 1922 the study of Reconstruction was dominated by the work of the Dunning School of historians at Columbia University. The proselytizing William A. Dunning wrote what became the first standard texts on the period. Possibly the best known of these was his influential *Reconstruction, Political and Economic, 1865–1877* (1907). Under his guidance Dunning's students undertook research on the Reconstruction era, often focusing in the experiences of individual southern states. Many of his pupils went on to teach in universities and colleges in their own right, ensuring the dissemination of his ideas over several generations.

Despite his northern background Dunning came to believe in what might be described as the classic southern white interpretation of Reconstruction. He was convinced that blacks were racially inferior to whites and that at the end of the Civil War in 1865, they were given rights that exceeded their intellectual capacities. The most important of these was the right to vote.

Unfit to exercise such a responsibility ignorant ex-slaves elected corrupt and unqualified state Republican administrations across the South. Political power was wielded by a triple alliance of embezzling northern "Carpetbaggers," unprincipled lowborn southern white "Scalawags," and ex-slaves themselves. In office these groups tried to enforce black and white social equality and plundered the pockets of already impoverished white southerners with ruinously high taxes and a series of ever more inventive and increasing financial swindles. This affront to the democratic process was finally ended only by the "Redemption" campaigns of 1875–1877, when desperate southern whites justifiably resorted to ballot rigging and intimidation to restore political propriety with the election of white Democratic Party state administrations.

The views of Dunning reflected, and reinforced, the racial conservatism of his era. The supposedly impartial academic findings of Dunning and his disciples provided further proof for southern whites, if such was needed, of the rightness of their actions in denying blacks access to the ballot box. In their own way professional historians thus contributed to the problems of African-American leaders who sought to defend the diminishing civil and political rights of black Americans in the early years of the twentieth century.

With a few honorable exceptions, perhaps most notably *Black Reconstruction* (1935) by the scholarly African-American W. E. B. Du Bois, the work of the Dunning school remained largely unchallenged until after World War II. In the early 1950s changing racial attitudes in America, reflected in the rise of the Civil Rights Movement, saw a new generation of historians, the Revisionists, question the Dunning interpretation. Works such as John Hope Franklin's *Reconstruction After the Civil War* (1961) and Kenneth M. Stampp's *The Era of Reconstruction* (1965) highlighted the positive achievements of the 1860s and 1870s, such as the modernizing of state constitutions and the widespread introduction of public schools in the South. The lurid images of vice and corruption evoked by Dunning were shown to be exaggerated.

Although marking an important change in the way that historians viewed the Reconstruction era, the writings of the Revisionists were still overly influenced by Dunning's ideas. Generally defensive, and sometimes almost apologetic, they viewed the history of the period from the perspective of southern whites more that that of freed black slaves. In analyzing the work of state Republican politicians Revisionists seemed more interested in proving that they were free from corruption than examining what they actually did to benefit their black constituents. The work of the Freedmen's Bureau was upheld because of its financial prudence and reluctance to interfere with the rights of planters, rather than condemned for the inadequate support it provided to freed slaves.

By the early 1970s a new group of historians, the Postrevisionists, aware of these limitations, sought to correct the imbalance. Studies such as Thomas Holt's *Black Over White: Negro Political Leadership in South Carolina During Reconstruction* (1977), and Leon Litwack's *Been in the Storm So Long* (1979), looked at Reconstruction from the viewpoint of freed black slaves. Early Postrevisionist writers, like Litwack, were, as students and young academics, often influenced by the antiwar radicalism and ideas of Black Power that were pervasive in the United States in the late 1960s and early 1970s.

Postrevisionist accounts dismissed the views of Dunning as dated and discredited. Instead, they stressed the extent to which the southern white planter class retained political, social, and economic power in the South after the Civil War. The system of sharecropping and the failure of Republican state and congressional leaders to provide freed slaves with an effective means of achieving independent land ownership were seen as condemning southern blacks to extreme poverty and neo-serfdom well into the 1930s.

The ascendancy of Postrevisionist thinking in the closing decades of the twentieth century was reflected in Eric Foner's *Reconstruction: America's Unfinished Revolution, 1863–1877* (1988). Highly regarded, and perhaps the most important book published on Reconstruction in the 1980s and 1990s, Foner's work all but ignored the writings of Dunning and his acolytes.

In contrast to the Reconstruction era, the experiences of black Americans between 1880 and 1915 have received comparatively little attention from historians. However, the publication of important new studies in the late 1980s and the 1990s began to alter the image of this period as the "Cinderella" years in black American historiography.

In 1989 Neil R. McMillen's *Dark Journey: Black Mississippians in the Age of Jim Crow* made available a scholarly and well-researched study of the lives of African Americans in Mississippi. In 1998 Leon Litwack's more ambitious work, *Trouble in Mind: Black Southerners in the Age of Jim Crow,* provided a richly detailed account of the social–economic life of ordinary black Americans across the South between 1890 and 1915.

Glenda Elizabeth Gilmore's *Gender and Jim Crow: Woman and the Politics of White Supremacy in North Carolina, 1896–1920* (1996) highlighted another significant development. By the mid-1990s historians had began to devote more time to studying the lives of African-American women, an area of research that had previously received little sustained attention. In the 1890s and early 1900s the black Women's Club Movement in the South and the National Association of Colored Woman (NACW) campaigned for greater black ownership of land, improved living conditions for blacks in the region, and better educational opportunities for their children. Historians like Gilmore began to recognize that the involvement of black women in such work constituted an important form of civil rights activity. Women's Club members were seen as the early pioneers of the struggle for black civil rights in the twentieth century.

Much of the debate on the origins and development of racial segregation has centered on the work of two historians, C. Vann Woodward and Joel Williamson. Woodward's *The Strange Career of Jim Crow* (1955) was published in the wake of the 1954 *Brown v. Board of Education* ruling by the U.S. Supreme Court. In the *Brown* decision the judges on the Court, in a unanimous 9–0 decision, reversed the separate but equal ruling of the 1896 *Plessy* case. Segregation in education was held to be unconstitutional because it created an innate sense of inferiority in the minds of black children.

The *Brown* decision met with prolonged and intense opposition in the white South. Woodward's work sought to allay the anxieties of white southerners by demonstrating that segregation was a comparatively recent feature of southern life. State segregation laws had not become widespread until the 1890s and, at that time, had marked a major departure from earlier southern custom and tradition. In previous decades blacks in the region had suffered from extreme discrimination, but there had not been a systematic physical separation of the races.

Albeit inspired by commendable motives, Vann Woodward's findings have been challenged by a number of other historians, most notably Joel Williamson. In his *The Crucible of Race* (1984), as well as in other writings, Williamson argued that segregation was already endemic in the South by the late 1860s and early 1870s. The 1896 *Plessy* ruling and southern segregation laws of the 1890s merely provided legal, or *de jure,* authority for the *de facto* segregation that already existed.

Discussion in the Vann Woodward–Williamson debate is complicated by the fact that patterns of segregation were often confusing and inconsistent. During Reconstruction, for example, it was common for white and black children to play together yet still attend separate schools. Moreover, segregation may have developed earlier in some parts of the South than others.

Specialized studies by historians have generally served to highlight the complexity of the issues rather than providing final clarification of them. Howard Rabinowitz's *Race Relations in the Urban South, 1865–1890* (1978) focused on five leading southern cities, Atlanta, Georgia, Montgomery, Alabama, Nashville, Tennessee, Raleigh, North Carolina, and Richmond, Virginia. His findings seemed to suggest that municipal segregation was widespread in the South in this period. John W. Graves's, *Town and Country: Race Relations in an Urban-Rural Context, Arkansas, 1865–1905* (1990) reached different conclusions. Graves found that in Little Rock, Arkansas, segregation became endemic in the 1890s only as a result of pressure from conservative rural politicians in the state. Prior to this the more cosmopolitan nature of city life had contributed to a more liberal and enlightened pattern of race relations in Little Rock. A concise overview of developments in the Vann Woodward–Williamson debate is provided in David Thelen (ed.), "Perspectives: The Strange Career of Jim Crow," *Journal of American History*, 75 (December 1988), 841–868.

A discussion of the reasons advanced by white southerners in the early twentieth century to justify racial segregation is provided by I. A. Newby, *Jim Crow's Defense: Anti-Negro Thought in America, 1900–1930* (1965). Adopting a different analytical framework John Cell, *The Highest Stage of White Supremacy* (1982), George M Frederickson, *White Supremacy: A Comparative Study in American and South African History* (1981), and George M. Frederickson, *Black Liberation: A Comparative History of Black Ideologies in the United States and South Africa* (1995), contrast black and white racial thought in the United States and South Africa.

On black education, good coverage of the Reconstruction era is provided by Ronald E. Butchart, *Northern Schools, Southern Blacks and Reconstruction: Freedmen's Education, 1862–1875* (1980), Robert C. Morris, *Reading, 'Riting and Reconstruction: The Education of Freedmen in the South, 1861–1870* (1981), and Henry L. Swint's older work *The Northern Teacher in the South, 1862–1870* (1967). The best study of the period 1865–1935 as a whole is James D. Anderson, *The Education of Blacks in the South, 1860–1935* (1988).

Examples of black economic success after emancipation are looked at in Carol Bleser, *The Promised Land: The History of the South Carolina Land Commission, 1869–1890* (1969), Elizabeth Raul Bethel, *Promiseland: A Century of Life in a Negro Community* (1981), and Janet Sharp Hermann, *The Pursuit of a Dream* (1981).

The experiences of most freedmen were unfortunately more depressing than uplifting. The economic problems faced by southern black sharecroppers between the 1880s and the 1930s are examined in a number of works. These include Roger A. Ransom and Richard L. Sutch, *One Kind of Freedom: The Economic Consequences of Emancipation* (1977), Robert Higgs, *Competition and Coercion: Blacks in the American Economy, 1865–1914* (1977), Jay R. Mandle, *The Roots of Black Poverty: The Southern Plantation Economy after the Civil War* (1978), Daniel A. Novak, *The Wheel of Servitude: Black Forced Labor After Slavery* (1978), and Peter Daniel, *The Shadow of Slavery: Peonage in the South, 1901–1969* (1990). These works all stress the enormous disadvantages suffered by blacks as small farmers and agricultural laborers in their economic relationships with white planters. By way of contrast Joseph D. Reid, "Sharecropping as an Understandable Market Response: The Post-bellum South," *Journal of Economic History*, XXXIII (1973), 106–130, is an unconvincing attempt to portray the sharecropping system as a natural free market compromise between the economic aspirations of freedmen and white landowners.

The attempts by black farmers to seek a political solution for their problems, through participation in the Populist movement of the 1890s, have received less than extensive coverage from historians. Individual state studies have generally highlighted the fragile nature of the biracial coalitions created by Populists. J. Abramovitz, "The Negro in the Populist Movement," *Journal of Negro History*, 38 (July 1953), 257–289, found that for all their efforts at interracial cooperation white Populist leaders were still prone to antiblack prejudices.

William M. Chafe, "The Negro in Populism: A Kansas Case Study," *Journal of Southern History*, 34 (August 1968), 402–419, argued that black and white Populists were divided because they pursued differing objectives. White Populists were primarily seeking redress for their economic grievances while blacks were more concerned with overcoming racial prejudices and obtaining protection from extralegal violence. More recently, Gregg Cantrell and D. Scott Barton, "Texas Populists and the Failure of Biracial Politics," *Journal of Southern History*, 55 (November 1989), 659–692, found that the more enlightened attitudes of Populist leaders in Texas were not shared by rank and file Populist members whose ingrained racial prejudices meant that efforts to form a biracial alliance were stillborn.

Much of the best work on the Great Migration has been in detailed studies of individual cities. These include Gilbert Osofsky, *Harlem: The Making of a Ghetto, New York, 1890–1930* (1971), Kenneth L. Kusmer, *A Ghetto Takes Shape: Black Cleveland, 1870–1930* (1976), Joe William Trotter, Jr., *Black Milwaukee: The Making of an Industrial Proletariat 1915–1945* (1985), Peter Gottlieb, *Making Their Own Way: Southern Blacks' Migration to Pittsburgh, 1916–1930* (1987), James R. Grossman, *Land of Hope: Chicago, Black Southerners and the Great Migration* (1989), and Richard W. Thomas, *Life For Us Is What We Make It: Building Black Community in Detroit, 1915–1945* (1992).

Good general overviews are provided by Florette Henri, *Black Migration, Movement North, 1900–1920: The Road from Myth to Man* (1976), Carole Marks, *Farewell—We're Good and Gone: The Great Black Migration* (1989), and the collected essays in Joe William Trotter (ed.), *The Great Migration in Historical Perspective* (1991). Milton C. Sernett, *Bound for the Promised Land: African Americans, Religion and the Great Migration* (1997), examines one particular aspect of the migratory experience.

Explanations of the causes of the Great Migration have traditionally taken the form of "push-pull" analysis; the negative or "push" features of the South that encouraged blacks to leave the region, and the positive or "pull" features of the North that made it more attractive. A useful attempt to broaden this framework of discussion is provided by Robert Higgs, "The Boll Weevil, the Cotton Economy and Black Migration, 1910–1930," *Agricultural History* (April 1976), 335–350.

The many problems faced by black migrants in the North have inclined some recent historians, like Gottlieb, Henri, and Marks, to the view that the migrants achieved little in the way of net gains as a result of their experience. Instead they traded one set of disadvantages, poverty, segregation, and discrimination, for another, high living costs, overcrowded accommodation, and more pressures on family life.

The thoughts of migrants themselves are preserved in Emmett J. Scott, "Letters of Negro Migrants of 1916–1918," *Journal of Negro History,* 4 (July and October 1919), 290–340, 412–465. This selection of correspondence from migrants to relatives in the South suggests that the urban newcomers, on the whole, felt the costs of migration to be outweighed by the benefits. However, a desire to reassure loved ones back home may have encouraged many to put a positive gloss on their experiences.

A good comparison of the experiences of black migrants and white European immigrants is Patrick Renshaw, "The Black Ghetto, 1890–1940," *Journal of American Studies,* 8 (1974), 41–59. In a thoughtful and perceptive essay Renshaw argues that the apparent advantages of black migrants over immigrants, their ability to speak English, and familiarity with American culture, may ultimately have worked to their disadvantage. These factors meant that African Americans lacked the clannishness and ethnic solidarity of their immigrant counterparts that was necessary to develop their own economic and community institutions in the cities of the North.

In respect to the cultural life of black Americans Eileen Southern, *The Music of Black Americans* (1997), remains the standard text on its subject, tracing the history of black American music from slavery up to the late twentieth century. Paul Oliver, *Blues Fell This Morning: Meaning in the Blues* (1990), provides a richly detailed and multifaceted account of black culture between the 1880s and the 1920s.

The portrayal of blacks in the emerging medium of Hollywood film is examined in Daniel Leab, *From Sambo to Superspade: The Black Experience in Motion Pictures* (1973), and Donald Bogle, *Toms, Coons, Mulattoes, Mammies and Bucks: An Interpretative History of Blacks in American Films* (1990). The increasingly negative and disturbing images of black Americans in white popular culture are discussed in George M. Frederickson, *The Black Image in the White Mind* (1972).

Concise overviews of black American history from the end of the Civil War through to the 1920s are contained in Mary Ellison, *The Black Experience: American Blacks since 1865* (1974), John Hope Franklin and Alfred A Moss, *From Slavery to Freedom: A History of Negro Americans,* 7th ed. (1994), and Kevern J. Verney, *Black Civil Rights in America* (2000).

On black leadership a number of good general texts are available. August Meier, *Negro Thought in America, 1880–1915* (1963), as its title implies, examines the differing philosophies of black spokesmen with particularly helpful coverage of the ideas of Booker T. Washington. Despite its age, Meier's work justly remains a key text on its period. Also of merit is August Meier and Elliott Rudwick, *Along the Color Line: Explorations in the Black Experience* (1976), which contains a thoughtful comparative analysis of the philosophy of Frederick Douglass and Booker T. Washington.

More recently Leon F. Litwack and August Meier (eds.), *Black Leaders of the Nineteenth Century* (1988), and John Hope Franklin and August Meier (eds.), *Black Leaders of the Twentieth Century* (1982), are useful collections of essays on individual black leaders and include studies of W. E. B. Du Bois, Frederick Douglass, Thomas Fortune, Marcus Garvey, William Monroe Trotter, and Booker T. Washington. Du Bois, Garvey, and Washington are also examined in John White's lucid *Black Leadership in America: From Booker T. Washington to Jesse Jackson* (1990). Howard N. Rabinowitz (ed.), *Southern Black Leaders of the Reconstruction Era* (1982), provides coverage of individuals from an earlier era. All of these works should be read in conjunction with one of the broader overviews of the period to set the ideas of the leaders considered in the context of the changing political, social, and economic conditions of their era.

Emma Lou Thornbrough, *T. Thomas Fortune: Militant Journalist* (1972), and Stephen R. Fox, *The Guardian of Boston: William Monroe Trotter* (1970), are the standard full length biographies on two important, but ultimately secondary, black American spokesmen of their day.

Frederick Douglass has, not surprisingly, received considerable coverage from historians. Douglass's autobiographies, *Narrative of the Life of an American Slave* (1845), *My Bondage and My Freedom* (1855), and *The Life and Times of Frederick Douglass* (1881 and a revised 1893 edition), have been helpfully published together in one volume as Frederick Douglass, *Autobiographies* (1994), compiled by Henry Louis Gates. The *Narrative* and *My Bondage and My Freedom* are also readily available as individual works. This is less true of *Life and Times*, which continues, as it was at the time of its original publication, to be the least widely read of Douglass's three autobiographical works.

In a broader context John W. Blassingame (ed.), *The Frederick Douglass Papers, Series One, Speeches, Debates and Interviews* (1979–1992), comprises the most extensive collection of primary source materials on Douglass. Published in five volumes, *1841–1846* (1979), *1847–1854* (1982), *1855–1863* (1986), *1864–1880* (1991), and *1881–1895* (1992), *The Frederick Douglass Papers* has effectively supplanted the earlier five-volume *The Life and Writings of Frederick Douglass* (1950–55), edited by Philip Foner. John W. Blassingame (ed.), *The Frederick Douglass Papers, Series Two: Autobiographical Writings*, is currently in the process of publication, with Volume One, *Narrative of the Life of an American Slave* (1999), already available.

A shorter, one-volume compilation of extracts from Foner's earlier collection can be found in Philip S. Foner (ed.), *Frederick Douglass: Selected Speeches and Writings* (1999). This need is also met by William Andrews (ed.), *The Oxford Frederick Douglass Reader* (1996). Philip S. Foner (ed.), *Frederick Douglass on Women's Rights* (1976), provides a compilation of Douglass's thoughts on one particular issue. Frederick S. Voss, *Majestic Wrath: A Pictorial Life of Frederick Douglass* (1995), makes available interesting source material of a different sort, including some rare photographs of Douglass interspersed with a narrative account of his life.

Booker T. Washington's *Frederick Douglass* (1906) is uninspired in style and provides little in the way of fresh information on its subject. Ghostwritten by Samuel Laing Williams, one of Washington's most trusted supporters, the book does, however, provide useful first hand insights into the Tuskegeean's own thoughts. By way of contrast, William S. McFeely's acclaimed *Frederick Douglass* (1991) is the best modern biography of the Sage of Anacostia. Well researched and balanced in judgment, McFeely's study has effectively replaced the earlier, though still worthy, biographies provided in Benjamin Quarles, *Frederick Douglass* (1948), and Philip S. Foner, *Frederick Douglass: A Biography* (1964).

Waldo E. Martin Jr, *The Mind of Frederick Douglass* (1984), provides perceptive insight into Douglass's thinking and the philosophical influences that helped shape it. David B. Cheseborough, *Frederick Douglass: Oratory from Slavery* (1998), looks at Douglass's abilities and techniques as a public speaker.

In the 1990s several important essay collections were published examining various aspects of Douglass's life and career. The first of these were Eric J. Sundquist (ed.), *Frederick Douglass: New Literary and Historical Essays* (1990), and William L. Andrews (ed.), *Critical Essays on Frederick Douglass* (1991).

More recently Bill E. Lawson and Frank M. Kirkland (eds.), *Frederick Douglass: A Critical Reader* (1999), comprised an examination of Douglass's thought by leading American philosophers. Alan J. Rice and Martin Crawford (eds.), *Liberating Sojourn: Frederick Douglass and Transatlantic Reform* (1999), was inspired by a conference at the University of Keele to mark the 150th anniversary of Douglass's extended visit to Great Britain from 1845–1847. The essays in the volume focus on Douglass's involvement in a range of nineteenth-century reform movements on both sides of the Atlantic. Reflecting the breadth of his interests, and the depth of his idealism, these included not only the crusade for the abolition of slavery but also the cause of women's rights, Irish home rule, Chartism, and the Temperance movement.

Booker T. Washington wrote numerous books designed to promote his philosophy and the work of Tuskegee. Uninspired in style and repetitive in content, many of these works are now largely forgotten. Still relevant, and the most important of Washington's writings, is his 1901 autobiography *Up From Slavery* which remains an essential text for any serious student or researcher. Available in its own right, the text of *Up From Slavery*, is also reprinted in full in the first of the 14 volumes of the *Booker T. Washington Papers* (1972–1989) together with his earlier autobiography *The Story of My Life and Work* and extracts from his later *My Larger Education* and other writings.

Compiled by Louis Harlan and a team of co-editors that includes some of the most highly respected historians in their field, the *Booker T. Washington Papers* ranks as one of the most important collections of primary source materials ever published on African-American history. The first 13 volumes of the papers, combined with the cumulative index that makes up Volume 14, make generally available to scholars an extensive selection of Washington's private correspondence, speeches, and articles from the collection of his papers housed in the Library of Congress and, to a lesser extent, at Tuskegee University.

Carefully chosen to present as full and as balanced a portrayal as possible of Washington the documents in the *Booker T. Washington Papers* are supported by detailed footnotes providing additional information on individuals and events. The meticulous preparation that went into the papers is indicated by the fact that every document chosen for publication was read out aloud not once, but twice, by Harlan and his editorial team to ensure correct punctuation and when to emphasize key words and phrases. Speaking of the project a few years after its completion, Harlan recalled that the job of editing had been "endless, laborious, and sometimes downright boring, mind-numbing work." Reading aloud the photocopies against the typescript, or galleys, for each volume was such a painstaking task that "we called it galley slavery." The selection of the documents in the first place was, if anything, an even more daunting task. Despite the fact that the *Booker T. Washington Papers* average more than 500 pages per volume, they represent less than five percent of the total amount of the material on Washington available in the Library of Congress.[1]

Washington's tireless resolve in preserving his personal documents and correspondence, combined with the dedication of Harlan and his co-editors, means that the *Booker T. Washington Papers* can be used to investigate almost every aspect of the Tuskegeean's life. In particular, they reveal the complex nature of his personality and details of his "secret life" of covert civil rights activity and persecution of his perceived enemies. Equally, they highlight the extent to which Washington sacrificed his private life to his mission as an educator and race leader. Duty, perseverance, and the fulfillment derived from work were seemingly his prime motivations in life, rather than the pursuit of love or personal happiness.

Some of the earliest studies of Washington and his ideas were written by individuals who had direct connections with Tuskegee Institute. These include *Tuskegee: Its Story and Its Work* (1901) by Washington's white ghostwriter Max Bennett Thrasher and Emmett J. Scott and Lyman Beecher Stowe, *Booker T. Washington: Builder of a Civilization* (1916). If useful as sources of first hand information, such works also demonstrate the extent to which Washington concealed his innermost thoughts even from his closest associates. Predictably, they are also more in the way of propaganda works on Washington's behalf rather than balanced appraisals of his strengths and weaknesses.

Continuing into the 1940s and the 1950s the principal studies of Washington, if worthy, remained sympathetic to their subject. These include Basil Matthews, *Booker T. Washington: Educator and Inter-Racial Interpreter* (1949), and Samuel J. Spencer, *Booker T. Washington and the Negro's Place in American Life* (1956). If acknowledging that Washington's leadership could be criticized as overly conservative, these accounts ultimately justified his program as the best that was available given the repressive racial conditions that prevailed in the United States at the start of the twentieth century.

A similar outlook prevailed in Bernard Weisberger's *Booker T. Washington* (1972). Weisberger also argued that Washington became more forthright in his criticisms of racial injustice in his speeches and writings during the last years of his life between 1911 and 1915. Hugh Hawkins (ed.), *Booker T. Washington and his Critics* (1974), provided a helpful collection of extracts from the writings of Washington's sympathizers and detractors, including the views of both his contemporaries and later historians. Readers were thus encouraged to make up their own minds as to Washington's place in history.

In recent years Louis Harlan has dominated the historiography on Booker T. Washington. In addition to editing the *Booker T. Washington Papers,* Harlan wrote a two-volume biography of the Tuskegeean, *Booker T. Washington: The Making of a Black Leader, 1865–1901* (1972), and *Booker T. Washington: The Wizard of Tuskegee, 1901–1915* (1983). A liberal thinker, Harlan was more critical of Washington than earlier biographers. His work also reflected the broader impact of the Civil Rights Movement and Black Power era in America since the 1950s. The rapid pace of change in these years made Washington's more patient conservatism appear unattractive.

The danger of this perspective was that it encouraged ahistorical thinking, judging Washington by the values of the 1960s and 1970s rather than those of his own day. An accomplished historian, Harlan took care to avoid this error and always strived to present the Tuskegeean's point of view even if he personally disagreed with it. His detailed knowledge of his subject, the result of more than 25 years of work on the collection of Washington's papers in the Library of Congress, gave him a depth of insight unequalled by previous and subsequent researchers. These factors combined meant that Harlan's two books remained unchallenged as the most authoritative biographical study of Washington at the end of the twentieth century.

Harlan's scholarly dedication is reflected in the fact that from the mid-1960s to the 1980s he also wrote a number of important articles on various aspects of Washington's life. Originally appearing in academic journals, these were made more generally available by their publication as a collection in Raymond W. Smock (ed.), *Booker T. Washington in Perspective: Essays of Louis Harlan* (1988). Harlan's lively 1997 autobiography, *All At Sea*, offers insights of a different sort, for readers seeking a better understanding of Harlan himself, and the experiences that shaped his early adult life during World War II.

In the 1990s Washington's enduring ability to inspire interest and controversy was confirmed by the appearance of new works. Virginia L. Denton's *Booker T. Washington and the Adult Education Movement* (1993) focused on Washington's contributions as an educator. Denton's study clearly benefited from her own experience in the teaching profession. Less positive is the imbalance created by the author's evident admiration for Washington and her determination to refute what she perceives as Harlan's "liberal revisionistic judgments" and his "general negativism towards the South."[2]

More recently Tunde Adeleke (ed.), *Booker T. Washington: Interpretative Essays* (1998), suggests that in the years leading up to the centenary of his death, the historical debate on Washington is still far from exhausted.

As with Washington, the catalogue of works on his most persuasive contemporary black critic, W. E. B. Du Bois, is extensive. Du Bois himself took care to preserve his private correspondence and papers from an early age, reflecting his early sense of destiny as a race leader and belief that the collection would be of value to later historians. Born in 1868 he was also a prolific writer for most of his long life. By his early teens he was contributing letters and articles to black newspapers like the New York *Globe* and New York *Freeman* and he was still an energetic author even when more than 90 years old, as was indicated by the publication of his *The Autobiography of W. E. B. Du Bois: A Soliloquy On viewing My Life from the Last Decade of Its First Century* (1962) only a year before his death. Moreover, the multitalented Du Bois made important contributions in a range of particular fields, as a historian, a sociologist, a novelist, and a poet, as well as in the more general roles of a journalist and race leader.

The Philadelphia Negro (1899), one of the first books written by Du Bois, demonstrates the conservatism of his social and economic thought in the years at the turn of the century. A sociological study of the lives of blacks in the city, many of Du Bois's conclusions could equally have been espoused by Booker T. Washington. He blamed the fecklessness of African Americans themselves for many of their problems and emphasized the need for thrift, hard work, and greater personal cleanliness.

Du Bois's famous essay "Of Mr Booker T. Washington and Others," published in *The Souls of Black Folk* (1903), was one of the first indications of his growing differences with Washington. The development of his ideas, and his rift with the Tuskegeean, are also dealt with by Du Bois in *The Negro* (1915), *Darkwater: Voices from Within the Veil* (1920), *Dusk of Dawn: An Essay Toward an Autobiography of a Race Concept* (1940), as well his 1962 *The Autobiography of W. E. B. Du Bois*.

Du Bois's principal works as a historian include *The Suppression of the African Slave Trade to the United States of America, 1638–1870* (1896), his biography of the radical abolitionist, *John Brown* (1909), and *Black Reconstruction in America: An Essay Toward a History of the Part Which Black Folk Played in the Attempt to Reconstruct Democracy in America, 1860–1880* (1935). Challenging the tired shibboleths of the Dunning school, *Black Reconstruction in America* preempted the thinking of later Revisionist and Postrevisionist historians. The Marxist analytical framework of the book, with its stress on class divisions, also attested to the radicalization of Du Bois's philosophy by the mid 1930s.

A two-volume compilation of Du Bois's public statements is provided by Philip S. Foner (ed.), *W. E. B. Du Bois Speaks: Speeches and Addresses 1890–1919*, and *Speeches and Addresses 1920–1963* (1970). Complimenting this work is the three-volume collection of Du Bois's private letters edited for publication by the white Marxist historian Herbert Aptheker as *The Correspondence of W. E. B. Du Bois, Volume I: 1877–1934, Volume II: 1934–1944*, and *Volume III: 1944–1963* (1973–1978).

A leading authority of his day on African-American history, Aptheker also edited the first American edition of *The Autobiography of W. E. B. Du Bois* (1968), *W. E. B. Du Bois, Against Racism: Unpublished Essays, Papers, Addresses, 1887–1961* (1985), and *Writings in Periodicals Edited by W. E. B. Du Bois: Selections from The Horizon* (1985).

An unofficial journal of the Niagara Movement from 1907 to 1910, The *Horizon* became defunct when Du Bois became editor of the NAACP journal, The *Crisis*. Extracts from Du Bois's work as *Crisis* editor from 1910 to 1934 can be found in W. E. B. Du Bois, *An ABC of Color* (1963). Some of Du Bois's most important *Crisis* editorials, together with extracts from his other writings, are available in David Levering Lewis (ed.), *W. E. B. Du Bois: A Reader* (1995), and Eric J. Sundquist (ed.), *The Oxford W. E. B. Du Bois Reader* (1996).

In their day the standard biographies of Du Bois, Francis L. Broderick, *W. E. B. Du Bois: Negro Leader in a Time of Crisis* (1959), and

Elliott Rudwick, *W. E. B. Du Bois: A Study in Minority Group Leadership*
(1960), have both began to show their age with the passage of the years.
The best modern studies are Manning Marable, *W. E. B. Du Bois: Black
Radical Democrat* (1986), David Levering Lewis, *W. E. B. Du Bois:
Biography of a Race, 1868–1919* (1993), and David Levering Lewis, The
Fight For Equality and the American Century, 1919–1963 (2000).

Lewis's magisterial study is both meticulously researched and rich in
detail. These works have justly earned him the reputation as the leading
living historian of Du Bois. At 735 pages and 715 pages in length respectively, they are, however, works that are likely to deter less committed
readers.

By way of contrast Marable's shorter work provides a readable full-
length biography of his subject. At the same time, Marable, a respected historian and left-wing thinker, has also been criticized for his portrayal of Du
Bois as a constant champion of the poor and the oppressed. Arguably, this
view gives insufficient attention to Du Bois's early conservatism and the
frequent apparent paradoxes and inconsistencies in his philosophy over
the years.

During the 1990s the seeming contradictions in Du Bois's thinking
were highlighted by a renewed debate of his conduct as *Crisis* editor during World War I. In a controversial 1918 editorial, "Close Ranks," he urged
African Americans to forget their grievances and unite in support of the
nation's war effort. At the time Du Bois was much criticized for this action
by more radical black spokespersons, like the socialist and labor leader A.
Philip Randolph. In a later 1919 editorial, "Returning Soldiers," Du Bois
appeared to reverse his position, urging returning black soldiers to fight as
vigorously for their rights at home as they had for the allied cause in
Europe.

In "'Closing Ranks' and 'Seeking Honors': W. E. B. Du Bois in World
War I," *Journal of American History,* 79 (June 1992), 96–124, the British
historian Mark Ellis sought to find an explanation for this inconsistency.
He argued that the *Crisis* editor's initial conservatism derived from the
fact that in 1918 Du Bois was seeking a commission as captain in the U.S.
Military Intelligence Branch (MIB) and thus needed to demonstrate his
patriotic credentials.

William Jordan, "'The Damnable Dilemma': African American
Accommodation and Protest During World War I," *Journal of American
History*, 81 (March 1995), 1562–1583, expressed a different point of view.
Taking issue with Ellis, Jordan argued that the "Close Ranks" article derived
from a periodic tendency toward calculated accommodationism by Du Bois
that predated World War I, most notably in the years before 1900.

Other works examining particular aspects of Du Bois's career include
Arnold Rampersad, *The Art and Imagination of W. E. B. Du Bois* (1976),

Shamoon Zamir, *Dark Voices: W. E. B. Du Bois and American Thought, 1888–1903* (1995), Rutledge M. Dennis (ed.), *W. E. B. Du Bois: The Scholar as Activist* (1996), and Michael B. Katz and Thomas J. Sugrue (eds.), *W. E. B. Du Bois and the City: The Philadelphia Negro and Its Legacy (1998).*

The far flung nature of the Garvey movement and the incompleteness of many UNIA records have been perennial problems for historians and other researchers on Garveyism.

For some years the most extensive and readily available published primary source material on Garvey was Amy Jacques Garvey (ed.), *Philosophy and Opinions of Marcus Garvey, Or Africa for the Africans* (1967), and E. U. Essien-Udom and Amy Jacques Garvey (eds.), *More Philosophy and Opinions of Marcus Garvey* (1977). Although providing a valuable collection of Garvey's speeches and writings, the documents in these works, edited by Garvey's widow, were clearly selected to portray the Jamaican in a favorable light. The two books would also have benefited from better presentation and organization and more detailed references providing factual background information on individuals and events mentioned in the text.

These criticisms could not be applied to the more recent *The Marcus Garvey and Universal Negro Improvement Association Papers* compiled by Robert Hill and a team of co-editors at the University of California. In the process of publication since 1983, this projected 10-volume collection, nine of which are presently available, represents an undertaking comparable to the *Booker T. Washington Papers* in its ambitious scope and meticulous presentation. The first six volumes focus on the activities of Garvey and the UNIA in the United States, with the other four devoted to the Garvey movement in Africa and the Caribbean. Additional material is made available in Robert A. Hill and Barbara Blair (eds.), *Marcus Garvey, Life and Lessons: A Centennial Companion to the Marcus Garvey and Universal Negro Improvement Association Papers* (1987). All of the volumes in the series are of incomparable value to Garvey scholars, drawing from source materials scattered across the world. The documents selected are clearly presented and benefit from extensive footnoting of relevant factual information.

Despite their impressive strengths the *Garvey Papers* are, in comparison, less satisfying than the *Booker T. Washington Papers.* Unlike Harlan, Hill and his editorial team were not able to make use of an extensive collection of Garvey's unpublished correspondence. Most of the surviving primary source material on the Jamaican rather takes the form of public writings and speeches by Garvey and commentaries by observers of the Garvey movement. At times such material can afford fascinating insights, as in the reports of U.S. secret service agents on UNIA meetings. Ultimately however, the reader is left with the impression of viewing

Garvey from a distance, rather than at close proximity, as is possible with the Tuskegeean.

A shorter, but still useful, collection of primary source extracts, including the thoughts of contemporary observers of the Garvey movement, is provided in E. David Cronon (ed.), *Marcus Garvey* (1973). John H. Clarke (ed.), *Marcus Garvey and the Vision of Africa* (1967), provides an informative selection of writings from both Garvey's contemporaries and later historians.

The most influential of the early academic biographies of Garvey is E. David Cronon, *Black Moses: the Story of Marcus Garvey and the Universal Negro Improvement Association* (1955). Although providing a clear narrative account of Garvey's life and career this work was marred by the author's negative perceptions of Garveyism. Cronon concluded that Garvey was an honest but incompetent leader, while the philosophy underpinning the Garvey movement was disturbingly right wing and reactionary.

Cronon's study reflects the fact that discussion of the impact and significance of Garvey as a race leader has generally divided historians into opposing camps of sympathetic and hostile critics. Supportive works include Tony Martin, *Race First: The Ideological and Organizational Struggles of Marcus Garvey and the Universal Negro Improvement Association* (1976), and Theodore G. Vincent, *Black Power and the Garvey Movement* (1972). These works portray Garvey as a visionary race leader who inspired later successful black independence movements in Africa after World War II. During his own lifetime Garvey's UNIA failed to achieve its objectives because the Jamaican's ideas were too far ahead of his time and because of the unremitting hostility of black opponents, U.S. authorities, and European colonial administrations in Africa and the Caribbean.

If Cronon can be criticized for being overly negative, Martin and Vincent arguably err at the other extreme, paying insufficient attention to divisions in the UNIA and Garvey's own failings as a race leader. Thoughtful and more balanced is Judith Stein, *The World of Marcus Garvey: Race and Class in Modern Society* (1986). Paying equal attention to Garvey's strengths and weaknesses, Stein's work is perhaps the best of the more recent studies of Garvey.

Studies on particular aspects of the Garvey movement include Randall K. Burkett, *Garveyism as a Religious Movement: The Institutionalization of a Black Civil Religion* (1978), Randall K. Burkett, *Black Redemption: Churchmen Speak for the Garvey Movement* (1978), and Emory J. Tolbert, *The UNIA and Black Los Angeles: Ideology and Community in the Garvey Movement* (1980).

Useful collections of essays on Garveyism are Rupert Lewis and Maureen Warner-Lewis, *Garvey, Africa, Europe, The Americas* (1986), and Rupert Lewis and Patrick Bryan (eds.), *Garvey: His Work and Impact*

(1991). These works examine Garveyism as an international phenomenon, looking at UNIA organization in Africa and the Caribbean as well as in the United States. Rupert Lewis, *Marcus Garvey: Anti Colonial Champion* (1987), takes the same approach, while Elton C. Fax, *Garvey: The Story of a Pioneer Black Nationalist* (1972), is useful for its insight into Garvey's early life in Jamaica.

The impact of West Indian immigrants in the United States is discussed in Harold Cruse, *The Crisis of the Negro Intellectual* (1984), and more fully in W. James, *Holding Aloft the Banner of Ethiopia: Caribbean Radicalism in Early Twentieth Century America* (1998). An older, but still useful, study is David J. Hellwig, "Black Meets Black: Afro American Reactions to West Indian Immigrants in the 1920s," *South Atlantic Quarterly*, 77 (1978), 206–224.

During the 1920s West Indians comprised a significant minority of the black population of New York City. Native black Americans held ambivalent attitudes toward this immigrant group. West Indians were respected for their strong family values and business acumen, being dubbed the "Jews of their race." Generally better educated than most black Americans West Indians were also seen as more robust in defending their civil and political rights. They made up an important nucleus of activists within the UNIA movement.

Less positively, West Indians were perceived as clannish, patronizing, and untrustworthy in business, as well as a source of competition in the labor market. They were also seen as being Un-American in values retaining artificial British notions of hierarchy and social deference, as reflected in Garvey's attempts to create a black UNIA nobility.

The pattern of race relations in Jamaica was notably different from that in the United States. Whites, who occupied the best jobs in the British colonial administration, made up only two percent of the island's population. They were assisted in this task by lesser civil servants and officials drawn mainly from a mixed race class that comprised around 18 percent of Jamaican inhabitants. Most of the remaining 80 percent of the island's population were politically and economically disadvantaged black laborers. These were generally regarded with disdain by mixed-race families who craved acceptance into the white ruling class.

Transplanted into the United States by West Indian immigrants, these social attitudes arguably added to the divisions within black American society. Garvey, who had all black ancestry, distrusted African Americans of mixed race backgrounds, such as W. E. B. Du Bois. In turn, they saw him as harboring Jamaican prejudices on race that were out of place in an American setting.

Notes

Chapter 1
Introduction: African-American History, 1865–1925

1. John H. Croushore and David M. Potter (eds.), *John William De Forest: A Union Officer in the Reconstruction* (New Haven: Yale University Press, 1948), 1, 39, 75–77.

2. George B. Tindall, *South Carolina Negroes, 1877–1900* (Columbia: University of South Carolina Press, 1952), 216.

3. Paul D. Escott et al. (eds.), *Major Problems in the History of the American South, Volume II: The New South*, 2nd ed. (Boston: Houghton Mifflin Company, 1999), 158–159.

4. Escott et al., *The New South*, 158–159.

5. Samuel R. Spencer, *Booker T. Washington and the Negro's Place in American Life* (Boston: Little Brown, 1956), 111; Lawrence J. Friedman, "Life 'in the Lion's Mouth': Another Look at Booker T. Washington," *Journal of Negro History*, 59 (1974), 344–345.

6. Bayrd Still, *Urban America: A History with Documents* (Boston: Little Brown, 1974), 210–211.

7. Alan M. Kraut, *The Huddled Masses: The Immigrant in American Society, 1880–1921* (Arlington Heights: Harlan Davidson Inc., 1982), 18, 20–21.

8. Carter Godwin Woodson, *A Century of Negro Migration* (Washington: n.p., 1918), 171.

9. Mary Ellison, *The Black Experience: American Blacks Since 1865* (London: B. T. Batsford Limited, 1974), 85–87; Thomas C. Holt and Elsa Barkley Brown (eds.), *Major Problems in African-American History, Volume II: From Freedom to "Freedom Now," 1865–1990s* (Boston:

Houghton Mifflin Company, 2000), 128; Ira Katznelson, *Black Men, White Cities* (Oxford: Oxford University Press, 1973), 62–63, 86–87.

10. Ellison, *The Black Experience*, 81, 85.

11. John Hope Franklin and Alfred A. Moss, *From Slavery to Freedom: A History of Negro Americans* (New York: McGraw-Hill, 1994), 313, 315.

12. Maldwyn A. Jones, *The Limits of Liberty: American History, 1607–1980* (Oxford: Oxford University Press, 1983), 439.

13. Allen W. Trelease, *White Terror: The Ku Klux Klan Conspiracy and Southern Reconstruction* (London: Secker and Warburg, 1972), 16.

14. Wyn Craig Wade, *The Fiery Cross: The Ku Klux Klan in America* (New York: Simon & Schuster Inc., 1987), 166, 253.

15. James Weldon Johnson, *Along This Way: The Autobiography of James Weldon Johnson* (Harmondsworth: Penguin Books Limited, 1990), 315; John Hope Franklin and August Meier, *Black Leaders of the Twentieth Century* (Urbana: University of Illinois Press, 1982), 89.

16. Liz Mackie, *The Great Marcus Garvey* (London: Hansib Printing Limited, 1987), 29.

17. Mackie, *The Great Marcus Garvey*, 32.

18. Mackie, *The Great Marcus Garvey*, 36.

19. Holt and Brown, *From Freedom to "Freedom Now,"* 144.

20. Wade, *The Fiery Cross*, 253.

Chapter 2
The Lion and the Lamb: Frederick Douglass and Booker T. Washington

1. William L. Andrews (ed.), *Critical Essays on Frederick Douglass* (Boston: G. K. Hall and Company, 1991), 35–36.

2. Timothy Thomas Fortune to Booker T. Washington, New York, 26 September 1895, in Louis R. Harlan (ed.), *The Booker T. Washington Papers, Volume 4, 1895–1898* (Urbana: University of Illinois Press, 1975), 31; A Speech by Emmett J. Scott, Houston, Texas, 29 December 1902, in Louis R. Harlan (ed.), *The Booker T. Washington Papers, Volume 6, 1901–1902* (Urbana: University of Illinois Press, 1977), 615.

3. Extracts from Booker T. Washington, *My Larger Education* (1911), in Louis R. Harlan (ed.), *The Booker T. Washington Papers, Volume 1, The Autobiographical Writings* (Urbana: University of Illinois Press, 1972), 422–426.

4. James Olney, "The Founding Fathers—Frederick Douglass and Booker T. Washington; or, The Idea of Democracy and a Tradition of Afro-American Autobiography," *Amerikastudien*, 35 (1990), 292.

5. Booker T. Washington, *Up From Slavery* (Harmondsworth: Penguin Books, 1986), 99–100.

6. Washington, *Up From Slavery*, 284, 288–289.

7. Samuel Laing Williams to Theodore Roosevelt, Chicago, 4/5th 1905, in The Booker T. Washington Papers, Library of Congress, Container 21 (Microfilm Reel 18), fl 5. Laing Williams, 1902–1914, n.d.; Wayne Mixon, "The Shadow of Slavery: Frederick Douglass, the Savage South, and the Next Generation," in Eric J. Sundquist (ed.), *Frederick Douglass: New Literary and Historical Essays* (Cambridge: Cambridge University Press, 1990), fn. 251.

8. Booker T. Washington, *Frederick Douglass* (New York: Argosy Antiquarian Limited, 1969), 5, 349.

9. See, for example, Booker T. Washington, "Christmas Days in Old Virginia," December 1907, in Harlan, *The Booker T. Washington Papers, 1*, 394–397.

10. Washington, *Frederick Douglass*, 18.

11. Washington, *Frederick Douglass*, 64–65.

12. Washington, *Frederick Douglass*, 339–340.

13. Washington, *Frederick Douglass*, 348.

14. Washington, *Frederick Douglass*, 306.

15. Washington, *My Larger Education*, in Harlan, *The Booker T. Washington Papers, 1*, 423–424.

16. Harlan, *The Booker T. Washington Papers, 6*, fn. 408; Booker T. Washington to Robert Heberton Terrell, Tuskegee, 19 February 1906, in Louis R. Harlan (ed.), *The Booker T. Washington Papers, Volume 8, 1904–1906* (Urbana: University of Illinois Press, 1979), 525–526; Booker T. Washington to Timothy Thomas Fortune, Tuskegee, 5 February 1907, Archibald Henry Grimke to Booker T. Washington, Boston, 14 September 1908, in Louis R. Harlan (ed.), *The Booker T. Washington Papers, Volume 9, 1906–1908* (Urbana: University of Illinois Press, 1980), 210–211, 623–625.

17. "An Appeal on Behalf of the Frederick Douglass Home," 15 January 1909, in Louis R. Harlan (ed.), *The Booker T. Washington Papers, Volume 10, 1909–1911* (Urbana: University of Illinois Press, 1981), 13–14.

18. Washington, *Frederick Douglass*, 178–179; Booker T. Washington, *The Story of My Life and Work* (1900), in Harlan, *The Booker T. Washington Papers, 1*, 56–57.

19. Washington, *Frederick Douglass*, 181.

20. August Meier, "Frederick Douglass's Vision for America: A Case Study in Nineteenth Century Negro Protest," in August Meier and Elliott Rudwick, *Along the Color Line: Explorations in the Black Experience* (Urbana: University of Illinois Press, 1976), 12.

21. Booker T. Washington to Frederick Douglass, New York, 2 April 1894, Frederick Douglass to Booker T. Washington, Cedar Hill, Anacostia, D.C., 19 February 1895, in Louis R. Harlan (ed.), *The Booker T. Washington Papers, Volume 3, 1889–1895* (Urbana: University of Illinois Press, 1974), 396, 520.

22. Washington, *Frederick Douglass*, 333.

23. E. W. Blake, "An Account of the Tuskegee Institute Commencement," 26 May 1892, in Harlan, *The Booker T. Washington Papers, 3*, 230–231; Frederick Douglass, "Self-Made Men: An Address Delivered in Carlisle, Pennsylvania in March 1893," in John W. Blassingame and John R. McKivigan (eds.), *The Frederick Douglass Papers: Series One: Speeches, Debates and Interviews, Volume 5, 1881–1895* (New Haven: Yale University Press, 1992), 545, 556.

24. Blassingame and McKivigan, *The Frederick Douglass Papers, 5*, 545–546.

25. Frederick Douglass, "Our Destiny is in Our Own Hands," An Address Delivered in Washington, D.C. on 16 April 1883, in Blassingame and McKivigan, *The Frederick Douglass Papers, 5*, 79.

26. Blassingame and McKivigan, *The Frederick Douglass Papers, 5*, 558.

27. Waldo E. Martin, Jr., *The Mind of Frederick Douglass* (Chapel Hill: University of North Carolina Press, 1984), 209; "Louis R. Harlan, Booker T. Washington and the White Man's Burden," in Raymond W. Smock (ed.), *Booker T. Washington in Perspective: Essays of Louis R. Harlan* (Jackson: University Press of Mississippi, 1988), 69, 72–73.

28. Frederick Douglass, "Strong to Suffer and Yet Strong to Survive," An Address Delivered in Washington, D.C. on 16 April 1886, in Blassingame and McKivigen, *The Frederick Douglass Papers 5*, 232.

29. Frederick Douglass, "The South Knows Us," An Address Delivered in Baltimore, Maryland, 4 May 1879, in John W. Blassingame and John R. McKivigen (eds.), *The Frederick Douglass Papers: Series One: Speeches, Debates and Interviews, Volume 4, 1864–1880*, 496–503.

30. Frederick Douglass, "The Negro Exodus From the Gulf States," An Address Delivered to the American Social Science Association, 12 September 1879, in Blassingame and McKivigen, *The Frederick Douglass Papers, 4*, 510–533.

31. Frederick Douglass, "In Law Free: In Fact a Slave," An Address Delivered in Washington, D.C. on 16 April 1888, in Blassingame and McKivigen, *The Frederick Douglass Papers, 5*, 357–373.

32. Douglass, "Strong to Suffer," in Blassingame and McKivigen, *The Frederick Douglass Papers, 5*, 233.

33. See, for example, Meier and Rudwick, *Along the Color Line*, 24; John White, *Black Leadership in America, 1895–1968* (London: Longman, 1985), 18–21.

34. Article in *Frederick Douglass's Paper*, 5 October 1855, quoted in Meier and Rudwick, *Along the Color Line*, 12.

35. Frederick Douglass, "This Decision Has Humbled the Nation," An Address Delivered in Washington, D.C. on 22 October 1883, in Blassingame and McKivigen, *The Frederick Douglass Papers, 5*, 110–123.

36. Frederick Douglass, "Lessons of the Hour," An Address Delivered

in Washington, D.C. on 9 January 1894, in Blassingame and McKivigen, *The Frederick Douglass Papers*, 5, 575–607.

37. Frederick Douglass, "I am a Radical Woman Suffrage Man," An Address Delivered in Boston, Massachusetts on 28 May 1888, in Blassingame and McKivigen, *The Frederick Douglass Papers*, 5, 378–387; William S. McFeely, *Frederick Douglass* (New York: W. W. Norton and Company, 1991), 135–156.

38. David Levering Lewis, *W.E.B. Du Bois: Biography of a Race, 1868–1919* (New York: Henry Holt and Company, 1993), fn 46, 671, cites "plentiful" rumors that Washington had a secret drinking problem, but these were based on hearsay and from unreliable, often downright hostile, sources. In the absence of hard evidence it is difficult to give much credence to such stories.

39. Booker T. Washington to Charles Monroe Lincoln, 14 December 1908, in Harlan, *The Booker T. Washington Papers*, 9, 700–701.

40. McFeely, *Frederick Douglass*, 291, 306, 359.

41. Frederick Douglass, *Autobiographies* (New York: The Library of America, 1994), 860–889.

42. Douglass, *Autobiographies*, 984–1017.

43. McFeely, *Frederick Douglass*, 377; Tommy L Lott, "Frederick Douglass and the Myth of the Black Rapist," in Bill E. Lawson and Frank M. Kirkland (eds.), *Frederick Douglass: A Critical Reader* (Oxford: Blackwell Publishers Limited, 1999), 314–315.

44. Washington, *Story of My Life and Work*, in Harlan, *The Booker T. Washington Papers*, 1, 56.

45. McFeely, *Frederick Douglass*, 377; Blassingame and McKivigen, *The Frederick Douglass Papers*, 5, 358.

46. Quoted in Andrews, *Critical Essays on Frederick Douglass*, 38.

47. Booker T. Washington to Oswald Garrison Villard, 1 January 1904, in The Booker T. Washington Papers, Library of Congress, Oswald Garrison Villard, Special Correspondence, 1904.

Chapter 3
Roads Not Taken: Booker T. Washington as a Race Leader

1. Andrew A. King, "Booker T. Washington and the Myth of Heroic Materialism," *Quarterly Journal of Speech*, 60 (October 1974), 324–325.

2. The best study on Fortune is Emma Lou Thornbrough, *T. Thomas Fortune: Militant Journalist* (Chicago: University of Chicago Press, 1972).

3. The standard biography of Trotter is Stephen R. Fox, *The Guardian of Boston: William Monroe Trotter* (New York: Atheneum, 1970).

4. For more information on Price see Paul Yandle, "Joseph Charles Price and His 'Peculiar Work', Part I and Part II," *North Carolina Historical Review*, LXX, Nos. 1 and 2 (January and April 1993), 40–56, 130–152.

5. Samuel R. Spencer, *Booker T. Washington and the Negro's Place in American Life* (Boston: Little Brown, 1956), 111; Lawrence J. Friedman, "Life 'in the Lion's Mouth': Another Look at Booker T. Washington," *Journal of Negro History*, 59 (1974), 344–345.

6. Booker T. Washington, An Address at the National Peace Jubilee, Chicago, Illinois, 16 October 1898; Booker T. Washington to the Editor of the Birmingham *Age Herald*, 10 November 1898; both in Louis R. Harlan (ed.), *The Booker T. Washington Papers, Volume 4, 1895–1898* (Urbana: University of Illinois Press, 1975), 490–493, 508–509.

7. Quoted in Dewey W. Grantham, "Dinner at the White House: Theodore Roosevelt, Booker T. Washington and the South," *Tennessee Historical Quarterly*, XVIII (June 1959), 122.

8. An Editorial in the Montgomery *Advertiser*, 16 August 1905; Booker T. Washington to Charles W. Hare, 22 August 1905; Booker T. Washington to Benjamin J. Davis, 29 August 1905; Booker T. Washington to Seth Low, 31 August 1905; Seth Low to the Editor of the Atlanta *Constitution*, 31 August 1905; Seth Low to Clark Howell, 1 September 1905; Hervey W. Laird to Booker T. Washington, 1 September 1905; Booker T. Washington to Charles W. Anderson, 13 September 1905; all in Louis R. Harlan (ed.), *The Booker T. Washington Papers, Volume 8, 1904–1906* (Urbana: University of Illinois Press, 1979), 341–352, 356–357.

9. Seth Low to Charles Fletcher Dole, 31 March 1911, in Louis R. Harlan (ed.), *The Booker T. Washington Papers, Volume 11, 1911–1912* (Urbana: University of Illinois Press, 1981), 71. Detailed accounts of the incident are given in William B Gatewood, "Booker T. Washington and the Ulrich Affair," *Phylon*, XXX (Fall 1969), 286–302, and Louis R. Harlan , *Booker T. Washington: The Wizard of Tuskegee, 1901–1915* (Oxford: Oxford University Press, 1983), 379–404.

10. Louis R. Harlan , "The Secret Life of Booker T. Washington," in Raymond W. Smock (ed.), *Booker T. Washington in Perspective: Essays of Louis R. Harlan* (Jackson: University Press of Mississippi, 1988), 110–132. Also highlighting the importance of Washington's covert civil rights action are August Meier, "Toward a Reinterpretation of Booker T. Washington," *Journal of Southern History*, XXIII (May 1957), 220–227, and Arvarh E. Strickland, "Booker T. Washington: The Myth and the Man," *Reviews in American History*, I (December 1973), 559–564.

11. Friedman, "Life 'in the Lion's Mouth,'" 343–351; Arthur L. Smith (ed.), *Language, Communication and Rhetoric in Black America* (New York: Harper & Row, 1972), 134–137; Emma Lou Thornbrough, "Booker T. Washington as Seen by His White Contemporaries," *Journal of Negro History*, 53 (1968), 181.

12. Booker T. Washington, A Speech in Montgomery, Alabama, 17 January 1890; Booker T. Washington to George Washington Cable, 7 April

1890; both in Louis R. Harlan (ed.), *The Booker T. Washington Papers, Volume 3, 1889–1895* (Urbana: University of Illinois Press, 1974), 24–25, 45; Felix James, "The Tuskegee Institute Movable School, 1906–1923," *Agricultural History*, XLV (July 1971), 201–209; Allen W. Jones, "The Role of Tuskegee Institute in the Education of Black Farmers," *Journal of Negro History*, 60 (1975), 252–267; Allen W. Jones, "Improving Rural Life for Blacks: The Tuskegee Negro Farmers' Conference, 1892–1915," *Agricultural History*, 65, No. 2 (Spring 1991), 105–114; B. D. Mayberry, "The Tuskegee Movable School: A Unique Contribution to National and International Agriculture and Rural Development," *Agricultural History*, 65, No. 2 (Spring 1991), 85–104.

13. Booker T. Washington, An Address Before the National Negro Business League, Academy of Music, Philadelphia, 20 August 1913; Booker T. Washington, A Speech at Western University, Quindara, Kansas, 4 March 1914; both in Louis R. Harlan (ed.), *The Booker T. Washington Papers, Volume 12, 1912–1914* (Urbana: University of Illinois Press, 1982), 264–265, 466–468.

14. Booker T. Washington, *The Future of the Negro* (1899), in Louis R. Harlan (ed.), *The Booker T. Washington Papers, Volume 5, 1899–1900* (Urbana: University of Illinois Press, 1976), 322; Friedman, "Life 'in the Lion's Mouth,'" 342–343; Don Quinn Kelley, "Ideology and Education: Uplifting the Masses in Nineteenth Century Alabama," *Phylon*, 40 (1979), 156–157; Alfred Young, "The Educational Philosophy of Booker T. Washington: A Perspective for Black Liberation," *Phylon*, 37 (1976), 231–232.

15. Spencer, *Booker T. Washington and the Negro's Place in American Life*, 152; Smith, *Language, Communication and Rhetoric*, 134–135; Thornbrough, "Booker T. Washington as Seen by His White Contemporaries," 181.

16. Leola Chambers to Booker T. Washington, 16 February 1914; Booker T. Washington to Leola Chambers, 25 February 1914; both in Harlan, *The Booker T. Washington Papers*, 12, 441, 451. An interesting analysis of Washington's folksy rhetoric is Frederick L. McElroy, "Booker T. Washington as Literary Trickster," *Southern Folklore*, 49 (1992), 89–107. McElroy is sympathetic to Washington's anecdotal speaking style, seeing it as part of the Tuskegeean's strategy of distraction when dealing with white audiences. However, he does not give consideration to the negative implications of Washington's imagery in reinforcing harmful racial stereotypes.

17. Washington, *The Future of the Negro*, in Harlan, *The Booker T. Washington Papers*, 5, 369.

18. Booker T. Washington, *The Story of the Negro* (1909), in Louis R. Harlan (ed.), *The Booker T. Washington Papers, Volume 1, the Autobiographical Writings* (Urbana: University of Illinois Press, 1972), 402.

19. Smith, *Language, Communication and Rhetoric*, 136–137.

20. Harlan, *The Wizard of Tuskegee*, 267; Booker T. Washington, *Up From Slavery* (Harmondsworth: Penguin Books Limited, 1987), 285.

21. Booker T. Washington as quoted in Friedman, "Life 'in the Lion's Mouth,'" 343; Booker T. Washington, "Christianizing Africa," December 1896, in Harlan, *The Booker T. Washington Papers*, *4*, 251–252; Booker T. Washington to the Editor of the Washington *Colored American*, 20 July 1899, in Harlan, *The Booker T. Washington Papers*, *5*, 164–166; Booker T. Washington, "Cruelty in the Congo Country," 8 October 1904, in Harlan, *The Booker T. Washington Papers*, *8*, 85–90; Booker T. Washington, An Article in the New York *Age*, 18 October 1913, in Louis R. Harlan , *The Booker T. Washington Papers, Volume 13, 1914–1915* (Urbana: University of Illinois Press, 1984), 394–401; Harlan, *The Wizard of Tuskegee*, 266–94; Louis R. Harlan, "Booker T. Washington and the White Man's Burden," in Smock, *Booker T. Washington in Perspective*, 68–97.

22. Harlan, *The Wizard of Tuskegee*, 267, 274; Smock, *Booker T. Washington in Perspective*, 69; Michael O. West, "The Tuskegee Model of Development in Africa: Another Dimension of the African/African American Connection," *Diplomatic History*, 16 (Summer 1992), 375.

23. Harlan, *The Wizard of Tuskegee*, 268–269; Smock, *Booker T. Washington in Perspective*, 72–73.

24. Washington, *Up From Slavery*, 98.

25. Arnold Cooper, "The Tuskegee Machine in Action: Booker T. Washington's Influence on Utica Institute, 1903–1915," *Journal of Mississippi History*, 48 (November 1986), 291–294; Harlan, *the Wizard of Tuskegee*, 32–106, 359–378; Charles F. Kellogg, *NAACP: A History of the National Association for the Advancement of Colored People, Volume I, 1909–1920* (Baltimore: John Hopkins University Press, 1967), 67–88; August Meier, "Booker T. Washington and the Negro Press, with Special Reference to the *Colored American Magazine*," *Journal of Negro History*, 37 (1958), 67–90; August Meier and Elliott Rudwick, *Along the Color Line: Explorations in the Black Experience* (Urbana: University of Illinois Press, 1976), 56–93; Elliott M. Rudwick, "Booker T. Washington's Relations with the National Association for the Advancement of Colored People," *Journal of Negro Education*, XXIX (Spring 1960), 134–44; Smock, *Booker T. Washington in Perspective*, 110–132; Daniel Walden, "The Contemporary Opposition to the Political and Educational Ideas of Booker T. Washington," *Journal of Negro History*, 45 (1960), 103–115.

26. Harlan, *The Wizard of Tuskegee*, 376–378; An Account of the Cosmopolitan Club Dinner in the New York *American*, 28 April 1908, in Louis R. Harlan (ed.), *The Booker T. Washington Papers, Volume 9, 1906–1908* (Urbana: University of Illinois Press, 1980), 515–521; Kellogg, *NAACP*, 71–72.

27. Harlan, *The Wizard of Tuskegee*, 359–378; August Meier, *Negro Thought in America, 1880–1915* (Ann Arbor: University of Michigan Press,

1963), 115–116; Booker T. Washington to Richard T. Greener, 11 August 1906; Booker T. Washington to Richard Carroll, 5 September 1906; both in Harlan, *The Booker T. Washington Papers, 9,* 55–56, 68–69.

28. Meier, *Negro Thought in America,* 115–116; Hugh Hawkins (ed.), *Booker T. Washington and His Critics: The Problem of Negro Leadership* (Boston: D. C. Heath and Company, 1962), 87–91.

29. Harlan, *The Wizard of Tuskegee,* 143–161; Maria A. Benson to Booker T. Washington, 20 May 1890; Booker T. Washington to Irene Bond, 16 February 1895; Booker T. Washington to Nathan B. Young, 25 February 1895; all in Harlan, *The Booker T. Washington Papers, 3,* 58, 519, 531–535; Booker T. Washington to Nathan B. Young, 26 March 1896, in Harlan, *The Booker T. Washington Papers, 4,* 145–149; Booker T. Washington to Wallace A. Rayfield, 30 April 1901; Leonara Love Chapman Kenniebrow to Booker T. Washington, 8 November 1901; Ida Bell Thompson McCall to Booker T. Washington, 11 November 1901; all in Louis R. Harlan , *The Booker T. Washington Papers, 6, 1901–1902* (Urbana: University of Illinois Press, 1977), 102, 297–298, 314.

30. Harlan, *The Wizard of Tuskegee,* 151–156.

31. Hawkins, *Booker T. Washington and His Critics,* 87; Meier, *Negro Thought in America,* 115–116.

32. Herbert Aptheker, "The Washington-Du Bois Conference of 1904," *Science and Society,* 13 (Autumn 1949), 344–351; Harlan, *The Wizard of Tuskegee,* 63.

33. Harlan, *The Wizard of Tuskegee,* 359–378; Oswald Garrison Villard to Booker T. Washington, 26 May 1909; Booker T. Washington to Oswald Garrison Villard, 28 May 1909; Booker T. Washington to Charles W. Anderson, 3 March 1911; all in Louis R. Harlan (ed.), *The Booker T. Washington Papers, 10, 1909–1911* (Urbana: University of Illinois Press, 1981), 116–120, 454, 614.

34. Louis R. Harlan, "Twenty Years With Booker T. Washington," in Genna Rae McNeil and Michael R. Winston (eds.), *Historical Judgments Reconsidered: Selected Howard University Lectures in Honor of Rayford W. Logan* (Washington, D.C.: Howard University Press, 1988), 135; Meier, *Negro Thought in America,* 116; Carl S. Matthews, "The Decline of the Tuskegee Machine, 1915–1925: The Abdication of Political Power," *South Atlantic Quarterly,* 75 (1976), 460–469.

35. Kelley, "Ideology and Education," 150–155; Howard N. Rabinowitz, *Race Relations in the Urban South, 1865–1890* (New York: Oxford University Press, 1978), 76–77, 248, 292–293; Strickland, "The Man and the Myth," 562; West, "The Tuskegee Model of Development in Africa," 371.

36. Bernard A. Weisberger, *Booker T. Washington* (New York: The New American Library Inc., 1972), 8; Preface by Oscar Handlin in Spencer, *Booker T. Washington and the Negro's Place in American Life,* ix.

37. West, "The Tuskegee Model of Development in Africa," 386.

38. Harlan, *The Wizard of Tuskegee*, 317–322.

39. Harlan, *The Wizard of Tuskegee*, 404; Meier, *Negro Thought in America*, 103; Spencer, *Booker T. Washington and the Negro's Place in American Life*, 190–192; Weisberger, *Booker T. Washington*, 122.

Chapter 4
As Separate as the Five Fingers: Booker T. Washington and the Age of Jim Crow

1. All quotations from Washington's 1895 Atlanta address are taken from the standard printed version of the speech as given in Booker T. Washington, *Up From Slavery* (Harmondsworth: Penguin Books, 1986), 218–225.

2. Washington, *Up From Slavery*, 225–226.

3. Robert L. Heath, "A Time for Silence: Booker T. Washington in Atlanta," *The Quarterly Journal of Speech*, 64 (1978), 385–399; Emma Lou Thornbrough, "Booker T. Washington as Seen by His White Contemporaries," *Journal of Negro History*, 53 (1968), 181; C. Vann Woodward, *The Strange Career of Jim Crow, 3rd rev. ed.* (Oxford: Oxford University Press, 1974), 82.

4. Heath, "A Time for Silence," 394.

5. Heath, "A Time for Silence," 388.

6. Booker T. Washington to Oswald Garrison Villard, New York City, 13 November 1904, The Booker T. Washington Papers, Tuskegee University, Box 6, Theodore Roosevelt Correspondence, fl. 59, November 1904.

7. Booker T. Washington, "Looking on the Bright Side of Life," A Sunday Evening Talk at Tuskegee Institute, 13 January 1907, in Louis R. Harlan (ed.), *The Booker T. Washington Papers, Volume 9, 1906–1908* (Urbana: University of Illinois Press, 1980), 183–7.

8. Booker T. Washington, A Speech at Hampton Institute, Hampton, Virginia, 13 October 1907, in Harlan, *The Booker T. Washington Papers, 9,* 375.

9. Booker T. Washington, "A Pitiable Spectacle in Georgia," 6 January 1900, Booker T. Washington to Timothy Thomas Fortune, 9 January 1900, in Louis R. Harlan (ed.), *The Booker T. Washington Papers, Volume 5, 1899–1900* (Urbana: University of Illinois Press, 1976), 403–405.

10. Booker T. Washington, "What I Am Trying to Do," November 1913, in Louis R. Harlan (ed.), *The Booker T. Washington Papers, Volume 12, 1912–1914* (Urbana: University of Illinois Press, 1982), 355–357.

11. Booker T. Washington to Ednah Dow Littlehale Cheney, Tuskegee, Alabama, 15 October 1895, in Louis R. Harlan (ed.), *The Booker T. Washington Papers, Volume 4, 1895–1898* (Urbana: University of Illinois Press, 1975), 56–57.

12. Booker T. Washington, "Christmas Days in Old Virginia," December 1907, in Louis R. Harlan (ed.), *The Booker T. Washington Papers, Volume 1, The Autobiographical Writings* (Urbana: University of Illinois Press, 1972), 398–399.

13. Booker T. Washington, *The Story of the Negro* (1909), in Harlan, *The Booker T. Washington Papers, 1,* 402.

14. Dickson D. Bruce, Jr., "Booker T. Washington's *The Man Farthest Down* and the Transformation of Race," *Mississippi Quarterly,* 48 (Spring 1995), 241–242, 248–249.

15. Booker T. Washington, A Speech Delivered Before the Women's New England Club, Boston, Massachusetts, 27 January 1890, in Louis R. Harlan (ed.), *The Booker T. Washington Papers, Volume 3, 1889–1895* (Urbana: University of Illinois Press, 1974), 25–32.

16. Booker T. Washington, An Address at the National Peace Jubilee, Chicago, 16 October 1898; Booker T. Washington to the Editor of the Birmingham *Age Herald,* 10 November 1898, in Harlan, *The Booker T. Washington Papers, 4,* 490–493, 508–509.

17. Booker T. Washington to Oswald Garrison Villard, 13 November 1904, The Booker T. Washington Papers, Tuskegee University.

18. Booker T. Washington, "Is the Negro Having a Fair Chance," November 1912, in Harlan, *The Booker T. Washington Papers, 12,* 64–82; Majority Opinion in *Plessy v. Ferguson* 1896; Opinion of the Court in *Brown v. Board of Education,* 17 May 1954, both as given in Waldo E. Martin, Jr., *Brown v Board of Education: A Brief History With Documents* (Boston: Bedford/St. Martin's, 1998), 76–80, 168–174.

19. Letters from Andrew Humphrey, Kelly Miller, and Archibald Grimke to Booker T. Washington, 20–28 May 1906; Booker T. Washington to Samuel Laing Williams, Tuskegee, Alabama, 28 May 1906, all in Harlan, *The Booker T. Washington Papers, 9,* 11–14.

20. Booker T. Washington, "My View of the Segregation Laws," December 1915, in Louis R. Harlan , *The Booker T. Washington Papers, Volume 13, 1914–1915* (Urbana: University of Illinois Press, 1984), 357–360.

21. Max Bennett Thrasher, *Tuskegee: Its Story and Its Work* (New York: Negro Universities Press, 1969), 29.

22. Louis R. Harlan, *Booker T. Washington: The Making of a Black Leader, 1856–1901* (Oxford: Oxford University Press, 1972), 163; Manning Marable, "Tuskegee and the Politics of Illusion in the New South," *The Black Scholar* (May, 1977), 14–15.

23. Neil R McMillen, *Dark Journey: Black Mississippians in the Age of Jim Crow* (Urbana: University of Illinois Press, 1989), 120–121.

24. Booker T. Washington, A Sunday Evening Talk, Tuskegee Institute, 6 May 1900, in Harlan, *The Booker T. Washington Papers, 5,* 503–504.

25. Booker T. Washington, *The Future of the Negro* (1899), in Harlan, *The Booker T. Washington Papers,* 5, 331.

26. Booker T. Washington to Portia Marshall Washington, Tuskegee, Alabama, 15 November 1906, in Harlan, *The Booker T. Washington Papers,* 9, 127.

27. Washington, "Is the Negro Having a Fair Chance?" in Harlan, *The Booker T. Washington Papers, 12*, 70–71.

28. Booker T. Washington, A Sunday Evening Talk, Tuskegee Institute, 28 October 1906, in Harlan, *The Booker T. Washington Papers,* 9, 111; Booker T. Washington as quoted in David J. Hellwig, "Building a Black Nation: The Role of Immigrants in the Thought and Rhetoric of Booker T. Washington," *Mississippi Quarterly* (Fall 1978), 539–540.

29. August Meier, "Booker T. Washington and the Town of Mound Bayou," *Phylon*, 15 (Fourth Quarter 1954), 396–401; Norman L. Crockett, "Witness to History: Booker T. Washington Visits Boley," *The Chronicles of Oklahoma*, 67 (Winter 1989–1990), 382–391.

30. Crockett, "Witness to History," 390.

31. Manning Marable, *Black Leadership* (New York: Columbia University Press, 1998), 37–38.

32. Booker T. Washington to Mrs. Mary Clement Leavitt, 3 November 1903, marked "Personal," The Booker T. Washington Papers, Tuskegee University, Box 6, Theodore Roosevelt Correspondence, fl 48, 1903.

Chapter 5
Realist or Reactionary? Booker T. Washington and the Great Migration

1. Booker T. Washington, The Standard Printed Version of the Atlanta Exposition Address, 18 September 1895, in Louis R. Harlan (ed.), *The Booker T. Washington Papers, Volume 3, 1889–1895* (Urbana: University of Illinois Press, 1974), 583–587.

2. Charles Vincent, "Booker T. Washington's Tour of Louisiana, April 1915," *Louisiana History*, XXII (Spring 1981), 195.

3. John Hope Franklin, *From Slavery To Freedom: A History of American Negroes* (New York: Alfred A. Knopf, 1961), 388–390; Raymond W. Smock (ed.), *Booker T. Washington in Perspective: Essays of Louis R. Harlan* (Jackson: University Press of Mississippi, 1988), 18–21.

4. Louis R. Harlan, *Booker T. Washington: The Wizard of Tuskegee, 1901–1915* (Oxford: Oxford University Press, 1983), 202.

5. Bernard A. Weisberger, *Booker T. Washington* (New York: The New American Library, Inc., 1972), 36.

6. An Entry in a Notebook of Ray Stannard Baker, New York City, 9 February 1915, in Louis R. Harlan (ed.), *The Booker T. Washington Papers, Volume 13, 1914–1915* (Urbana: University of Illinois Press, 1984), 237–238.

7. Booker T. Washington, "Christmas Days in Old Virginia," December 1907, in Louis R. Harlan (ed.), *The Booker T. Washington Papers, Volume 1, The Autobiographical Writings* (Urbana: University of Illinois Press, 1972), 394; Booker T. Washington, A Draft of an Article on Fishing in Mobile Bay, circa October 1915, in Harlan, *The Booker T. Washington Papers, 13,* 420.

8. Booker T. Washington, A Sunday Evening Talk on the Subject of Work, Tuskegee Institute, 4 February, 1900, quoted in Max Bennett Thrasher, *Tuskegee: Its Story and Its Work* (New York: Negro Universities Press, 1969), 87; Weisberger, *Booker T. Washington,* 49.

9. August Meier, "Booker T. Washington and the Negro Press," *Journal of Negro History,* 38 (January 1953), 67–70.

10. Gilbert Osofsky, *Harlem: The Making of a Ghetto: New York, 1890–1930* (New York: Harper Torchbooks, 1971), 162–164.

11. Henry S. Enck, "Tuskegee Institute and Northern White Philanthropy: A Case Study in Fund Raising, 1900–1915," *Journal of Negro History,* 65 (Fall 1980), 338; Harlan, *The Wizard of Tuskegee,* 436; Weisberger, *Booker T. Washington,* 120.

12. Edwin D. Hoffman, "From Slavery to Self-Reliance: The Record of Achievement of the Freedmen of the Sea Island Region," *Journal of Negro History,* XLI (January 1956), 8–42; Carol Bleser, *The Promised Land: The History of the South Carolina Land Commission, 1869–1890* (Columbia: University of South Carolina Press, 1969), 146–156; Kevern J Verney, "'Trespassers in the Land of Their Birth': Blacks and Landownership in South Carolina and Mississippi During the Civil War and Reconstruction, 1861–1877," *Slavery and Abolition,* IV (May 1983), 64–78; Elizabeth Raul Bethel, *Promiseland: A Century of Life in a Negro Community* (Philadelphia: Temple University Press, 1981).

13. Janet Sharp Hermann, *The Pursuit of a Dream* (Oxford: Oxford University Press, 1981), 3–34; Verney, "'Trespassers in the Land of Their Birth,'" 67–69.

14. Florette Henri, *Black Migration, Movement North, 1900–1920: The Road From Myth to Man* (New York: Anchor Press/Doubleday, 1976), 26–27.

15. W. E. B. Du Bois, *The Philadelphia Negro: A Social Study* (New York: Schocken Books, 1967), 147.

16. Booker T. Washington, "Is The Negro Having a Fair Chance?" November 1912, in Louis R. Harlan (ed.), *The Booker T. Washington Papers, Volume 12, 1912–1914* (Urbana: University of Illinois Press, 1982), 70; Booker T. Washington, "The Negro in the North: Are His Advantages as Great as in the South?" 28 September 1907, in Louis R. Harlan (ed.), *The Booker T. Washington Papers, Volume 9, 1906–1908* (Urbana: University of Illinois Press, 1980), 342.

17. Booker T. Washington, *Up From Slavery* (Harmondsworth: Penguin Books, 1986), 68–69.

18. Booker T. Washington, *The Future of the Negro* (1899), in Louis R. Harlan (ed.), *The Booker T. Washington Papers, Volume 5, 1899–1900* (Urbana: University of Illinois Press, 1976), 376; Booker T. Washington to the Editor of the New York *Age*, circa 7 March 1913, in Harlan, *The Booker T. Washington Papers, 12*, 137; Washington, "The Negro in the North," in Harlan, *The Booker T. Washington Papers, 9*, 344.

19. Claude McKay, *Harlem: Negro Metropolis* (New York: Harcourt, Brace Jovanovich Inc., 1968), 97–99.

20. Emmett J. Scott and Lyman Beecher Stowe, *Booker T. Washington: Builder of a Civilization* (London: T. Fisher Unwin Limited, 1916), 31–32; An Account of a Speech in New York, 21 September 1906, in Harlan, *The Booker T. Washington Papers, 9*, 73–74.

21. Booker T. Washington to the Editor of the New York *Age*, circa 7 March 1913, in Harlan, *The Booker T. Washington Papers, 12*, 137.

22. Kenneth L. Kusmer, *A Ghetto Takes Shape: Black Cleveland, 1870–1930* (Urbana: University of Illinois Press, 1976), 190.

23. Peter Gottlieb, *Making Their Own Way: Southern Blacks' Migration to Pittsburgh, 1916–1930* (Urbana: University of Illinois Press, 1987), 91; Allan H. Spear, *Black Chicago: The Making of a Negro Ghetto, 1890–1920* (Chicago: University of Chicago Press, 1967), 151.

24. Gottlieb, *Making Their Own Way*, 89, 206; James Weldon Johnson, *Black Manhattan* (New York: Arno Press and the *New York Times*, 1968), 161; Spear, *Black Chicago*, 155; Joe William Trotter, *Black Milwaukee: The Making of an Industrial Proletariat, 1915–1945* (Urbana: University of Illinois Press, 1985), 14, 47.

25. Gottlieb, *Making Their Own Way*, 104–105; Kusmer, *Black Cleveland*, 195; Richard W. Thomas, *Life For Us Is What We Make It: Building Black Community in Detroit, 1915–1945* (Bloomington: Indiana University Press, 1992), 32; James R. Grossman, *Land of Hope: Chicago, Black Southerners and the Great Migration* (Urbana: University of Chicago Press, 1989), 128–129; Spear, *Black Chicago*, 151.

26. Gottlieb, *Making Their Own Way*, 146–149; Grossman, *Land of Hope*, 210–213; Kusmer, *Black Cleveland*, 197; Spear, *Black Chicago*, 159–166; Joe William Trotter (ed.), *The Great Migration in Historical Perspective* (Bloomington: Indiana University Press, 1991), 83–105.

27. McKay, *Harlem*, 89–93; Patrick Renshaw, "The Black Ghetto, 1890–1940," *Journal of American Studies*, 8 (1974), 41–47; Spear, *Black Chicago*, 181.

28. Scott and Stowe, *Builder of a Civilization*, 32; Booker T. Washington, An Address Before the National Negro Business League, Philadelphia, 20 August 1913, and Booker T. Washington, Extracts from an Address Before the National Negro Baptist Convention, Nashville, Tennessee, 19 September 1913, both in Harlan, *The Booker T. Washington Papers, 12*, 262, 289.

29. Scott and Stowe, *Builder of a Civilization*, 32; Washington, *Up From Slavery*, 119.

30. Letter from Pittsburgh, Pa., 11 May 1917, in Emmett J. Scott, "Additional Letters of Negro Migrants of 1916–1918," *Journal of Negro History* (October, 1919), 459–460.

31. Thomas, *Life For Us Is What We Make It*, 46; Henri, *Black Migration*, 140.

32. Du Bois, *The Philadelphia Negro*, 178.

33. Osofsky, *The Making of a Ghetto*, 147–149; Thomas, *Life For Us Is What We Make It*, 112; Letter from Cleveland, Ohio, 28 August 1917, in Scott, "Additional Letters of Negro Migrants," 460–461.

34. Harlan, *The Booker T. Washington Papers*, 9, 344; Booker T. Washington, "Destitute Colored Children of the South," An Address Before the White House Conference on the Care of Dependent Children, Washington, D.C., 25 January 1909, in Louis R. Harlan (ed.), *The Booker T. Washington Papers, Volume 10, 1909–1911* (Urbana: University of Illinois Press, 1981), 18–21; Scott and Stowe, *Builder of a Civilization*, 33.

35. Gottlieb, *Making Their Own Way*, 69; Thomas, *Life For Us Is What We Make It*, 99; Du Bois, *The Philadelphia Negro*, 148; Grossman, *Land of Hope*, 130–138; Osofsky, *The Making of a Ghetto*, 137–142; Spear, *Black Chicago*, 24–25, 147–148; Trotter, *Black Milwaukee*, 24.

36. .Kusmer, *A Ghetto Takes Shape*, 221–227; Osofsky, *The Making of a Ghetto*, 8, 137–141; Du Bois, *The Philadelphia Negro*, 152; Roi Ottley, *New World A-Coming: Inside Black America* (Boston: Houghton Mifflin Company, 1943), 27–28; Thomas, *Life For Us Is What We Make It*, 102–110; Trotter, *Black Milwaukee*, 70.

37. Du Bois, *The Philadelphia Negro*, 160–161; Osofsky, *The Making of a Ghetto*, 143.

38. Trotter, *The Great Migration in Historical Perspective*, 3.

39. Washington, "The Standard Version of the Atlanta Exposition Address," in Harlan, *The Booker T. Washington Papers*, 3, 584; Kusmer, *A Ghetto Takes Shape*, 161–162, 174–175, 178–184; Spear, *Black Chicago*, 201–216; Thomas, *Life For Us Is What We Make It*, 125, 127–135.

40. Washington, *Up From Slavery*, 83; Du Bois, *The Philadelphia Negro*, 368–384; Kusmer, *A Ghetto Takes Shape*, 175–178; McKay, *Harlem*, 125; Osofsky, *The Making of a Ghetto*, 159–178; Thomas, *Life For Us Is What We Make It*, 252.

41. Ira Katznelson, *Black Men: White Cities* (London: Oxford University Press, 1973), 86–101; Spear, *Black Chicago*, 191–192.

42. Harlan, *The Booker T. Washington Papers*, 9, 344.

43. Carole Marks, *Farewell—We're Good and Gone: The Great Black Migration* (Bloomington: Indiana University Press, 1989), 173–174.

44. Gottlieb, *Making Their Own Way*, 110; Henri, *Black Migration*, ix;

Marks, *Farewell—We're Good and Gone*, 172–176; Spear, *Black Chicago*, 226–227; Thomas, *Life For Us Is What We Make It*, 108; Booker T. Washington, An Address Before the Afro-American Council, New York, 11 October 1906, in Harlan, *The Booker T. Washington Papers*, *9*, 95.

Chapter 6
The Realist and the Dreamer?
Booker T. Washington and W. E. B. Du Bois

1. Jas C. Lucky to John E. Bruce, Jersey, Channel Islands, 22 April 1910, in the John Edward Bruce Collection, Schomburg Center, Reel 1, 22 February 1856–1857 August 1924.

2. Samuel R. Spencer, *Booker T. Washington and the Negro's Place in American Life* (Boston: Little Brown, 1956), 152.

3. Elliott Rudwick, "The Niagara Movement," *Journal of Negro History*, 42 (1957), 178–180.

4. "An Open Letter to the People of Great Britain and Europe," by William Edward Burghardt Du Bois and Others, New York, 26 October 1910, in Louis R. Harlan (ed.), *The Booker T. Washington Papers, Volume 10, 1909–1911* (Urbana: University of Illinois Press, 1981), 422–425.

5. More detailed accounts of the tactics used by Washington against Du Bois and other critics of the Tuskegee philosophy can be found in August Meier, "Booker T. Washington and the Negro Press," *Journal of Negro History*, 38 (January 1953), 67–90; Rudwick, "The Niagara Movement," 181–185; Louis R. Harlan, "The Secret Life of Booker T. Washington," in Raymond W Smock (ed.), *Booker T. Washington in Perspective: Essays of Louis R. Harlan* (Jackson: University Press of Mississippi, 1988), 110–132.

6. Booker T. Washington to Richard Le Roy Stokes, Tuskegee, Alabama, 27 August 1906, in Louis R. Harlan (ed.), *The Booker T. Washington Papers, Volume 9, 1906–1908* (Urbana: University of Illinois Press, 1980), 62.

7. Oswald Garrison Villard to Booker T. Washington, New York, 26 May 1909, in Harlan, *The Booker T. Washington Papers, 10*, 116–118.

8. Booker T. Washington to Hugh Mason Browne, New York, 1 May 1909, in Harlan, *The Booker T. Washington Papers, 10*, 93; Booker T. Washington to the Editor of the Indianapolis *Star*, Tuskegee, Alabama, 15 April 1912, in Louis R. Harlan (ed.), *The Booker T. Washington Papers, 11, 1911–1912* (Urbana: University of Illinois Press, 1981), 517–518.

9. Booker T. Washington, *Up From Slavery* (Harmondsworth: Penguin Books Limited, 1986), 1–3; W. E. B. Du Bois, *Darkwater: Voices From Within the Veil* (New York: Schocken Books, 1972), 5–6.

10. Washington, *Up From Slavery*, 74–75.

11. Du Bois, *Darkwater*, 110–113, 115.

12. Francis L. Broderick, *W. E. B. Du Bois: Negro Leader in a Time of Crisis* (Stanford: Stanford University Press, 1959), 70; W. E. B. Du Bois, *Dusk of Dawn: An Essay Toward an Autobiography of a Race Concept* (London: Transaction Publishers, 1984), 78–79.

13. W. E. B. Du Bois to Dr. Horace Bumstead, Brookline Massachusetts, 7 January 1914, in the W. E. B. Du Bois Papers, Library of Congress, Microfilm Reel 4, 1025; Joel E. Spingarn to W. E. B. Du Bois, 24 October 1914, in Herbert Aptheker (ed.), *The Correspondence of W. E. B. Du Bois, Volume I, 1877–1934* (Amherst: University of Massachusetts Press, 1973), 200–202.

14. Mary White Ovington, *Black and White Sat Down Together: The Reminiscences of an NAACP Founder* (New York: The Feminist Press, 1995), 19–20.

15. Du Bois, *Dusk of Dawn*, 70.

16. Report by W. E. B. Du Bois to the United States Commission on Industrial Education, 1915, in the W. E. B. Du Bois Papers, Library of Congress, Washington, D.C., Reel 5, 210–215.

17. Report by W. E. B. Du Bois to the United States Commission on Industrial Education, 1915; W. E. B. Du Bois, "A Negro Nation Within the Nation," June 1935, in Philip S. Foner (ed.), *W. E. B. Du Bois Speaks: Volume II, Speeches and Addresses, 1920–1963* (New York: Pathfinder, 1970), 80–81.

18. W. E. B. Du Bois, *The Negro* (London: Oxford University Press, 1970), 135; W. E. B. Du Bois, *The Souls of Black Folk* (New York: Dover Publications Inc., 1994), 30–31; Du Bois, *Dusk of Dawn*, 72; W. E. B. Du Bois, "Politics and Industry," An Address to the Conference on the Status of the Negro, New York, 31 May 1909, in the W. E. B. Du Bois Papers, Library of Congress, Reel 80, 186–190.

19. Louis R. Harlan, *Booker T. Washington: The Wizard of Tuskegee, 1901–1915* (Oxford: Oxford University Press, 1983), 117, 119, 121; An Interview with Portia Marshall Washington in the Birmingham *Age Herald*, 23 November 1901, in Louis R. Harlan (ed.), *The Booker T. Washington Papers, Volume 6, 1901–1902* (Urbana: University of Illinois Press, 1977), 326.

20. Booker T. Washington to the Editor of the Indianapolis *Star*, Tuskegee, Alabama, 15 April 1912, in Harlan, *The Booker T. Washington Papers, 11*, 517–518.

21. Washington, *Up From Slavery*, 119; Alfred Young, "The Educational Philosophy of Booker T. Washington: A Perspective for Black Liberation," *Phylon*, 37 (1976), 233.

22. Booker T. Washington to Oswald Garrison Villard, Tuskegee, Alabama, 13 November 1904, in the Booker T. Washington Papers, Tuskegee University, Box 6: Theodore Roosevelt Correspondence, fl. 59, November 1904.

23. Booker T. Washington to Charles William Eliot, Tuskegee, Alabama, 20 October 1906; Booker T. Washington to Samuel Laing Williams, Tuskegee, Alabama, 18 February 1908; both in Harlan, *The Booker T. Washington Papers*, 9, 96–98, 453.

24. Booker T. Washington to Oswald Garrison Villard, Tuskegee, Alabama, 13 November 1904, in the Booker T. Washington Papers, Tuskegee University.

25. Booker T. Washington to Oswald Garrison Villard, Tuskegee, Alabama, 13 November 1904, in the Booker T. Washington Papers, Tuskegee University; Du Bois, "Politics and Industry."

26. Booker T. Washington to Oswald Garrison Villard, Tuskegee, Alabama, 13 November 1904, in the Booker T. Washington Papers, Tuskegee University.

27. W. E. B. Du Bois, *The Philadelphia Negro: A Social Study* (New York: Schocken Books, 1967), 368; Washington, *Up From Slavery*, 237.

28. David Levering Lewis, *W. E. B. Du Bois: Autobiography of a Race, 1868–1919* (New York: Henry Holt and Company, 1993), 221, 245, 297; Du Bois quoted in Broderick, *W. E. B. Du Bois*, 67.

29. W. E. B. Du Bois, "The Problem of Negro Crime," An Address to the Emancipation Celebration of the Colored Citizens of Atlanta, 1 January 1899, in The W. E. B. Du Bois Papers, Library of Congress, Reel 80.

30. W. E. B. Du Bois, "A Pageant in Seven Decades, 1878–1938," in Philip S. Foner (ed.), *W. E. B. Du Bois Speaks*, *II*, 41.

31. Du Bois, *Dusk of Dawn*, 55; W. E. B. Du Bois to Booker T. Washington, Wilberforce, 24 September 1895, in Aptheker, *Correspondence of W. E. B. Du Bois*, *I*, 39; W. E. B. Du Bois to Booker T. Washington, Atlanta, Georgia, 16 May 1900, in the W. E. B. Du Bois Papers, Library of Congress, Reels 43–44.

32. Booker T. Washington, *The Future of the Negro* (1899); Booker T. Washington to W. E. B. Du Bois, Tuskegee, Alabama, 26 October 1899; both in Louis R. Harlan (ed.), *The Booker T. Washington Papers, Volume 5, 1899–1900* (Urbana: University of Illinois Press, 1976), 245, 386; Du Bois, *Dusk of Dawn*, 78–79; Lewis, *W. E. B. Du Bois*, 297.

33. W. E. B. Du Bois, "Close Ranks," July 1918, in David Levering Lewis (ed.), *W. E. B. Du Bois: A Reader* (New York: Henry Holt and Company, 1995), 697; William Jordan, "'The Damnable Dilemma': African American Accommodation and Protest During World War I," *Journal of American History*, 81, No. 4 (March 1995), 1565. Lewis, *W. E. B. Du Bois*, 552–557, and Mark Ellis, "'Closing Ranks' and 'Seeking Honors'": W. E. B. Du Bois in World War I," *Journal of American History*, 79 (June 1992), 96–124, both view Du Bois's "Close Ranks" editorial as an attempt by Du Bois to demonstrate his patriotism, to aid his application for a commission in the U.S. Military Intelligence Branch. Even if correct, this does not alter

the fact that in 1918, Du Bois was prepared to use accommodationist tactics to further his objectives. Such an interpretation only raises questions about what those objectives actually were.

34. Asa Philip Randolph, as quoted in John White, *Black Leadership in America from Booker T. Washington to Jesse Jackson, 2nd ed.* (London: Longman, 1990), 55.

35. W. E. B. Du Bois, "The Pan African Congresses: The Story of a Growing Movement," October 1927, in Lewis, *W. E. B. Du Bois: A Reader*, 670–675; W. E. B. Du Bois to Charles Evans Hughes, U.S. Secretary of State, New York, 23 June 1921, in Robert A. Hill (ed.), *The Marcus Garvey and UNIA Papers, Volume IX: Africa for the Africans, June 1921–December 1922* (Berkeley: University of California Press, 1995), 3–6; Harlan, *The Wizard of Tuskegee*, 267–274; Louis R. Harlan, "Booker T. Washington and the White Man's Burden," in Smock, *Booker T. Washington in Perspective*, 68–97.

36. W. E. B. Du Bois, An Editorial in the *Crisis*, December 1915, in Louis R. Harlan (ed.), *The Booker T. Washington Papers, Volume 13, 1914–1915* (Urbana: University of Illinois Press, 1984), 492–493.

37. Du Bois, *Dusk of Dawn*, 74, 76–77; An Address Delivered by W. E. B. Du Bois in Boston, February 1910, in Herbert Aptheker (ed.), *Writings in Periodicals Edited by W. E. B. Du Bois: Selections from the Horizon* (New York: Kraus Thompson Organization Limited, 1985), 112; W. E. B. Du Bois to Rev. D. J. Jenkins, Charleston, South Carolina, 30 March 1905, in the W. E. B. Du Bois Papers, Library of Congress, Reel 3, 574–575.

38. Du Bois, *Dusk of Dawn*, 73; Aptheker, *Selections from the Horizon*, 112.

39. Lewis, *W. E. B. Du Bois*, 233–237.

40. Booker T. Washington to W. E. B. Du Bois, 11 March 1900, in Aptheker, *Correspondence of W. E. B. Du Bois, I*, 44.

41. Du Bois, *Dusk of Dawn*, 94.

42. Lewis, *W. E. B. Du Bois*, 235–236, 242; Du Bois, *Dusk of Dawn*, 78–79.

43. Foner, *W. E. B. Du Bois Speaks, I*, 29–30; W. E. B. Du Bois to Kelly Miller, undated letter; W. E. B. Du Bois to Miss A. P. Moore, 2 April 1907; both in the W. E. B. Du Bois Papers, Library of Congress, Reel 2, 649. For more detailed secondary accounts of the conference see Harlan, *The Wizard of Tuskegee*, 63–83, and Herbert Aptheker, "The Washington-Du Bois Conference of 1904," *Science and Society*, 13 (Fall 1949), 344–351.

44. W. E. B. Du Bois to Hugh M. Browne, Atlanta, Georgia, 10 November 1904, in the Booker T. Washington Papers, Tuskegee University, "Committee of Twelve," Box 8 fl. 22, 87; Du Bois, *Dusk of Dawn*, 81.

45. Du Bois, *Dusk of Dawn*, 86–87.

46. Booker T. Washington to Allerton D. Hitch, Tuskegee, Alabama, 28 January 1904, in Louis R. Harlan (ed.), *The Booker T. Washington*

Papers, Volume 7, 1903–1904 (Urbana: University of Illinois Press, 1977), 416–417; Booker T. Washington to the Editor of the Indianapolis *Star*, Tuskegee, Alabama, 15 April 1912, in Harlan, *The Booker T. Washington Papers, 11*, 517.

47. Booker T. Washington to Mrs Mary Clement Leavitt, Tuskegee, Alabama, 3 November 1903, in the Booker T. Washington Papers, Tuskegee University, Box 6: Theodore Roosevelt Correspondence, fl. 48, 1903.

48. Albert Bushell Hart to W.E.B. Du Bois, Cambridge, Massachusetts, 24 April 1904, in the W. E. B. Du Bois Papers, Library of Congress, Reel 2, 148.

49. Seth Low to Oswald Garrison Villard, New York, 9 April 1913, in Louis R. Harlan (ed.), *The Booker T. Washington Papers, Volume 12, 1912–1914* (Urbana: University of Illinois Press, 1982), 166–167.

50. Booker T. Washington to Oswald Garrison Villard, Tuskegee, Alabama, 13 November 1904, in the Booker T. Washington Papers, Tuskegee University, Box 6: Theodore Roosevelt Correspondence, fl. 59, November 1904.

Chapter 7
The Wizard and the Goat: Booker T. Washington,
Ralph W. Tyler, and the National Negro Business League

1. The best account of the origins and early years of the League is Louis R. Harlan, "Booker T. Washington and the National Negro Business League," in Raymond W. Smock (ed.), *Booker T. Washington in Perspective: Essays of Louis R. Harlan* (Jackson: University Press of Mississippi, 1988), 98–109.

2. Smock, *Booker T. Washington in Perspective*, 101; Charles W. Chapelle to Emmett J. Scott, 21 April 1914, Container 1059, fl. C, NNBL, 1914, in the Booker T. Washington Papers, Library of Congress.

3. Louis R. Harlan (ed.), *The Booker T. Washington Papers, Volume 6, 1901–1902* (Urbana: University of Illinois Press, 1977), fn. 338; Louis R. Harlan, *Booker T. Washington: The Wizard of Tuskegee, 1901–1915* (Oxford: Oxford University Press, 1983), 30, 327–328, 351–352.

4. Ralph W. Tyler to Booker T. Washington, 30 September, 1895, Container 530 (R400), fl. Ralph W. Tyler 1895, 1905–15, n.d.; Ralph W. Tyler to Booker T. Washington, 25 February 1905; Emmett J. Scott to Ralph W. Tyler, 5 June 1907; Ralph W. Tyler to Booker T. Washington, 3 October 1907; Container 20 (R17), fl. Ralph W. Tyler, 1905–1907; all in the Booker T. Washington Papers, Library of Congress; Harlan, *The Wizard of Tuskegee*, 324.

5. Booker T. Washington to Ralph W. Tyler, 13 May 1913, Container 530 (R400), fl. Ralph W. Tyler, 1895, 1904–15, n.d.; Ralph W. Tyler to

Booker T. Washington, 8 May 1913; Booker T. Washington to J. C. Napier, 29 April 1913, Container 1057, fl. NNBL 19133; all in the Booker T. Washington Papers, Library of Congress.

6. Booker T. Washington to Ralph W. Tyler, 12 May 1913; Booker T. Washington to Ralph W. Tyler, 14 May 1913; Ralph W. Tyler to Booker T. Washington, 17 May 1913; Ralph W. Tyler to Booker T. Washington, 7 June 1913; Container 1057, fl. NNBL 1913; Ralph W. Tyler, May–July 1913; all in the Booker T. Washington Papers, Library of Congress.

7. Ralph W. Tyler to Booker T. Washington, 19 September 1913, Container 1057, fl. NNBL 1913; Ralph W. Tyler to Booker T. Washington, 3 March 1914; Ralph W. Tyler to Emmett J. Scott, 19 March 1914, Container 1061, fl. NNBL 1914; J. E. Bush to Booker T. Washington, 30 September 1913, Container 1056, fl. NNBL 1913; all in the Booker T. Washington Papers, Library of Congress.

8. Booker T. Washington to Ralph W. Tyler, 24 September 1913, in Louis R. Harlan (ed.), *The Booker T. Washington Papers, Volume 12, 1912–1914* (Urbana: University of Illinois Press, 1982), 292–293.

9. Booker T. Washington to Ralph W. Tyler, 24 September 1913, in Harlan, *The Booker T. Washington Papers, 12*, 293.

10. Ralph W. Tyler to Emmett J. Scott, 23 June 1913; Ralph W. Tyler to Emmett J. Scott, 13 July 1913; both in Container 1057, fl. NNBL 1913, the Booker T. Washington Papers, Library of Congress.

11. Ralph W. Tyler to Emmett J. Scott, 24 November 1913; Ralph W. Tyler to Emmett J. Scott, 19 December 1913; Ralph W. Tyler to Emmett J. Scott, 25 December 1913; all in Container 1057, fl. NNBL 1913, the Booker T. Washington Papers, Library of Congress.

12. C. H. Moore to Emmett J. Scott, 22 March 1910, Box 62, fl. 365; C. H. Moore to Emmett J. Scott, 13 April 1910; C. H. Moore to J. Cochran, 20 April 1910, Box 63, fl. 369; all in the National Negro Business League Papers, Tuskegee University; Tyler as quoted in Harlan, *The Wizard of Tuskegee*, 419–420.

13. W. C. Gordan to Emmett J. Scott, 8 November 1913; T J Elliott to Emmett J. Scott, 21 November 1913; both in Container 1056, fl. NNBL 1913, the Booker T. Washington Papers, Library of Congress.

14. Perry W. Howard to Booker T. Washington, 23 December 1913, Container 1056, fl. NNBL 1913; Emmett J. Scott to Ralph W. Tyler, 1 December 1913, Container 1057, fl. NNBL 1913, both in the Booker T. Washington Papers, Library of Congress; Theodore Hemmingway, "Booker T. Washington in Mississippi, October 1908," *Journal of Mississippi History* (February 1984), 30–31.

15. Ralph W. Tyler to Booker T. Washington, 23 June 1913; Ralph W. Tyler to Emmett J. Scott, 7 July 1913; Ralph W. Tyler to Booker T. Washington, 18 October 1913; Ralph W. Tyler to Booker T. Washington, 26

October 1913; Container 1057, fl. NNBL 1913, the Booker T. Washington Papers, Library of Congress.

16. Ralph W. Tyler to Booker T. Washington, 19 June 1913; Ralph W. Tyler to Booker T. Washington, 26 October 1913; Container 1057, fl. NNBL 1913, the Booker T. Washington Papers, Library of Congress.

17. Ralph W. Tyler to Emmett J. Scott, 12 July 1913; Ralph W. Tyler to Booker T. Washington, 12 October 1913; Ralph W. Tyler to Booker T. Washington, 23 June 1913; Report of National Organizer, 12 July 1913; Container 1057, fl. NNBL 1913, the Booker T. Washington Papers, Library of Congress.

18. Fred Moore to Booker T. Washington, 26 June 1906, Box 24, fl. 206; James G. Cook to Booker T. Washington, 21 July 1906, Box 26, fl. 211; both in the Booker T. Washington Papers, Tuskegee University.

19. Smock, *Booker T. Washington in Perspective*, 101; Ralph W. Tyler to Emmett J. Scott, 13 July 1913; Tyler's Report from 25 June to 5 July 1913; Container 1057, fl. NNBL 1913; Ralph W. Tyler to Emmett J. Scott, 12 June 1914; Ralph W. Tyler to Booker T. Washington, 29 June 1914; Container 1061, fl. NNBL 1914, the Booker T. Washington Papers, Library of Congress.

20. Ralph W. Tyler to Emmett J. Scott, 19 September 1913, Container 1056, fl. NNBL 1913; Ralph W. Tyler to Emmett J. Scott, 28 July 1913, Container 1057, fl. NNBL 1913; Ralph W. Tyler to Emmett J. Scott, 15 February 1914, Container 1061, fl. NNBL, Ralph W. Tyler 1914; all in the Booker T. Washington Papers, Library of Congress.

21. Ralph W. Tyler to Emmett J. Scott, 12 June 1914, Container 1061, fl. NNBL, Ralph W. Tyler 1914, Booker T. Washington Papers, Library of Congress.

22. John H. Dickerson to Booker T. Washington, 4 April 1914, Container 1059, fl. NNBL, 1914; A. N. Johnson to Booker T. Washington, 4 May 1914, Container 1060, fl. NNBL 1914; Ralph W. Tyler to Booker T. Washington, 15 May 1914, Container 1061, fl. NNBL 1914; "A National Organizer Should Organize or . . . !" Anonymous Typed Manuscript, Container 1065, fl. NNBL 1916; the Booker T. Washington Papers, Library of Congress.

23. R. W. Thompson to Emmett J. Scott, 27 September 1914, Container 1064, fl. NNBL 1915, the Booker T. Washington Papers, Library of Congress.

24. Ralph W. Tyler to Emmett J. Scott, 29 December 1913, Container 1057, fl. NNBL 1913; Charles H. Anderson to Emmett J. Scott, 16 January 1914; Charles H. Brooks to Booker T. Washington, 6 October 1914; J. E. Bush to Booker T. Washington, 25 September 1914; Container 1058, fl. NNBL 1914, the Booker T. Washington Papers, Library of Congress.

25. Ralph W. Tyler to Booker T. Washington, 16 December 1912,

Container 94 (R86), fl. Ralph W. Tyler; Ralph W. Tyler to Emmett J. Scott, 19 September 1913; Charles H. Anderson to Emmett J. Scott, 25 September 1913; Container 1056, fl. NNBL 1914, the Booker T. Washington Papers, Library of Congress.

26. R. W. Thompson to Emmett J. Scott, 27 March 1914, Container 1061, fl. NNBL 1914, the Booker T. Washington Papers, Library of Congress.

27. Charles W. Anderson to Booker T. Washington, 13 September 1913; Charles W. Anderson to Hon. James A. Cobb, 20 September 1913; Charles W. Anderson to Booker T. Washington, 25 September 1913; Charles W. Anderson to Booker T. Washington, 26 September 1913; Charles W. Anderson to Booker T. Washington, 12 January 1914; Charles W. Anderson to Booker T. Washington, 22 January 1914; Container 26 (R22), fl. Charles W. Anderson Correspondence, the Booker T. Washington Papers, Library of Congress.

28. Booker T. Washington to Ralph W. Tyler, 17 September 1913; Booker T. Washington to Ralph W. Tyler, 28 November 1913; "List of Persons Receiving Attached Copy of Letter Relative to Tour of Hon. Ralph W. Tyler . . . Through State of Mississippi During Month of December, 1913"; Ralph W. Tyler to Booker T. Washington, 3 March 1914; Container 1061, fl. NNBL 1914, the Booker T. Washington Papers, Library of Congress.

29. Booker T. Washington to Charles W. Anderson, 6 October 1913; Booker T. Washington to Charles W. Anderson, 3 March 1914; Container 26 (R22), fl. Charles W. Anderson Correspondence; Emmett J. Scott to Charles W. Anderson, 16 January 1914, Container 7 (R16), fl. Charles W. Anderson Correspondence, the Booker T. Washington Papers, Library of Congress.

30. Booker T. Washington to Ralph W. Tyler, 29 September 1913, Container 530 (R400); Emmett J. Scott to Ralph W. Tyler, 20 February 1914; Booker T. Washington to Ralph W. Tyler, 20 February 1914; Container 1061, fl. NNBL 1914; Booker T. Washington to Charles W. Anderson, 6 October 1913, Container 26 (R22), fl. Charles W. Anderson Correspondence, the Booker T. Washington Papers, Library of Congress.

31. Ralph W. Tyler to Emmett J. Scott, 21 January 1914, Container 20 (R17), fl. Ralph W. Tyler Correspondence; Charles W. Anderson to Emmett J. Scott, 17 February 1914, Container 26 (R22), fl. Charles W. Anderson Correspondence, the Booker T. Washington Papers, Library of Congress.

32. Ralph W. Tyler to Emmett J. Scott, 4 January 1914, Container 1061, fl. NNBL 1914, the Booker T. Washington Papers, Library of Congress.

33. Ralph W. Tyler to Booker T. Washington, 29 June 1914, Container 1061, fl. NNBL 1914, the Booker T. Washington Papers, Library of Congress.

34. Emmett J. Scott to William C. Graves, 11 March 1915, Container 1063, fl. NNBL 1915, the Booker T. Washington Papers, Library of

Congress; Samuel E. Courtney to Booker T. Washington, 4 October 1906, Box 41; Charles H. Moore to Warren Logan, 17–19 August 1910, Box 69, fl. 395; both in the Booker T. Washington Papers, Tuskegee University.

35. Booker T. Washington to Charles W. Anderson, 20 February 1914, Container 1058, fl. NNBL 1914, the Booker T. Washington Papers, Library of Congress.

36. Ralph W. Tyler to Booker T. Washington, 26 August 1914, Container 1061, fl. NNBL 1914, the Booker T. Washington Papers, Library of Congress.

37. R. W. Thompson to Emmett J. Scott, 27 September 1914, Container 1064, fl. NNBL 1915, the Booker T. Washington Papers, Library of Congress.

38. Ralph W. Tyler to Emmett J. Scott, 10 October 1914, Container 20 (R17), fl. Ralph W. Tyler Correspondence, the Booker T. Washington Papers, Library of Congress.

39. Booker T. Washington to Ralph W. Tyler, 2 September 1914, Container 1061, fl. NNBL 1914, the Booker T. Washington Papers, Library of Congress.

40. Booker T. Washington to Ralph W. Tyler, 16 January 1915; Ralph W. Tyler to Booker T. Washington, 20 January 1915; Container 530 (R400), fl. Ralph W. Tyler Correspondence; Ralph W. Tyler to Emmett J. Scott, 20 January 1915, Container 20 (R17), fl. Ralph W. Tyler Correspondence, the Booker T. Washington Papers, Library of Congress.

41. Virginia Lantz Denton, *Booker T. Washington and the Adult Education Movement* (Gainesville: University Press of Florida, 1993), 121.

42. Undated Circular, Container 1054, fl. NNBL 1903–1904, the Booker T. Washington Papers, Library of Congress.

43. See, for example, Louis R. Harlan, "The Secret Life of Booker T. Washington," in Smock, *Booker T. Washington in Perspective*, 110–132.

44. Ralph W. Tyler to Booker T. Washington, 26 August 1914, Container 1061, fl. NNBL 1914, the Booker T. Washington Papers, Library of Congress.

45. Harlan, *The Booker T. Washington Papers*, 6, fn. 338.

Chapter 8
The Sorcerer and the Apprentice:
Booker T. Washington and Marcus Garvey

1. Quoted in Raymond W Smock (ed.), *Booker T. Washington in Perspective: Essays of Louis R. Harlan* (Jackson: University Press of Mississippi, 1988), 169; W.E.B. Du Bois, "Back To Africa," *Century Magazine*, 105 (February 1923), W. E. B. Du Bois, "A Lunatic or a Traitor," *Crisis* (May 1924), both reprinted in David Levering Lewis (ed.), *W. E. B. Du Bois: A Reader* (New York: Henry Holt and Company, 1995), 333, 340.

2. Marcus Garvey, "The Negro's Greatest Enemy," September 1923, in Robert A. Hill (ed.), *The Marcus Garvey and Universal Negro Improvement Association Papers, Volume I, 1826–August 1919* (Berkeley: University of California Press, 1983), 5.

3. Rupert Lewis, *Marcus Garvey: Anti-Colonial Champion* (London: Karin Press, 1987), 34, 51–53; Elton C. Fax, *Garvey: The Story of a Pioneer Black Nationalist* (New York: Dodd, Mead and Company, 1972), 46–49.

4. Report in the *Gleanor*, 23 October 1914; "Negroes Loyal Message," *The Times*, 27 October 1914; Lewis Harcourt to Sir William Henry Manning, Downing St., London, 2 November 1914; Address by Marcus Garvey, 26 August 1915; all in Hill, *The Marcus Garvey and UNIA Papers, I*, 82, 86, 89, 135.

5. Louis R. Harlan (ed.), *The Booker T. Washington Papers, Volume 13, 1914–1915* (Urbana: University of Illinois Press, 1984), 126–127, 133–134, 261, 284, 354–355, 372–373, 376. This correspondence is also given in Hill, *The Marcus Garvey and UNIA Papers, I*, 66–69, 71, 116–118, 141, 153–154, 156–157.

6. Hill, *The Marcus Garvey and UNIA Papers, I*, 166, 173–183, 185–186; Carl S. Matthews, "Documents: Marcus Garvey Writes From Jamaica on the Mulatto Escape Hatch," *Journal of Negro History*, 59 (1974), 170–176.

7. Convention Reports, New York, 21 August and 31 August 1922, in Robert A. Hill (ed.), *The Marcus Garvey and Universal Negro Improvement Association Papers, Volume IV, 1 September 1921–2 September 1922* (Berkeley: University of California Press, 1985), 939–940, fn. 942, 1036.

8. Marcus Garvey to R. R. Moton, Oakland, California, 23 October 1923; Address by Marcus Garvey, The Chapel, Tuskegee Institute, 1 November 1923; Marcus Garvey to R. R. Moton, Tuskegee, Alabama, 2 November 1923; R. R. Moton to Marcus Garvey, Tuskegee Institute, Alabama, 6 November 1923, in Robert A. Hill (ed.), *The Marcus Garvey and Universal Negro Improvement Association Papers, Volume V, 1 September 1922–August 1924* (Berkeley: University of California Press, 1986), 484, 490–497; Amy Jacques Garvey, *Garvey and Garveyism* (London: Collier Macmillan, 1970), 130–131.

9. Robert A. Hill (ed.), *The Marcus Garvey and Universal Negro Improvement Association Papers, Volume II, 27 August 1919–31 August 1920* (Berkeley: University of California Press, 1983), fn. 15, 133.

10. Editorials by Marcus Garvey, the *Black Man*, London, June 1935, in Robert A. Hill (ed.), *The Marcus Garvey and Universal Negro Improvement Association Papers, Volume VII, November 1927–August 1940* (Berkeley: University of California Press, 1990), 625.

11. R. R. Moton to Marcus Garvey, Tuskegee Institute, Alabama, 30 November 1921, in Hill, *The Marcus Garvey and UNIA Papers, IV*, fn. 2, 162, 228–229.

12. Report of Angus Fletcher, British Library of Information, on his

American Tour, 12 June 1923, in Hill, *The Marcus Garvey and UNIA Papers, V*, 321–322.

13. Speech by Marcus Garvey, Philadelphia, 13 November 1921, in Hill, *The Marcus Garvey and UNIA Papers, IV*, 183; Interview with Frederick Moore by Charles Mowbray White, New York, 23 August 1920, in Hill, *The Marcus Garvey and UNIA Papers, IV*, 622–623.

14. Opening Convention Speech by Marcus Garvey, New York, 1 August 1921, in Robert A. Hill (ed.), *The Marcus Garvey and Universal Negro Improvement Association Papers, Volume IX: Africa For The Africans, June 1921–December 1922* (Berkeley: University of California Press, 1995), 133; Editorial Letter by Marcus Garvey, New York, 17 October 1922, in Hill, *The Marcus Garvey and UNIA Papers, V*, 51–54.

15. Florent de Selys-Fanson, Change d' Affaires, to Henri Jasper, Belgian Embassy, Washington, D.C., 27 October 1922, in Hill, *The Marcus Garvey and UNIA Papers, V*, 56–57; Report by Charles Hallaert, Belgian Vice Consul, New York City, 16 August 1922, in Hill, *The Marcus Garvey and UNIA Papers, IX*, 59.

16. Emmett J. Scott to Marcus Garvey, Tuskegee Institute, Alabama, 2 March 1916, in Hill, *The Marcus Garvey and UNIA Papers, I*, 185–186; Tony Martin, *Race First: The Ideological and Organizational Struggles of Marcus Garvey and the UNIA* (Westport: Greenwood Press, 1976), 282.

17. Emmett J. Scott, Memorandum for the Military Intelligence Division, Washington, D.C., 11 December 1918, in Hill, *The Marcus Garvey and UNIA Papers, I*, 322.

18. See, for example, E David Cronon, *Black Moses: The Story of Marcus Garvey and the UNIA* (Madison: University of Wisconsin Press, 1969), 69–70.

19. Emmett J. Scott to W. E. Mullinson, Washington, D.C., 12 September 1922, in Hill, *The Marcus Garvey and UNIA Papers, V*, 12.

20. Interview with Frederick Moore by Charles Mowbray White, New York, 23 August 1920, in Hill, *The Marcus Garvey and UNIA Papers, II*, 622–624.

21. Hill, *The Marcus Garvey and UNIA Papers, VII*, 975–975; Martin, *Race First*, 93.

22. Marcus Garvey to Frederick Fortune, London 25 July 1928, in Hill, *The Marcus Garvey and UNIA Papers, VII*, 211–212.

23. Marcus Garvey to Earnest S. Cox, Box 1733, Atlanta, Georgia, 27 August 1925; Marcus Garvey to Freda Toote, Atlanta Georgia, 26 October 1926, in Robert A. Hill (ed.), *The Marcus Garvey and Universal Negro Improvement Association Papers, Volume VI, September 1924–December 1927* (Berkeley: University of California Press, 1989), 229, 461.

24. Marcus Garvey to Norton G. Thomas, Atlanta, Georgia, circa 9 December 1926, in Hill, *The Marcus Garvey and UNIA Papers, VI*, 283.

25. Hill, *The Marcus Garvey and UNIA Papers, II*, fn. 3, 258–259.

26. Marcus Garvey, "The Negro's Greatest Enemy," in Hill, *The Marcus Garvey and UNIA Papers, I*, 3–4.

27. Editorials by Marcus Garvey, the *Black Man*, London, June 1935, in Hill, *The Marcus Garvey and UNIA Papers, VII*, 625.

28. Marcus Garvey to Earnest S. Cox, Box 1733, Atlanta, Georgia, 27 August 1925, in Hill, *The Marcus Garvey and UNIA Papers, VI*, 229.

29. Judith Stein, *The World of Marcus Garvey: Race and Class in Modern Society* (Baton Rouge: Louisiana State University Press, 1986), 166, 171–174.

30. Quoted in Martin, *Race First*, 33.

31. Quoted in Martin, *Race First*, 32; An Article in the New York *World*, 18 August 1922, in Hill, *The Marcus Garvey and UNIA Papers, IV*, 918.

32. Speech by Marcus Garvey, Liberty Hall, New York, 11 February 1921, in Hill, *The Marcus Garvey and UNIA Papers, III*, 181.

33. Arthur L. Tolson, "Booker T. Washington's Philosophy and Oklahoma's African American Towns," in Tunde Adeleke (ed.), *Booker T. Washington: Interpretative Essays* (Lampeter: The Edwin Mellen Press Limited, 1998), 21–33; Norman L. Crockett, "Witness to History: Booker T. Washington Visits Boley," *The Chronicles of Oklahoma*, 67 (Winter 1989–1990), 382–391.

34. Booker T. Washington, *Up From Slavery* (Harmondsworth: Penguin Books Limited, 1986), 68–69.

35. Booker T. Washington, *The Future of the Negro* (1899), in Louis R. Harlan (ed.), *The Booker T. Washington Papers, Volume 5, 1899–1900* (Urbana: University of Illinois Press, 1976), 332, 366–367.

36. Elton G. Fax, *Garvey: The Story of a Pioneer Black Nationalist* (New York: Dodd, Mead and Company, 1972), 18–20; Newspaper Report, 16 October 1914, in Hill, *The Marcus Garvey and UNIA Papers, I*, 79–80.

37. Report of UNIA Meeting, New York, 7 November 1920, in Hill, *The Marcus Garvey and UNIA Papers, III*, 75.

38. Jonathan Earle (ed.), *The Routledge Atlas of African American History* (London: Routledge, 2000), 104; Martin, *Race First*, 15; Judith Stein, *The World of Marcus Garvey: Race and Class in Modern Society* (Baton Rouge: Louisiana State University Press, 1986), 154–155.

39. Washington, *Up From Slavery*, 79.

40. Stein, *The World of Marcus Garvey*, 153–160; Theodore Vincent, *Black Power and the Garvey Movement* (Berkeley: The Ramparts Press, 1971), 168.

41. Booker T. Washington, "Christianizing Africa," an Article in *Our Day*, December 1896, in Harlan, *The Booker T. Washington Papers, 4*, 251–252; Booker T. Washington to the Editor of the Washington *Colored American*, London, England, 20 July 1899, in Harlan, *The Booker T. Washington Papers, 5*, 164–166; Booker T. Washington, "Cruelty in the Congo

Country," an Article in *Outlook*, 8 October 1904, in Harlan, *The Booker T. Washington Papers, 8*, 85–90; Louis R. Harlan, "Booker T. Washington and the White Man's Burden," in Raymond W. Smock (ed.), *Booker T. Washington in Perspective: Essays of Louis R. Harlan* (Jackson: University Press of Mississippi, 1988), 69–73; Michael West, "The Tuskegee Model of Development in Africa: Another Dimension of the African/African-American Connection," *Diplomatic History*, 16 (Summer 1992), 374.

42. West, "The Tuskegee Model of Development in Africa," 375–376.

43. Booker T. Washington, *The Story of My Life and Work* (1900), in Harlan, *The Booker T. Washington Papers, 1*, 149.

44. Booker T. Washington to Joseph Booth, Tuskegee Institute, Alabama, 13 November 1913, in Harlan, *The Booker T. Washington Papers, 12*, 330–331.

45. Manning Marable, "Booker T. Washington and African Nationalism," *Phylon*, 35 (December 1974), 400–401; West, "The Tuskegee Model of Development in Africa," 377–379.

46. Marable, "Booker T. Washington and African Nationalism," 403–404; West, "The Tuskegee Model of Development in Africa," 374.

47. Speech by Marcus Garvey, New York 7 September 1921, in Hill, *The Marcus Garvey and UNIA Papers, IV*, 36–37.

48. Editorial in the *Negro World*, 6 February 1926, quoted in Rupert Lewis, *Marcus Garvey: Anti-Colonial Champion* (London: Karin Press, 1987), 71–72; Theodore Vincent, *Black Power and the Garvey Movement*, 16.

49. Marcus Garvey, an Article in the Jamaica *Times*; First UNIA Report, 21 August 1915; both in Hill, *The Marcus Garvey and UNIA Papers, I*, 104, 129; Conference Reports, New York, 31 August 1922, in Hill, *The Marcus Garvey and UNIA Papers, IV*, 1036; Amy Jacques Garvey, *Garvey and Garveyism* (London: Collier Macmillan, 1970), 13.

50. Reports by Special Agent P-138, New York City, 19 and 21 August 1920, in Hill, *The Marcus Garvey and UNIA Papers, II*, 607–608, 612.

51. NAACP Press Release, August 10 1923, in The NAACP Papers (UPA Microfilm), Library of Congress, Washington, D.C., Part II, Series A, Reel 35, 832.

52. Lewis, *Marcus Garvey: Anti-Colonial Champion*, 78–80.

53. Vincent, *Black Power and the Garvey Movement*, 18.

Chapter 9
Booker T. Washington and African-American Autobiography

1. Louis R. Harlan (ed.), *The Booker T. Washington Papers, Volume 1, The Autobiographical Writings* (Urbana: University of Illinois Press, 1972), xxviii, xxx.

2. Edward Elder Cooper to Booker T. Washington, Washington, D.C., 7 November 1901; Charles W. Anderson to Booker T. Washington, New

York, 7 April 1902; both in Louis R. Harlan (ed.), *The Booker T. Washington Papers, Volume 6, 1901–1902* (Urbana: University of Illinois Press, 1977), 295–296, 438–439.

3. Emily Howland to Booker T. Washington, Sherwood, New York, 27 January 1901; Walter Hines Page to Booker T. Washington, New York, 19 March 1902; both in Harlan, *The Booker T. Washington Papers, 6*, fn. 202, 419–420.

4. George Eastman to Booker T. Washington, Rochester, New York, 2 January 1902, in Harlan, *The Booker T. Washington Papers, 6*, 370; David Page Morehouse to Booker T. Washington, Oswego, New York, 26 December 1913; P. C. Jackson to Booker T. Washington, Lometa, Texas, circa 15 December 1913; both in Louis R. Harlan (ed.), *The Booker T. Washington Papers, Volume 12, 1912–1914* (Urbana: University of Illinois Press, 1982), 372, 382–383.

5. Grace W. Minns to Booker T. Washington, 24 May 1901, in Harlan, *The Booker T. Washington Papers, 6*, 123–125; W. A. Johnson to Booker T. Washington, New York, 16 November 1904, in Louis R. Harlan (ed.), *The Booker T. Washington Papers, Volume 8, 1904–1906* (Urbana: University of Illinois Press, 1979), 134–135; Mahadev Hari Modak to Booker T. Washington, Bombay-Khandala, India, 9 May 1913, in Harlan, *The Booker T. Washington Papers, 12*, 178–179; Emmett J. Scott to Edwin L. Baker, Tuskegee, Alabama, 18 October 1915, in Louis R. Harlan (ed.), *The Booker T. Washington Papers, Volume 13, 1914–1915* (Urbana: University of Illinois Press, 1984), 401.

5. Estelle du Bois-Raymond to Booker T. Washington, Berlin, SW, 12 April 1902, in Harlan, *The Booker T. Washington Papers, 6*, 443.

7. Robert Elliott Speer to Booker T. Washington, New York, 19 September 1902; Heinrich Albert Wilhelm, Prince of Prussia, to Booker T. Washington, Dormstadt, 4 April 1902; both in Harlan, *The Booker T. Washington Papers, 6*, 433, 524–525; Booker T. Washington to the Archbishop of Canterbury, Tuskegee, Alabama, 27 October 1904, in Harlan, *The Booker T. Washington Papers, 8*, 118.

8. Harlan, *The Booker T. Washington Papers, 1*, xxxv; Emmett J. Scott to J. S. Johnson, Tuskegee, Alabama, 22 October 1914; Harry Centennial Oppenheimer to Emmett J. Scott, New York, 1 October 1915; Emmett J. Scott to Edwin L. Barker, Tuskegee, Alabama, 18 October 1915; Emmett J. Scott to Harry Centennial Oppenheimer, Tuskegee, Alabama, 23 October 1915; all in Harlan, *The Booker T. Washington Papers, 13*, 147–148, 374–375, 401–402, 408–409; Robert A. Hill (ed.), *The Marcus Garvey and Universal Negro Improvement Association Papers, Volume V, September 1922–August 1924* (Berkeley: University of California Press, 1986), fn. 761.

9. Introduction by Louis R. Harlan, in Booker T. Washington, *Up From Slavery* (Harmondsworth: Penguin Books Limited, 1986), xliii.

10. Emily Howland to Booker T. Washington, Sherwood, New York, 27 January 1901, in Harlan, *The Booker T. Washington Papers, 6*, 20–21.

11. Mary Fletcher Mackie to Booker T. Washington, Newburgh, New York, 21 November 1900, in Louis R. Harlan (ed.), *The Booker T. Washington Papers, Volume 5, 1899–1900* (Urbana: University of Illinois Press, 1976), 675; Robert Elliott Speer to Booker T. Washington, New York, 19 September, 1902, in Harlan, *The Booker T. Washington Papers, 6*, 524–625.

12. Harlan, *The Booker T. Washington Papers, 1*, xxxviii.

13. Harlan, *The Booker T. Washington Papers, 1*, xvi–xvii, xx; Donald B. Gibson, "Strategies and Revisions of Self-Representation in Booker T. Washington's Autobiographies," *American Quarterly*, 45 (September 1993), 377; Booker T. Washington to J. L. Nichols and Company, Tuskegee, Alabama, 26 April 1901, in Harlan, *The Booker T. Washington Papers, 6*, 95–97.

14. Charlotte D. Fitzgerald, "*The Story of My Life and Work*: Booker T. Washington's Other Autobiography," *The Black Scholar*, 21, No. 4 (1991), 38–39.

15. Booker T. Washington to Robert Heberton Terrell, Tuskegee, Alabama, 4 April 1911, in Louis R. Harlan (ed.), *The Booker T. Washington Papers, Volume 11, 1911–1912* (Urbana: University of Illinois Press, 1981), 78.

16. Harlan, *The Booker T. Washington Papers, 1*, xxv.

17. Introduction by St Clair Drake, in Booker T. Washington and Robert E. Park, *The Man Farthest Down* (New Brunswick: Transaction Publishers, Inc., 1984), xviii–xix; Robert Ezra Park to Booker T. Washington, Tuskegee Institute, Alabama, 25 February 1905, in Harlan, *The Booker T. Washington Papers, 8*, fn. 203; Fred H. Matthews, "Robert Park, Congo Reform and Tuskegee: The Molding of a Race Relations Expert, 1905–1913," *Canadian Journal of History*, 8 (March 1973), 37–65.

18. Harlan, *The Booker T. Washington Papers, 1*, xvii; Fitzgerald, "*The Story of My Life and Work*," 35.

19. Fitzgerald, "*The Story of My Life and Work*," 35; Harlan, *The Booker T. Washington Papers, 1*, xvii–xviii.

20. Timothy Thomas Fortune to Booker T. Washington, New York, 1 June 1900, in Harlan, *The Booker T. Washington Papers, 5*, 549; Harlan, *The Booker T. Washington Papers, 1*, xviii–xix.

21. Edgar Webber to Margaret James Murray Washington, Guthrie, O.T., 26 November 1901, in Harlan, *The Booker T. Washington Papers, 6*, 329–330.

22. In any event *The Story of My Life and Work* outsold *Up From Slavery* for some years, due to the aggressive marketing techniques of Nichols and Co. Harlan, *The Booker T. Washington Papers, 1*, xxxiv.

23. Harlan, *The Booker T. Washington Papers, 1*, xx, xxiii, xxxiv; Booker T. Washington to J. L. Nichols and Company, Tuskegee, Alabama, 14 May 1901, in Harlan, *The Booker T. Washington Papers, 6*, 109–110.

24. Booker T. Washington to Lyman Abbott, Tuskegee, Alabama, circa 8 October 1900, in Harlan, *The Booker T. Washington Papers, 5*, 653–654.

25. Harlan, *The Booker T. Washington Papers, 1*, xxxi–xxxii.

26. James M. Cox, "Autobiography and Washington," *Sewanee Review* (Spring 1977), 249, 260–261; Booker T. Washington to Lyman Abbott, Tuskegee, Alabama, circa 8 October 1900, in Harlan, *The Booker T. Washington Papers, 5*, 653.

27. Harlan, *The Booker T. Washington Papers, 1*, xxvi; Introduction by Louis R. Harlan, in Washington, *Up From Slavery*, xxii–xxiii.

28. Gibson, "Strategies and Revisions of Self-Representation," 381–384.

29. Washington, *The Story of My Life and Work*, in Harlan, *The Booker T. Washington Papers, 1*, 12.

30. Washington, *The Story of My Life and Work*, and *Up From Slavery*, in Harlan, *The Booker T. Washington Papers, 1*, 10, 216.

31. Harlan, *The Booker T. Washington Papers, 1*, 221–223.

32. Fitzgerald, "*The Story of My Life and Work*," 39.

33. Harlan, *The Booker T. Washington Papers, 1*, 25–26, 260–264.

34. Washington, *Up From Slavery*, 81–82, 128.

35. Asa Leland Duncan to Booker T. Washington, Missoula, Montana, 23 July 1913; Booker T. Washington to Asa Leland Duncan, Tuskegee, Alabama, 15 August 1913; John Henry Washington to Asa Leland Duncan, Tuskegee, Alabama, 20 August 1913, all in Harlan, *The Booker T. Washington Papers, 12*, 240–242, 253, 265–269.

36. Mary Fletcher Mackie to Booker T. Washington, Newburgh, New York, 21 November 1900, in Harlan *The Booker T. Washington Papers, 5*, 675–677.

37. Washington, *Up From Slavery*, 267–268.

38. Washington, *Up From Slavery*, 146–147.

39. Washington, *Up From Slavery*, 198–199.

40. Washington, *Up From Slavery*, 264–265, 268–269.

41. Max Bennett Thrasher to Booker T. Washington, New York, 9 January 1900; Lyman Abbott to Booker T. Washington, New York, 1 October 1900, both in Harlan, *The Booker T. Washington Papers, 5*, 409, 646.

42. Emmett J. Scott and Lyman Beecher Stowe, *Booker T. Washington: Builder of a Civilization* (London: T. Fisher Unwin Limited, 1916), 279–280; Maria A. Benson to Booker T. Washington, Nashville, Tennessee, 20 May 1890, in Louis R. Harlan (ed.), *The Booker T. Washington Papers, Volume 3, 1889–1895* (Urbana: University of Illinois Press, 1974), 58.

43. Horace Bumstead to Booker T. Washington, Brookline, Massachusetts, 10 April 1907, in Louis R. Harlan (ed.), *The Booker T. Washington Papers, 9, 1906–1908* (Urbana: University of Illinois Press, 1980), 257–261; Louis R. Harlan, *Booker T. Washington: The Wizard of Tuskegee, 1901–1915* (Oxford: Oxford University Press, 1983), 320–321.

44. Harlan, *The Wizard of Tuskegee*, 107–108.

45. Washington, *Up From Slavery*, 263, 266, 269–270.

46. James Olney, "The Founding Fathers—Frederick Douglass and Booker T. Washington: or, The Idea of Democracy and a Tradition of Afro-American Autobiography," *Amerikastudien*, 35 (1990), 281.

47. Olney, "The Founding Fathers," 282–283; Gibson, "Strategies and Revisions of Self-Representation," 380.

48. Washington, *Up From Slavery*, 99–100, 284, 288.

49. Frederick Douglass, *Narrative of the Life of Frederick Douglass: An American Slave* (Harmondsworth: Penguin Books Limited, 1986), 47, Washington, *Up From Slavery*, 1; Harriet Beecher Stowe, *Uncle Tom's Cabin, or, Life Among the Lowly* (Harmondsworth: Penguin Books Limited, 1986), 355–356.

50. William L. Andrews (ed.), *Critical Essays on Frederick Douglass* (Boston: G. K. Hall and Company, 1991), 2; David B. Chesebrough, *Frederick Douglass: Oratory From Slavery* (Westport: Greenwood Press, 1998), 74–75.

51. Gibson, "Strategies and Revisions of Self-Representation," 387–388.

52. Alex Haley and Malcolm X, *The Autobiography of Malcolm X* (Harmondsworth: Penguin Books Limited, 1968), 84; Washington, *Up From Slavery*, 1.

53. Washington, *Up From Slavery*, 267–319.

54. Haley and Malcolm X, *The Autobiography of Malcolm X*, 457, 464–476.

55. Washington, *Up From Slavery*, 74–75.

56. Haley and Malcolm X, *The Autobiography of Malcolm X*, 305.

57. Haley and Malcolm X, *The Autobiography of Malcolm X*, 266–268; Washington, *Up From Slavery*, 314.

58. Haley and Malcolm X, *The Autobiography of Malcolm X*, 118, 206–207.

59. Harold Cruse, *Rebellion or Revolution?* (New York: William Morrow, 1968), 201–202, 211.

Chapter 10
Booker T. Washington and African-American History:
A Historiographical Perspective

1. Louis R. Harlan, "Twenty Years With Booker T. Washington," in Genna Rae McNeil and Michael R. Winston (eds.), *Historical Judgments Reconsidered: Selected Howard University Lectures in Honor of Rayford W. Logan* (Washington, D.C.: Howard University Press, 1988), 133.

2. Virginia Lantz Denton, *Booker T. Washington and the Adult Education Movement* (Gainesville: University Press of Florida, 1993), 165.

Bibliography

Unpublished Sources

The John Edward Bruce Collection, The Schomburg Center, Harlem, New York City.

The Booker T. Washington Papers, The Schomburg Center, Harlem, New York City.

The Booker T. Washington Papers, Tuskegee University, Tuskegee, Alabama.

The W.E.B. Du Bois Papers (Microfilm), Library of Congress, Washington, D.C.

The NAACP Papers, Library of Congress, Washington, D.C.

The Booker T. Washington Papers, Library of Congress, Washington, D.C.

Published Sources

Abromovitz, Jack. "The Emergence of Booker T. Washington as a National Negro Leader," *Social Education*, XXXII (May 1968), 445–451.

———. "The Negro in the Populist Movement," *Journal of Negro History*, 38 (July 1953), 257–289.

Adeleke, Tunde, ed. *Booker T. Washington: Interpretative Essays*. Lampeter: The Edwin Mellen Press Limited, 1998.

Anderson, James D. *The Education of Blacks in the South, 1860–1935*. Chapel Hill: University of North Carolina Press, 1988.

Andrews, William L., ed. *Critical Essays on Frederick Douglass*. Boston: G. K. Hall and Company, 1991.

———. *The Oxford Frederick Douglass Reader*. Oxford: Oxford University Press, 1996.

Aptheker, Herbert. "The Washington-Du Bois Conference of 1904," *Science and Society*, 13 (Fall 1949), 344–351.

— — —, ed. *The Correspondence of W. E. B. Du Bois*, Three Volumes. Amherst: University of Massachusetts Press, 1973–1978.

— — —. *The Negro in the South: Booker T. Washington and W. E. B. Du Bois*. New York: Carol Publishing Group, 1970.

— — —. *W. E. B. Du Bois, Against Racism: Unpublished Essays, Papers, Addresses, 1887–1961*. Amherst: University of Massachusetts Press, 1985.

— — —. *Writings in Periodicals Edited by W. E. B. Du Bois: Selections from The Horizon*. New York: Kraus-Thomson Organization Limited, 1985.

Berman, Edward H. "Tuskegee In Africa," *Journal of Negro Education*, 41 (Spring 1972), 99–112.

Bethel, Elizabeth Raul. *Promiseland: A Century of Life in a Negro Community*. Philadelphia: Temple University Press, 1981.

Blassingame, John W. and John R. McKivigen, eds. *The Frederick Douglass Papers, Series One: Speeches, Debates and Interviews*, 5 Volumes. New Haven: Yale University Press, 1979–1992.

— — —. *The Frederick Douglass Papers, Series Two: Autobiographical Writings, Volume 1: Narrative*. New Haven: Yale University Press, 1999.

Bleser, Carol. *The Promised Land: The History of the South Carolina Land Commission, 1869–1890*. Columbia: University of South Carolina Press, 1969.

Blumenthal, Henry. "Woodrow Wilson and the Race Question," *Journal of Negro History*, XLVIII (January 1963), 1–21.

Bodnor, John, Roger Simon, and Michael P. Weber. *Lives of Their Own: Blacks, Italians, and Poles in Pittsburgh, 1900–1960*. Chicago: University of Illinois Press, 1982.

Bogle, Donald. *Toms, Coons, Mulattoes, Mammies and Bucks: An Interpretative History of Blacks in American Films*. New York: Continuum, 1990.

Brisbane, Robert Hughes. "Some New Light on the Garvey Movement," *Journal of Negro History*, 36 (1951), 53–62.

Broderick, Francis L. *W. E. B. Du Bois: Negro Leader in a Time of Crisis*. Stanford: Stanford University Press, 1959.

Bruce, Dickson D. "Booker T. Washington's *The Man Farthest Down* and the Transformation of Race," *Mississippi Quarterly*, 48 (Spring 1995), 239–253.

Bullock, Henry A. *A History of Negro Education in the South: From 1619 to the Present*. New York: Praeger, 1967.

Burkett, Randall K. *Garveyism as a Religious Movement: The*

Institutionalization of a Black Civil Religion. London: The Scarecrow Press, Inc., 1978.

— — —, ed. *Black Redemption: Churchmen Speak for the Garvey Movement.* Philadelphia: Temple University Press, 1978.

Butchart, Ronald E. *Northern Schools, Southern Blacks and Reconstruction: Freedmen's Education, 1862–1875.* Westport: Greenwood Press, 1980.

Calista, Donald J. "Booker T. Washington: Another Look," *Journal of Negro History,* 49 (1964), 240–255.

Cantrell, Gregg, and D. Scott Barton. "Texas Populists and the Failure of Biracial Politics." *Journal of Southern History,* LV, No. 4 (November 1989), 659–692.

Capeci, Dominic J., and Jack C. Knight. "Reckoning With Violence: W. E. B. Du Bois and the 1906 Atlanta Race Riot," *Journal of Southern History,* LXII, No. 4 (November 1996), 727–766.

Cell, John. *The Highest Stages of White Supremacy: The Origins of Segregation in South Africa and the American South.* Cambridge: Cambridge University Press, 1982.

Chafe, William M. "The Negro and Populism: A Kansas Case Study," *Journal of Southern History,* 34 (August 1968), 402–419.

Chaffee, Mary Law. "William E. B. DuBois' Concept of the Racial Problem in the United States." *Journal of Negro History,* 41 (1956), 241–258.

Chesebrough, David B. *Frederick Douglass: Oratory from Slavery.* Westport: Greenwood Press, 1998.

Clarke, John H., ed. *Malcolm X: The Man and His Times.* New York: African World Press, 1990.

— — —. *Marcus Garvey and the Vision of Africa.* New York: Random House, 1974.

Cohen, William. "Negro Involuntary Servitude in the South, 1865–1940: A Preliminary Analysis," *Journal of Southern History,* XLII (February 1976), 31–60.

Cone, James H. *Martin and Malcolm and America: A Dream or a Nightmare.* New York: Orbis Books, 1996.

Contee, Clarence G. "Du Bois, The NAACP and the Pan-African Congress of 1919," *Journal of Negro History,* 57 (1972), 13–28.

— — —. "The Emergence of Du Bois as an African Nationalist," *Journal of Negro History,* 54 (1969), 48–63.

Cook, Mercer. "Booker T. Washington and the French," *Journal of Negro History,* XL (October 1955), 318–340.

Cooper, Arnold. "Booker T. Washington and William J. Edwards of Snow Hill Institute, 1893–1915," *The Alabama Review,* 40 (April 1987), 111–132.

— — —. "The Tuskegee Machine in Action: Booker T. Washington's

Influence on Utica Institute, 1903–1915." *Journal of Mississippi History*, 48 (November 1986), 283–295.

Cox, James M. "Autobiography and Washington," *Sewanee Review* (Spring 1977), 235–261.

Cox, Oliver C. "The Leadership of Booker T. Washington," *Social Forces*, XXX (October 1951), 91–97.

Crockett, Norman L. "Witness to History: Booker T. Washington Visits Boley," *The Chronicles of Oklahoma*, 67 (Winter 1989–1990), 382–391.

Crofts, Daniel W. "The Warner-Foraker Amendment to the Hepburn Bill: Friend or Foe of Jim Crow?" *Journal of Southern History*, 39 (August 1973), 341–358.

Cronon, E. David. *Black Moses: The Story of Marcus Garvey and the Universal Negro Improvement Association.* Madison: University of Wisconsin Press, 1969.

– – –, ed. *Great Lives Observed: Marcus Garvey.* Englewood Cliffs: Prentice-Hall, Inc., 1973.

Croushore, John H., and David M. Potter, eds. *John William De Forest: A Union Army Officer in the Reconstruction.* New Haven: Yale University Press, 1948.

Cruse, Harold. *The Crisis of the Negro Intellectual.* New York: William Morrow, 1984.

– – –. *Rebellion or Revolution?* New York: William Morrow, 1968.

Cummings, Melbourne. "Historical Setting for Booker T. Washington and the Rhetoric of Compromise, 1895." *Journal of Black Studies*, 8, No. 1 (September 1977), 75–82.

Daniel, Peter. *The Shadow of Slavery: Peonage in the South, 1901–1909.* Urbana: University of Illinois Press, 1990.

DeCanio, Stephen J. *Agriculture in the Postbellum South: The Economics of Production and Supply.* Cambridge, Massachusetts: MIT Press, 1974.

DeCaro, L. A. *On the Side of My People: A Religious Life of Malcolm X.* New York: New York University Press, 1996.

Dennis, Rutledge M., ed. *Research in Race and Ethnic Relations. W. E. B. Du Bois: The Scholar as Activist.* London: JAI Press Inc., 1996.

Denton, Virginia Lantz. *Booker T. Washington and the Adult Education Movement.* Gainesville: University Press of Florida, 1993.

Dixon, Thomas. *The Clansman: An Historical Romance of the Ku Klux Klan.* Lexington: University of Kentucky Press, 1970.

Douglass, Frederick. *Autobiographies.* New York: The Library of America, 1994.

Du Bois, W. E. B. *An ABC of Color.* New York: International Publishers, 1989.

———. *The Autobiography of W. E. B. Du Bois: A Soliloquy on Viewing My Life from the Last Decade of Its First Century*. USA: New World Paperbacks, 1979.

———. *Black Reconstruction in America: An Essay Toward a History of the Part Which Black Folk Played in the Attempt to Reconstruct Democracy in America, 1860–1880*. New York: Atheneum, 1971.

———. *Darkwater: Voices From Within the Veil*. New York: Schocken Books, 1972.

———. *Dusk of Dawn: An Essay Toward an Autobiography of a Race Concept*. London: Transaction Publishers, 1984.

———. *The Negro*. London: Oxford University Press, 1970.

———. *The Philadelphia Negro: A Social Study*. New York: Schocken Books, 1967.

———. *The Souls of Black Folk*. New York: Dover Publications Inc., 1994.

Dunn, Frederick. "The Educational Philosophies of Washington, Du Bois, and Houston: Laying the Foundations for Afrocentrism and Multiculturalism." *Journal of Negro Education*, 62 (Winter 1993), 24–34.

Dunning, William A. *Reconstruction, Political and Economic*. New York: Harper & Row, 1906.

Dyer, Thomas G. *Theodore Roosevelt and the Idea of Race*. Baton Rouge: Louisiana State University Press, 1980.

Dyson, Michael E. *Making Malcolm: The Myth and Meaning of Malcolm X*. Oxford: Oxford University Press, 1995.

Earle, Jonathan. *The Routledge Atlas of African American History*. London: Routledge, 2000.

Edwards, Adolph. *Marcus Garvey, 1887–1940*. London: New Beacon Books, 1967.

Eisenstadt, Peter, ed. *Black Conservatism: Essays in Intellectual and Political History*. New York: Garland Publishing, Inc., 1999.

Elder, Arlene A. "Chesnutt on Washington: An Essential Ambivalence," *Phylon*, XXXVIII, No. 1 (Spring 1977), 1–8.

Ellis, Mark. "'Closing Ranks' and 'Seeking Honors': W. E. B. Du Bois in World War I," *Journal of American History*, 79 (June 1992), 96–124.

———. "W. E. B. Du Bois and the Formation of Black Opinion in World War I: A Commentary on 'The Damnable Dilemma,'" *Journal of American History*, 81, No. 4 (March 1995), 1584–1590.

Ellison, Mary. *The Black Experience: American Blacks Since 1865*. London: B. T. Batsford Limited, 1974.

Enck, Henry S. "Black Self-Help in the Progressive Era: The 'Northern Campaigns' of Smaller Southern Black Industrial Schools, 1900–1915," *Journal of Negro History* (January 1976), 73–87.

———. "Tuskegee Institute and Northern White Philanthropy: A Case

Study in Fund Raising, 1900–1915," *Journal of Negro History*, 65 (Fall 1980), 336–348.

Escott, Paul D., David R. Goldfield, Sally McMillen, and Elizabeth Hayes Turner. *Major Problems in the History of the American South, Volume II: The New South, 2nd ed.* Boston: Houghton Mifflin, 1999.

Essien–Udom, E. U., and Amy Jacques Garvey, eds. *More Philosophy and Opinions of Marcus Garvey.* London: Frank Cass, 1977.

Fax, Elton G. *Garvey: The Story of a Pioneer Black Nationalist.* New York: Dodd, Mead and Company, 1972.

Ferguson, Karen J. "Caught in 'No Man's Land': The Negro Cooperative Demonstration Service and the Ideology of Booker T. Washington, 1900–1918," *Agricultural History*, 72, No. 1 (Winter 1998), 33–54.

Fitzgerald, Charlotte D. "*The Story of My Life and Work*: Booker T. Washington's Other Autobiography," *The Black Scholar*, 21, No. 4 (1991), 35–40.

Flynn, John P. "Booker T. Washington: Uncle Tom or Wooden Horse?" *Journal of Negro History*, 54 (1969), 262–274.

Foner, Eric. *Reconstruction: America's Unfinished Revolution, 1863–1877.* New York: Harper & Row, 1988.

Foner, Philip S. *Frederick Douglass: A Biography.* New York: The Citadel Press, 1964.

———. "Is Booker T. Washington's Idea Correct?" *Journal of Negro History*, 55 (1970), 343–347.

———. *The Life and Writings of Frederick Douglass*, 5 Volumes, New York: International Publishers, 1950–1955.

———, ed. *Frederick Douglass on Women's Rights.* Westport: Greenwood Press, 1976.

———. *Frederick Douglass: Selected Speeches and Writings.* Chicago: Lawrence Hill, 1999.

———. *W. E. B. Du Bois Speaks: Speeches and Addresses, 1890–1919.* New York: Pathfinder, 1970.

———. *W. E. B. Du Bois Speaks: Speeches and Addresses, 1920–1963.* New York: Pathfinder, 1970.

Fox, Stephen R. *The Guardian of Boston: William Monroe Trotter.* New York: Atheneum, 1970.

Frank, Andrew K. *The Routledge Historical Atlas of the American South.* London: Routledge, 1999.

Franklin, John Hope. *Reconstruction After the Civil War, 2nd ed.* Chicago: University of Chicago Press, 1961.

Franklin, John Hope, and Alfred A. Moss. *From Slavery to Freedom: A History of Negro Americans*, 7th Ed. New York: McGraw-Hill, 1994.

Franklin, John Hope, and August Meier, eds. *Black Leaders of the Twentieth Century.* Urbana: University of Illinois Press, 1982.

Frederickson, George M. *The Black Image in the White Mind.* New York: Harper & Row, 1972.

———. *Black Liberation: A Comparative History of Black Ideologies in the United States and South Africa.* Oxford: Oxford University Press, 1995.

———. *White Supremacy: A Comparative Study in American and South African History.* Oxford: Oxford University Press, 1981.

Friedman, Lawrence J. "Life 'in the Lion's Mouth': Another Look at Booker T. Washington," *Journal of Negro History,* 59 (1974), 337–351.

Garvey, Amy Jacques. *Garvey and Garveyism.* London: Collier Macmillan, 1970.

Gatewood, William B. "Booker T. Washington and the Ulrich Affair," *Phylon,* XXX (Fall 1969), 286–302.

Gibson, Donald B. "Strategies and Revisions of Self-Representation in Booker T. Washington's Autobiographies," *American Quarterly,* 45 (September 1993), 370–393.

Gill, Walter Arthur Harris. "Booker T. Washington's Philosophy of Black Education: A Reassessment," *Western Journal of Black Studies,* 16, No. 4 (1992), 214–220.

Gilmore, Glenda Elizabeth. *Gender and Jim Crow: Women and Politics of White Supremacy in North Carolina, 1896–1920.* Chapel Hill: University of North Carolina Press, 1996.

Glazier, Kenneth M. "W. E. B. Du Bois's Impressions of Woodrow Wilson," *Journal of Negro History,* 58 (1973), 452–459.

Gottlieb, Peter. *Making Their Own Way: Southern Black's Migration to Pittsburgh, 1916–1930.* Urbana: University of Illinois Press, 1987.

Grantham, Dewey W. "Dinner at the White House: Theodore Roosevelt, Booker T. Washington and the South," *Tennessee Historical Quarterly,* XVIII (June 1958), 112–130.

Graves, John William. "Jim Crow in Arkansas: A Reconsideration of Urban Race Relations in the Post-Reconstruction South," *Journal of Southern History,* LV (August 1989), 421–448.

———. *Town and Country: Race Relations in an Urban-Rural Context, Arkansas, 1865–1905.* Fayetteville: University of Arkansas Press, 1990.

Grossman, James R. *Land of Hope: Chicago, Black Southerners, and the Great Migration.* Urbana: University of Chicago Press, 1989.

Haley, Alex, and Malcolm X. *The Autobiography of Malcolm X.* London: Penguin Books, 1968.

Harlan, Louis R. *All At Sea: Coming of Age in World War II.* Urbana: University of Illinois Press, 1997.

———. *Booker T. Washington: The Making of a Black Leader, 1856–1901.* Oxford: Oxford University Press, 1972.

———. *Booker T. Washington: The Wizard of Tuskegee, 1901–1915.* Oxford:

Oxford University Press, 1983.

———, ed. *The Booker T. Washington Papers* 14 volumes. Urbana: University of Illinois Press. 1972–1989.

Harris, Joel Chandler. *Uncle Remus: His Songs and Sayings.* Harmondsworth: Penguin Books Limited, 1982.

Harrison, Alferteen, ed. *Black Exodus: The Great Migration from the American South.* Jackson: University Press of Mississippi, 1991.

Hawkins, Hugh, ed. *Booker T. Washington and his Critics: The Problem Of Negro Leadership.* Boston: D.C. Heath and Company, 1974.

Heath, Robert L. "A Time For Silence: Booker T. Washington in Atlanta," *The Quarterly Journal of Speech*, 64 (1978), 385–399.

Hellwig, David J. "Black Meets Black: Afro American Reactions to West Indian Immigrants in the 1920s," *South Atlantic Quarterly*, 77 (1978), 206–224.

———."Building a Black Nation: The Role of Immigrants in the Thought and Rhetoric of Booker T. Washington," *Mississippi Quarterly* (Fall 1978), 529–550.

Hemmingway, Theodore. "Booker T. Washington in Mississippi, October 1908," *Journal of Mississippi History* (February 1984), 29–42.

Henri, Florette. *Black Migration: Movement North, 1900–1920: The Road from Myth to Man.* New York: Anchor/Doubleday, 1976.

Hermann, Janet Sharp. *The Pursuit of a Dream.* Oxford: Oxford University Press, 1981.

Higgs, Robert. "The Boll Weevil, The Cotton Economy, and Black Migration, 1910–1930," *Agricultural History* (April 1976), 335–50.

———. *Competition and Coercion: Blacks in the American Economy, 1865–1914.* Cambridge: Cambridge University Press, 1977.

Hill, Robert A. "'The Foremost Radical Among His Race': Marcus Garvey and the Black Scare, 1918–1921." *Prologue* (Winter 1984), 215–231.

———, ed. *The Marcus Garvey and Universal Negro Improvement Association Papers, Volumes i–ix.* Berkeley: University of California Press, 1983–1995.

Hill, Robert A. and Barbara Blair, eds. *Marcus Garvey Life and Lessons: A Centennial Companion to The Marcus Garvey and Universal Negro Improvement Association Papers.* Berkeley: University of California Press, 1987.

Hoffman, Edwin D. "From Slavery to Self-Reliance: The Record of Achievement of the Freedmen of the Sea Island Region," *Journal of Negro History*, XLI (January 1956), 8–42.

Holt, Thomas J. *Black Over White: Negro Political Leadership in South Carolina During Reconstruction.* Urbana: University of Illinois Press, 1977.

Holt, Thomas C., and Elsa Barkley Brown. *Major Problems in African-*

American History, Volume II: From Freedom To "Freedom Now." *1865–1990s.* Boston: Houghton Mifflin Company, 2000.

Huber Patrick J., and Gary R. Kramer. "Nathanial C. Bruce, Black Education and the 'Tuskegee of the Midwest,'" *Missouri Historical Review*, 86 (October 1991), 35–54.

James, Felix. "The Tuskegee Institute Movable School, 1906–1923," *Agricultural History*, XLV (July 1971), 201–209.

James, Winston. *Holding Aloft the Banner of Ethiopia: Caribbean Radicalism in Early Twentieth Century America.* London: Verso Books, 1998.

Johnson, G. B. "The Negro Migration and Its Consequences," *Journal of Social Forces*, 11 (March 1924), 404–408.

Johnson, James Weldon. *Along This Way: The Autobiography of James Weldon Johnson.* Harmondsworth: Penguin Books Limited, 1990.

— — —. *Black Manhattan.* New York: Arno Press and the *New York Times*, 1968.

Jones, A. W. "The Role of Tuskegee Institute in the Education of Black Farmers," *Journal of Negro History*, 60 (1975), 252–267.

Jones, Allen. "Improving Rural Life for Blacks: The Tuskegee Negro Farmers' Conference, 1892–1915," *Agricultural History*, 65, No. 2 (Spring 1991), 105–114.

Jones, Maldwyn A. *The Limits of Liberty: American History, 1607–1980.* Oxford: Oxford University Press, 1983.

Jordan, William. "'The Damnable Dilemma': African American Accommodation and Protest During World War I," *Journal of American History*, 81, No. 4 (March 1995), 1562–1583.

Katz, Michael B., and Thomas J. Sugrue. *W. E. B. Du Bois, Race, and the City: The Philadelphia Negro and Its Legacy.* Philadelphia: University of Pennsylvania Press, 1998.

Katznelson, Ira. *Black Men: White Cities.* London: Oxford University Press, 1973.

Kelley, Don Quinn. "Ideology and Education: Uplifting the Masses in Nineteenth Century Alabama," *Phylon*, 40 (1979), 147–158.

— — —. "The Political Economy of Booker T. Washington: A Bibliographic Essay," *Journal of Negro Education* (Fall 1977), 403–418.

Kellogg, Charles F. *NAACP: A History of the National Association for the Advancement of Colored People, Volume I, 1909–1920.* Baltimore: The Johns Hopkins University Press, 1967.

King, Andrew A. "Booker T. Washington and the Myth of Heroic Materialism," *Quarterly Journal of Speech*, 60 (October 1974), 323–327.

Kirby, John Temple. "The Southern Exodus, 1910–1960: A Primer for Historians," *Journal of Southern History*, XLIX (November 1983), 585–600.

Kornweibel, Theodore. "Apathy and Dissent: Black America's Negative Responses to World War I," *South Atlantic Quarterly*, 80 (1981), 322–338.

Kraut, Alan M. *The Huddled Masses: The Immigrant in American Society, 1880–1921.* Arlington Heights: Harlan Davidson Inc., 1982.

Kusmer, Kenneth L. *A Ghetto Takes Shape: Black Cleveland, 1870–1930.* Urbana: University of Illinois Press, 1976.

Lawson, Bill E., and Frank M. Kirkland, eds. *Frederick Douglass: A Critical Reader.* Oxford: Blackwell, 1999.

Leab, Daniel J. *From Sambo to Superspade: The Black Experience in Motion Pictures.* London: Secker and Warburg, 1973.

Lewis, David Levering. *W. E. B. Du Bois: Biography of a Race, 1868–1919.* New York: Henry Holt, 1993.

———. *W. E. B. DuBois: The Fight for Equality and the American Century, 1919–1963.* New York: Henry Holt, 2000.

———, ed. *W. E. B. Du Bois: A Reader.* New York: Henry Holt, 1995.

Lewis, Rupert. *Marcus Garvey: Anti-Colonial Champion.* London: Karin Press, 1987.

Lewis, Rupert, and Maureen Warner-Lewis, eds. *Garvey, Africa, Europe, The Americas.* Jamaica: University of the West Indies, 1986.

Lewis, Rupert, and Patrick Bryan, eds. *Garvey: His Work and Impact.* Trenton: Africa World Press, Inc., 1991.

Litwack, Leon F. *Been in the Storm So Long: The Aftermath of Slavery.* New York: Alfred A. Knopf, Inc., 1979.

———. *Trouble in Mind: Black Southerners in the Age of Jim Crow.* New York: Alfred A. Knopf, 1998.

Litwack, Leon F., and August Meier, eds. *Black Leaders of the Nineteenth Century.* Urbana: University of Illinois Press, 1988.

Logan, Rayford W., ed. *W. E. B. Du Bois: A Profile.* New York: Hill and Wang, 1971.

Mackie, Liz. *The Great Marcus Garvey.* London: Hansib Publishing Limited, 1987.

Mandle, Jay R. *The Roots of Black Poverty: The Southern Plantation Economy After the Civil War.* Durham: Duke University Press, 1978.

Marable, Manning. *Black Leadership.* New York: Columbia University Press, 1998.

———. "Booker T. Washington and African Nationalism," *Phylon*, 35 (December 1974), 398–406.

———. "Tuskegee and the Politics of Illusion in the New South," *The Black Scholar* (May 1977), 13–24.

———. *W. E. B. Du Bois: Black Radical Democrat.* Boston: Twayne Publishers, 1986.

Marks, Carole. *Farewell—We're Good and Gone: The Great Black*

Migration. Bloomington: Indiana University Press, 1989.

Martin, Tony. *Race First: The Ideological and Organizational Struggles of Marcus Garvey and the Universal Negro Improvement Association*. Westport: Greenwood Press, 1976.

Martin, Waldo E. *The Mind of Frederick Douglass*. Chapel Hill: The University of North Carolina Press, 1984.

———, ed. *Brown v Board of Education: A Brief History With Documents*. Boston: Bedford/St. Martin's, 1998.

Matthews, Basil. *Booker T. Washington: Educator and Inter-Racial Interpreter*. Cambridge, Mass: Harvard University Press, 1948.

Matthews, Carl S. "The Decline of the Tuskegee Machine, 1915–1925: The Abdication of Political Power," *South Atlantic Quarterly*, 75 (1976), 460–469.

———, ed. "Documents: Marcus Garvey Writes from Jamaica on the Mulatto Escape Hatch," *Journal of Negro History*, 59 (1974), 170–176.

Matthews, Fred H. "Robert Park, Congo Reform and Tuskegee: The Molding of a Race Relations Expert, 1905–1913," *Canadian Journal of History*, 8 (March 1973), 37–65.

Mayberry, B. D. "The Tuskegee Movable School: A Unique Contribution to National and International Agriculture and Rural Development," *Agricultural History*, 65, No. 2 (Spring 1991), 85–104.

McElroy, Frederick L. "Booker T. Washington as Literary Trickster," *Southern Folklore*, 49, No. 2 (1992), 89–107.

McFeely, William S. *Frederick Douglass*. New York: W. W. Norton and Company, 1991.

McKay, Claude. *Harlem: Negro Metropolis*. New York: Harcourt, Brace Jovanovich, Inc., 1968.

McMillen, Neil R. *Dark Journey: Black Mississippians in the Age of Jim Crow*. Urbana: University of Illinois Press, 1989.

McNeil, Genna Rae, and Michael R. Winston (eds.). *Historical Judgments Reconsidered: Selected Howard University Lectures in Honor of Rayford W. Logan*. Washington, D.C.: Howard University Press, 1988.

Meier, August. "Booker T. Washington and the Negro Press," *Journal of Negro History*, 38 (January 1953), 67–90.

———. "Booker T. Washington and the Negro Press: With Special Reference to the *Colored American Magazine*," *Journal of Negro History*, 37 (1958), 67–90.

———. "Booker T. Washington and the Town of Mound Bayou," *Phylon*, 15 (1954), 396–401.

———. "Negro Class Structure and Ideology in the Age of Booker T. Washington," *Phylon*, 23 (Fall 1962), 258–266.

———. *Negro Thought in America, 1880–1915*. Ann Arbor: University of Michigan Press, 1963.

———. "Towards a Reinterpretation of Booker T. Washington," *Journal of Southern History*, XVIII (May 1957), 220–227.

Meier, August, and Elliott M. Rudwick. *Along the Color Line: Explorations in the Black Experience*. Urbana: University of Chicago Press, 1976.

———. "The Boycott Movement Against Jim Crow Street Cars in the South, 1900–1916," *Journal of American History*, 55 (1969), 756–776.

Miller, Zana L. "Race-ism and the City: The Young Du Bois and the Role of Place in Social Theory," *American Studies*, 30 (Fall 1989), 89–102.

Moore, Jack B. *W. E. B. Du Bois*. Boston: Twayne Publishers, 1981.

Morris, Robert C. *Reading, 'Riting and Reconstruction: The Education of Freedmen in the South, 1861–1870*. Chicago: University of Chicago Press, 1981.

Moses, William J. *Black Messiahs and Uncle Toms: Social and Literary Manipulations of a Religious Myth*. Philadelphia: Pennsylvania State University Press, 1982.

Moses, Wilson J. "The Politics of Ethiopianism: W.E.B. Du Bois and Literary Black Nationalism," *American Literature*, 47 (1975), 411–426.

Nembhard, Len S. *Trials and Triumphs of Marcus Garvey*. Millwood: Kraus Reprint Co., 1978.

Newby, I. A. *Jim Crow's Defense: Anti-Negro Thought in America, 1900–1930*. Baton Rouge: Louisiana State University Press, 1965.

Norrell, Robert. *Reaping the Whirlwind: The Civil Rights Movement in Tuskegee*. New York: Vintage Books, 1986.

Novak, Daniel A. *The Wheel of Servitude: Black Forced Labor After Slavery*. Lexington: University of Kentucky Press, 1978.

Oliver, Paul. *Blues Fell This Morning: Meaning in the Blues*. Cambridge: Cambridge University Press, 1990.

———. *The Story of the Blues*. London: Barrie and Jenkins Limited, 1970.

Olney, James. "The Founding Fathers—Frederick Douglass and Booker T. Washington; or, The Idea of Democracy and a Tradition of Afro-American Autobiography," *Amerikastudien*, 35 (1990), 281–296.

O'Reilly, Kenneth. *Nixon's Piano: Presidents and Racial Politics from Washington to Clinton*. New York: The Free Press, 1995.

Osofsky, Gilbert. *Harlem: The Making of a Ghetto. Negro New York, 1890–1930*. New York: Harper Torchbooks, 1971.

Ottley, Roi. *"New World A-Coming": Inside Black America*. Boston: Houghton Mifflin Company, 1943.

Ovington, Mary White. *Black and White Sat Down Together: The Reminiscences of an NAACP Founder*. New York: The Feminist Press, 1995.

Painter, Nell I. *Exodusters: Black Migration to Kansas After*

Reconstruction. New York: Alfred A. Knopf, 1977.

Perry, Bruce. *Malcolm: The Life of a Man Who Changed America.* New York: Station Hill, 1991.

Pfeffer, Paula A. *A. Philip Randolph: Pioneer of the Civil Rights Movement.* Baton Rouge: Louisiana State University Press, 1990.

Pinckney, Alphonse. *Red, Black and Green: Black Nationalism in the United States.* Cambridge: Cambridge University Press, 1976.

Pitre, Merline. Review of John H. Burrows, *The Necessity of Myth: The National Negro Business League.* Auburn, Alabama: Hickory Hill Press, 1988, in *Journal of Southern History,* LVII (February 1991), 130–131.

———. "Robert Lloyd Smith: A Black Lawmaker in the Shadow of Booker T. Washington," *Phylon,* 46 (September 1985), 262–268.

Pole, J. R. *Paths to the American Past.* Oxford: Oxford University Press, 1979.

Puttkamer, C. W., and R. Worthy. "William Monroe Trotter, 1872–1934," *Journal of Negro History,* 43 (1958), 298–316.

Quarles, Benjamin. *Frederick Douglass.* New York: Da Capo Press, 1997.

Rabinowitz, Howard N. *Race Relations in the Urban South, 1865–1890.* New York: Oxford University Press, 1978.

———. *Southern Black Leaders of the Reconstruction Era.* Urbana: University of Illinois Press, 1982.

Rampersad, Arnold. *The Art and Imagination of W. E. B. Du Bois.* New York: Schocken Books, 1990.

Ransom, Roger L., and Richard Sutch. *One Kind of Freedom: The Economic Consequences of Emancipation.* Cambridge: Cambridge University Press, 1977.

Rath, Richard C. "Echo and Narcissus: The Afrocentric Pragmatism of W. E. B. Du Bois," *Journal of American History* (September 1997), 461–495.

Reed, Adolph L. *W. E. B. Du Bois and American Political Thought: Fabianism and the Color Line.* Oxford: Oxford University Press, 1997.

Reid, Joseph D. "Sharecropping as an Understandable Market Response: The Post-Bellum South," *Journal of Economic History,* XXXIII (1973), 106–130.

Renshaw, Patrick. "The Black Ghetto, 1890–1940," *Journal of American Studies,* 8 (1974), 41–59.

Rice, Alan J., and Martin Crawford, eds. *Liberating Sojourn: Frederick Douglass and Transatlantic Reform.* Athens: University of Georgia Press, 1999.

Rogers, Ben F. "William E. B. DuBois, Marcus Garvey, and Pan-Africa," *Journal of Negro History,* 40 (1955), 154–165.

Rouse, Jaqueline Anne. "Out of the Shadow of Tuskegee: Margaret

Murray Washington, Social Activism, and Race Vindication," *Journal of Negro History* (Spring-Fall 1996), 31–46.

Rudwick, Elliott M. "Booker T. Washington's Relations with the National Association for the Advancement of Colored People," *Journal of Negro Education*, XXIX (Spring 1960), 134–144.

———. "The Niagara Movement," *Journal of Negro History*, 42 (1957), 177–200.

———. "W. E. B. Du Bois in the Role of *Crisis* Editor," *Journal of Negro History*, 43 (1958), 214–240.

———. *W.E.B. Du Bois: A Study in Minority Group Leadership.* Philadelphia: University of Pennsylvania Press, 1960.

Runcie, John. "Black Music and the Garvey Aesthetic," *Afro-Americans in New York Life and History* (July, 1987), 7–23.

———. "Marcus Garvey and the Harlem Renaissance," *Afro-Americans in New York Life and History* (July 1987), 7–28.

Scheiner, Seth M. "President Theodore Roosevelt and the Negro, 1901–1908," *Journal of Negro History*, 47 (1962), 169–82.

Schweninger, Loren. *Black Property Owners in the South, 1790–1915.* Urbana: University of Illinois Press, 1990.

Scott, Emmett J. "Letters of Negro Migrants of 1916–1918," *Journal of Negro History*, 4 (July and October 1919), 290–340, 412–465.

———. "Twenty Years After: An Appraisal of Booker T. Washington," *Journal of Negro Education*, 5 (October 1936), 543–554.

Scott, Emmett J., and Lyman Beecher Stowe. *Booker T. Washington: Builder of a Civilization.* London: T. Fisher Unwin Limited, 1916.

Sernett, Milton. *Bound for the Promised Land: African American Religion and the Great Migration.* Durham: Duke University Press, 1997.

Severn, John K., and William Warren Rogers. "Theodore Roosevelt Entertains Booker T. Washington: Florida's Reaction to the White House Dinner," *Florida Historical Quarterly* (January, 1976), 306–318.

Smith, Arthur L., ed. *Language, Communication and Rhetoric in Black America.* New York: Harper & Row, 1972.

Smock, Raymond W., ed. *Booker T. Washington in Perspective: Essays of Louis R. Harlan.* Jackson: University Press of Mississippi, 1988.

Socken, J. *The Black Man and the American Dream.* Chicago: Quadrangle Books, 1971.

Southern, Eileen. *The Music of Black Americans: A History*, 3rd ed. New York: W. W. Norton and Company, 1997.

Spear, Allan H. *Black Chicago: The Making of a Negro Ghetto, 1890–1920.* Chicago: University of Chicago Press, 1967.

Spencer, Samuel R. *Booker T. Washington and the Negro's Place in American Life.* Boston: Little, Brown and Company, 1956.

Spivey, Donald. "The African Crusade for Black Industrial Schooling,"

Journal of Negro History, 63 (January 1978), 1–17.

Stampp, Kenneth M. *The Era of Reconstruction.* London: Eyre and Spottiswoode 1965.

Stein, Judith. "'Of Mr. Booker T. Washington and Others': The Political Economy of Racism in the United States," *Science and Society*, 38 (1974–1975), 422–463.

— — —. *The World of Marcus Garvey: Race and Class in Modern Society.* Baton Rouge: Louisiana State University Press, 1986.

Still, Bayard. *Urban America: A History with Documents.* Boston: Little Brown, 1974.

Stone, Donald P. *Fallen Prince: William James Edwards, Black Education and the Quest for Afro American Nationality.* Snow Hill, Alabama: The Snow Hill Press, 1990.

Stowe, Harriet Beecher. *Uncle Tom's Cabin, or, Life Among the Lowly.* Harmondsworth: Penguin Books Limited, 1986.

Strickland, Arvarh E. "Booker T. Washington: The Myth and the Man," *Reviews in American History*, 1 (December 1973), 559–564.

Stueck, William. "Progressivism and the Negro: White Liberals and the Early NAACP," *The Historian* (November 1975), 58–78.

Stull, Bradford T. *Amid the Fall, Dreaming of Eden: Du Bois, King, Malcolm X, and Emancipatory Composition.* Carbondale: Southern Universities Press, 1999.

Suggs, Henry Lewis. "P. B. Young of the Norfolk *Journal and Guide*: A Booker T. Washington Militant, 1904–1928," *Journal of Negro History* (Fall 1979), 365–376.

Sundquist, Eric J., ed. *Frederick Douglass: New Literary and Historical Essays.* Cambridge: Cambridge University Press, 1990.

— — —. *The Oxford W. E. B. Du Bois Reader.* Oxford: Oxford University Press, 1996.

Swint, Henry L. *The Northern Teacher in the South, 1862–1870.* New York: Octagon Books, Inc., 1967.

Thelen, David, ed. "Perspectives: The Strange Career of Jim Crow," *Journal of American History*, 75 (December 1988), 841–868.

Thomas, Richard W. *Life For Us Is What We Make It: Building Black Community in Detroit, 1915–1945.* Bloomington: Indiana University Press, 1992.

Thornbrough, Emma Lou. "Booker T. Washington as Seen By His White Contemporaries," *Journal of Negro History*, 53 (1968), 161–182.

— — —. "The Brownsville Episode and the Negro Vote," *Mississippi Valley Historical Review*, 44 (December 1957), 469–493.

— — —. "More Light on Booker T. Washington and the New York *Age*," *Journal of Negro History*, XLIII (1958), 34–49.

— — —. "The National Afro-American League, 1887–1908," *Journal of*

Southern History, 27 (1961), 494–512.

— — —. *T. Thomas Fortune: Militant Journalist.* Chicago: University of Chicago Press, 1972.

Thrasher, Max Bennett. *Tuskegee: Its Story and Its Work.* New York: Negro Universities Press, 1969.

Tindall, George B. *South Carolina Negroes, 1877–1900.* Columbia: University of South Carolina Press, 1952.

Tinsley, James A. "Roosevelt, Foraker, and the Brownsville Affray," *Journal of Negro History*, 41 (1956), 43–65.

Tolbert, Emory J. *The UNIA and Black Los Angeles: Ideology and Community in the American Garvey Movement.* Los Angeles: University of California Center for Afro-American Studies, 1980.

Trelease, Allen W. *White Terror: The Ku Klux Klan Conspiracy and Southern Reconstruction.* London: Secker and Warburg, 1972.

Trotter, Joe William. *Black Milwaukee: The Making of an Industrial Proletariat, 1915–1945.* Urbana: University of Illinois Press, 1985.

— — —. "The Shifting Historiography of African American Urban History," *Journal of Urban History*, 21, No. 4 (May 1995), 438–457.

— — —, ed. *The Great Migration in Historical Perspective.* Bloomington: Indiana University Press, 1991.

Tuttle, William M. *Race Riot: Chicago in the Red Summer of 1919.* New York: Atheneum, 1970.

Verney, Kevern. *Black Civil Rights in America.* London: Routledge, 2000.

— — —. "'Roads Not Taken': Booker T. Washington and Black Leadership in the United States, 1895–1915," *Borderlines*, 3, No. 2 (Winter 1996–1997), 144–158.

— — —. "'Trespassers in the Land of their Birth': Blacks and Landownership in South Carolina and Mississippi during the Civil War and Reconstruction, 1861–1877," *Slavery and Abolition*, 4, No. 1 (May 1983), 66–78.

Vincent, Charles. "Booker T. Washington's Tour of Louisiana, April 1915," *Louisiana History*, XXII (Spring 1981), 189–198.

Vincent, Theodore G. *Black Power and the Garvey Movement.* Berkeley: The Ramparts Press, 1971.

Voss, Frederick S. *Majestic Wrath: A Pictorial Life of Frederick Douglass.* Washington, D.C.: Smithsonian Institute Press, 1995.

Wade, Wyn Craig. *The Fiery Cross: The Ku Klux Klan in America.* New York: Simon & Schuster Inc., 1987.

Walden, Daniel. "The Contemporary Opposition to the Political and Educational Ideas of Booker T. Washington," *Journal of Negro History*, 45 (1960), 103–115.

Walker, Clarence E. "Heirs of the Wizard," *Journal of Policy History*, 4, No. 3 (1992), 339–349.

Washington, Booker T. *Frederick Douglass*. New York: Argosy Antiquarian Limited, 1969.

———. *Up From Slavery*. Harmondsworth: Penguin Books, 1986.

Washington, Booker T., and Robert E. Park. *The Man Farthest Down: A Record of Observation and Study in Europe*. London: Transaction Books, 1984.

Waskow, Arthur I. *From Race Riot to Sit-In, 1919 and the 1960s*. Gloucester, Massachusetts: Peter Smith, 1975.

Watson, Elwood. "Marcus Garvey's Garveyism: Message from a Forefather," *Journal of Religious Thought*, 51 (1994), 77–94.

Weinberg, Meyer, ed. *The World of W.E.B. Du Bois: A Quotation Sourcebook*. Westport: Greenwood Press, 1992.

Weisberger, Bernard A. *Booker T. Washington*. New York: The New American Library Inc., 1972.

Weisbrod, Robert G. *Ebony Kinship: Africa, Africans and the Afro-American*. Westport: Greenwood Press, 1974.

Weiss, Nancy J. "The Negro and the New Freedom: Fighting Wilsonian Segregation," *Political Science Quarterly*, LXXIV (1968), 61–79.

Wesley, Charles H. "W. E. B. DuBois—The Historian," *Journal of Negro History*, 50 (1965), 147–162.

West, Michael O. "The Tuskegee Model of Development in Africa: Another Dimension of the African/African American Connection," *Diplomatic History*, 16 (Summer 1992), 371–387.

White, Arthur O. "Booker T. Washington's Florida Incident, 1903–1904," *Florida Historical Quarterly*, LI (January 1973), 227–249.

White, John. *Black Leadership in America from Booker T. Washington to Jesse Jackson*, 2nd ed. London: Longman, 1990.

Williams, Yvonne. "William Monroe Trotter: Race Man, 1872–1934," *Afro-American Studies*, 1 (1971), 243–251.

Williamson, Joel. *The Crucible of Race: Black-White Relations in the American South Since Emancipation*. Oxford: Oxford University Press, 1984.

Wolfenstein, Eugene. *The Victims of Democracy: Malcolm X and the Black Revolution*. London: Free Association Books, 1989.

Wolgemuth, Kathleen Long. "Woodrow Wilson's Appointment Policy and the Negro," *Journal of Southern History*, 24 (1958), 457–471.

Woodson, Carter G. *A Century of Negro Migration*. Washington, D.C.: 1918.

Woodward, C. Vann. *The Strange Career of Jim Crow*, 3rd Edition. Oxford: Oxford University Press, 1974.

Woofter, Thomas Jackson. *Negro Migration: Changes in Rural Organization and Population of the Cotton Belt*. New York: AMS Press, 1971.

Yandle, Paul. "Joseph Charles Price and His 'Peculiar Work', Part I and

Part II," *The North Carolina Historical Review*, LXX, Nos. 1 and 2 (January and April 1993), 40–56, 130–152.

Yellin, Jean F. "Du Bois, *Crisis* and Woman's Suffrage," *Massachusetts Review*, 14 (1973), 365–375.

Young, Alfred. "The Educational Philosophy of Booker T. Washington: A Perspective for Black Liberation," *Phylon*, 37 (1976), 224–235.

Zamir, Shamoon. *Dark Voices: W. E. B. Du Bois and American Thought, 1888–1903*. Chicago: University of Chicago Press, 1995.

Index